Liberalism in an Illiberal Age

Recent titles in
Contributions in Intercultural and Comparative Studies
Series Editor: Ann M. Pescatello

Power and Pawn: The Female in Iberian Families, Societies, and Cultures
Ann M. Pescatello

Tegotomono: Music for the Japanese Koto
Bonnie C. Wade

Historical Archaeology: A Structural Approach in an African Culture
Peter R. Schmidt

Sacred Words: A Study of Navajo Religion and Prayer
Sam D. Gill

Liberalism in an Illiberal Age

New Culture Liberals in Republican China, 1919–1937

EUGENE LUBOT

Contributions in Intercultural and Comparative Studies, Number 5

Greenwood Press
Westport, Connecticut • London, England

Library of Congress Cataloging in Publication Data

Lubot, Eugene.
Liberalism in an illiberal age.

(Contributions in intercultural and comparative studies, ISSN 0147-1031 ; no. 5)
Bibliography: p.
Includes index.
1. Liberalism—China—History. I. Title. II. Series.
JC599.C6L83 320.5'12'0951 81-13409
ISBN 0-313-23256-3 (lib. bdg.) AACR2

Library of Congress Catalog Card Number: 81-13409
ISBN: 0-313-23256-3
ISSN: 0147-1031

First published in 1982

Greenwood Press
A division of Congressional Information Service, Inc.
88 Post Road West, Westport, Connecticut 06881

Printed in the United States of America

10 9 8 7 6 5 4 3 2 1

For Donna, Karen, and Keven

Contents

Illustrations

Acknowledgments

I would like to express my thanks to a number of people. Lloyd Eastman and Allen Linden read my work at an early stage in its development, offering encouragement and many helpful suggestions. Much of my conceptualizing took place during two National Endowment for the Humanities Summer Seminars. These seminars have provided considerable benefit to teachers such as myself who have been located at small colleges and universities. The stimulating atmosphere and outstanding library resources are partly responsible. But for me, at least, equally important was the opportunity to watch some outstanding minds at work. The directors of the two seminars in which I participated, Ho Ping-ti of the University of Chicago and David Jarovsky of Northwestern University, were exemplary in this respect. Their immense learning, powers of analysis, and intellectual integrity were models for the highest standards of scholarly research. Much of the writing of this book was completed during a sabbatical from Wheaton College (Massachusetts), and some final checking and revisions were facilitated by a research grant from the University of Tennessee at Chattanooga. I would like to thank both institutions for their support. The photographs were provided by the Historical Commission of the Central Committee of the Kuomintang, Republic of China, and are reprinted by permission. I appreciate their assistance. Finally, I am grateful to Nancy Shepardson, at Wheaton, and Elke Lawson, at Chattanooga, who typed early versions of this work; and especially to Olga Mohn of Albright College who typed the final version. Needless to say, I alone am responsible for any errors of fact or analysis which remain.

Liberalism in an Illiberal Age

1. Introduction

Liberalism, so the conventional wisdom observes, is a Western concept with little relevance to Asia. Distinctive historical conditions spawned it, and Asian cultures developed along different lines. This study seeks to dispute that contention, arguing that liberal values did play a role in modern China and that Chinese liberals faced many of the dilemmas common to liberalism in other historical settings.

The word liberalism, in the context of modern China, immediately evokes the name Hu Shih. He has become identified as the archetypical liberal critic, protesting sincerely but ineffectually against the evils of his time. But Hu Shih was not alone. Others committed themselves to similar views, articulating them in such journals as Endeavor (Nu-li chou-pao), Contemporary Review (Hsien-tai p'ing-lun), Crescent Moon (Hsin-yueh yueh-k'an), and Independent Critic (Tu-li p'ing-lun). A representative list would include, in addition to Hu Shih: Ts'ai Yuan-p'ei, Chiang Meng-lin, T. F. Tsiang, Lo Lung-chi, T'ao Meng-ho, Fu Ssu-nien, Chang Po-ling, Liang Shih-ch'iu, T'ao Hsi-sheng, Ting Wen-chiang, and Ch'en Heng-che.

Certainly some legitimate questions might be raised about the accuracy of the liberal label for this group. In what ways were these individuals liberal? First, they maintained an attitude of optimism about the inherent rationality of mankind and the amenability of China's problems to gradual, peaceful, and rational solutions. Their cast of mind, in other words, was liberal in the sense of looking for moderate, nonviolent ways to make reforms. They reacted negatively to class conflict, hoping to bring conflicting classes into harmony through education and patient reforms. Second, they exhibited a genuine concern for protecting basic civil liberties such as freedom of speech and of the press. For them, diversity of opinion was a necessary ingredient of a healthy society. Finally, they favored a constitutional government, which would support the democratic process and provide institutional checks on authoritarianism. They possessed only limited confidence in the ability of people to govern themselves, at least until educational reforms were implemented, but they wanted to end China's long tradition of dictatorships.

While upholding these fundamental liberal principles, Chinese liberals were distinctly a product of their own culture. The liberal values that emerged in modern China came from traditional Chinese sources and from the ideas of the New Culture movement (ca. 1915-1919), rather than from any conscious imitation of a Western model. Indeed, the most appropriate label for Hu Shih and the other individuals listed above is "New Culture liberals," because New Culture values exerted as much influence on their behavior as did liberal principles. In one sense this is a study of the dilemmas confronted by those who maintained New Culture views in the post-May Fourth years. But this is also a study of the dilemmas of modern liberalism. Regardless of the sources, New Culture liberals did uphold liberal principles in an illiberal age. Their experience warrants a place in the comparative history of modern liberalism.

Liberalism East and West

From many sources there evolved in the West a certain pattern of ideas and institutions which might be labeled classical liberalism. A suggestive, though certainly not exhaustive, list would include rationalism, pragmatism, faith in science and progress, guarantees of civil liberties, protection of property by law, tolerance of dissent and openness to new ideas, concern for representative government, and laissez-faire economics. There was also a spirit of individualism, based partly on a commitment to liberating the individual (inherent in liberalism) and partly on the conviction that the unfettered individual would act creatively and productively in ways that benefited society. As John Stuart Mill said, " . . . a state which dwarfs its men, in order that they may be more docile instruments in its hands even for beneficial purposes--will find that with small men no great things can really be accomplished."[1]

The liberal experience was different in modern China, and it needs to be put in a broad perspective before making any historical assessments. It is, for example, important to appreciate how recently liberal values have received general acceptance even in the West. The idea of law as natural or universal is very old in the West, but the concept of natural rights only began to assume an important role in the West in the late seventeenth century.[2] It represented a shift in emphasis from the community and social order in favor of the wishes of the individual. This shift, which came comparatively recently in Western society, was not inevitable. The proper balance between individual and social needs has been a recurring question in political theory, and there is much justification (especially in a crowded society such as China) for coming down on the side of social order. Also, the location of sovereignty in the people, with state authority justified only so long as it satisfies the needs of the people, was a quite recent and explosive idea in the West. The Divine Right of Kings enjoyed longevity, and persuasive arguments (within the accepted frame of reference) provided its underpinnings.

Some questions might also be raised about just how liberal Western liberalism has been. Strong evidence can be adduced to argue that Western liberalism has always had a class bias, that it was designed to protect the interests of the propertied classes against governmental interference. Under the smoke screen of freedom for all, the rich and powerful were able to enhance their interests at the expense of the poor and the weak. The result was a sham in which the privileged enjoyed the fruits of individualism and freedom, while the disadvantaged had freedom only to work hard and suffer. This interpretation of liberalism would further argue that liberal principles were always carefully limited by the need to maintain social order. Unlimited freedom of action was granted to the "safe" people, but the state was quick to clamp down on any dissent or unconventional behavior which threatened the interests of the privileged or the social stability from which they prospered. The record of the United States in this regard may be better than some countries, but only a Pollyanna would deny that some element of class bias exists in the American application of liberal values. Moreover, in times of national crisis American governments have curtailed civil rights without much protest by the general population. The Alien and Sedition Acts; the Civil War suspension of the writ of habeas corpus; the arrest of Eugene Debs and other acts of Woodrow Wilson's government during World War I; the Smith Act; and the internment of Japanese-Americans during World War II are just some of the most visible examples in support of this proposition.

If the existence of liberalism has been so problematic in

the West, one could hardly expect to find it securely established in China where social harmony was considered more important than individual rights. Confucian principles reinforced these priorities, producing individuals very aware of their insignificant place in the scheme of things. From this perspective it is no surprise that the concept of human rights was slow to appear on the Chinese scene, carefully qualified even by those who were its sponsors. In fact the surprising thing is that such an idea gained any currency at all in the Chinese setting.

China never experienced the European Renaissance, which apotheosized man and gloried in his potential for achievement. China's world view logically assumed that such an exaggerated perception of man's importance would jeopardize the harmony of the universe. Equally significant is the fact that China never experienced the scientific revolution of the seventeenth century, with its great discoveries and consequent confidence in man's ability to control his own fate. China has a magnificent record of scientific achievement, but the mental habits associated with scientific investigation were not respectable for Confucian gentlemen until late in the Ming dynasty. Given the Confucian cosmology, the idea of mastering the laws of nature and utilizing them for the benefit of mankind could only be viewed as threatening. Consequently, the boundless confidence in man's creative potential unleashed by the scientific revolution was delayed in China. One might even argue that the delay lasted until the establishment of the People's Republic of China. Thus, this basic rationale for liberalism--that is, a confidence in the creative ability of the individual and optimism regarding the future--was missing from China until quite recently.

Also absent from China was the industrial revolution which accompanied the scientific revolution. Consequently, no powerful middle class developed in China, capable of protecting its property and safeguarding itself against governmental interference. And even had industrial development occurred more rapidly in China, there is no assurance that an independent or powerful middle class could have developed. The Chinese state has historically been watchful regarding the appearance of any independent source of economic power. Merchants who became too powerful might have their wealth confiscated. Commercial enterprises that were especially lucrative would be run by state monopolies. So effective was this policy that successful merchants invariably tried to educate their sons to become officials, so that they could make the transition from merchant family to the scholar-gentry. Thus, China, for more than one reason, was without the powerful middle class which provided another element in the evolution of Western liberalism.

Finally, there is the social contract idea enunciated by John Locke and others, which argued that governmental authority rested on the consent of the governed. There existed a similar idea in China with the concept of a Mandate of Heaven, utilized by the Chou dynasty and later elucidated by Mencius. This principle stated that if an emperor (or the officials for whom he was responsible) failed to act appropriately or to preserve order, then Heaven would withdraw its mandate and the people had the right of rebellion. There are common elements in the Western and Chinese concepts, but there is also a fundamental difference. In China the authority is vested in Heaven, and the people act as its agents. In the West authority rests with the people who voluntarily delegate it to the government. The Chinese concern is basically for an orderly society. Unless society is well ordered and the people well governed, the harmony in the universe is jeopardized. In the West there is at least the presumption that the needs of the people are important for their own sake. One theory, thus, is a mechanism to help assure social order; while the other presupposes that the people are entitled to certain rights which are intrinsically worth preserving.

Indigenous Sources of Chinese Liberalism

Although most of the conditions which spawned Western liberalism were absent in traditional China, there were some indigenous sources for the New Culture liberalism which did emerge. One was the Confucian article of faith that man was perfectible through proper guidance and moral education. Indeed, faith in the redemptive qualities of education is one of the most enduring characteristics of Chinese culture.[3] Hu Shih and Chiang Meng-lin paid tribute to the influence of John Dewey's ideas on education, yet this merely added a Western imprimatur to their Confucian predilections. In essence, many New Culture liberals assumed the role of Confucian chün-tzu (gentlemen), paternalistically drawing the proper moral lessons from which others might benefit.

Beginning in the early Ch'ing period other indigenous developments served as precursors of later New Culture liberalism.[4] The devastating impact of conquest by the Manchus led many Chinese to reexamine their own assumptions in search of an explanation. Many concluded that they had lost touch with reality and that Confucianism had become too abstract. This led to lessening the emphasis on the self-cultivation (hsiu-shen) aspect of neo-Confucianism in favor of "practical statesmanship." Ultimately this evolved into the scholasticism of the "school of empirical research," but in the seventeenth and eighteenth centuries many notable Confucian scholars began employing much more empirical, and even scientific, methods in their study of the classics. Scholarship emphasized critical, textual comparisons rather than moralistic commentaries, and the reverence traditionally directed at the classics was replaced by a critical objectivity. In many ways these Ch'ing scholars began the process of liberating Chinese minds from the fetters of Confucian conventions. A new spirit of inquiry and new standards of evidence, which can arguably be called protoscientific, emerged as a totally indigenous force.

This trend continued in the nineteenth century, with individuals such as Wei Yuan and Kung Tzu-chen, and culminated with K'ang Yu-wei and the New Text school. When events revealed the inadequacies of the t'i-yung self-strengthening approach to China's problems, this setting produced advocates of more far-reaching reforms and even revolution. However, these terms are loaded ones, and both radical reformers (such as K'ang Yu-wei and Liang Ch'i-ch'ao) and revolutionaries (such as Sun Yat-sen) can be considered precursors of the New Culture viewpoint which developed later. In the early twentieth century, China's political spectrum was extremely imprecise. Certain ideas were shared by both revolutionaries and reformers.[5] Both groups wanted far-reaching political, social, and intellectual reforms in order to bring wealth and power to China. Both were highly critical of the Confucian tradition for its repressiveness, citing with approval the Western emphasis on freedom and equality. Moreover, conditions were so volatile that individuals frequently shifted positions, rarely maintaining a logically consistent revolutionary or reformist posture on all issues.

Recent studies have helped clarify the continuities and discontinuities between the 1898 reformers (Liang Ch'i-ch'ao, K'ang Yu-wei, et al.) and the May Fourth generation.[6] The May Fourth period (or the May Fourth movement) is generally considered to stretch from 1915 to 1921, although some prefer the more limited definition of 1917 to 1921. The period takes its name from the May Fourth incident, which refers to student demonstrations of 4 May 1919 against the Versailles Conference. These protested news that the Shantung Peninsula (Chinese territory which had become part of the German Concession in China) would be transferred to Japan rather than restored to Chinese control. The broader May Fourth period was characterized by considerable intellectual and cultural ferment, and these developments are usually identified as the New Culture movement. Compared with the reformers of 1898, the May Fourth generation seems more totalistic in its rejection of Chinese traditions. Many wanted a total overthrow of Confucius and sons, preferring to seek solutions to China's problems from the West. Lu Hsün ridiculed Ah-Q, Ch'en Tu-hsiu wrote of Mr. Democracy and Mr. Science, and Ibsen's plays fired people's imaginations about the heroic individual. In a general way this dichotomy has some validity. But the particular individuals analyzed in this study, who clung to New Culture viewpoints in the illiberal 1920s and 1930s, shared much in common with Liang Ch'i-ch'ao.[7]

Liang wanted change within the system, was generally averse to violence, and advocated a blend of old and new values. But, most important, he stressed the need for new citizens, articulating a vision of comprehensive intellectual reform which played so large a part in the thinking of New Culture liberals. Liang's new citizens would have a spirit of individualism and initiative, moral and physical courage, and a sense of civic responsibility. They would provide the foundation for representative government. Liang very strongly stood for liberating Chinese minds from the conventions of the past, opening them to ideas from everywhere. Like many of his contemporaries he felt Western strength was rooted in its assertive individuals, freedom of thought, and representative institutions. And he thought these were necessary for China to become strong. Like the New Culture liberals, he advocated a qualified form of individualism as a means toward the goal of national strength. Also, like them he placed high hopes on the value of education as a vehicle of social reform.

New Culture values were most clearly articulated in the early years of the May Fourth period, from about 1915 to 1919. During the years preceding the May Fourth incident a considerable degree of consensus existed among Chinese intellectuals regarding the proper approach to China's problems. There was widespread agreement that China's malady was so intertwined in the very fabric of the society that the most thoroughgoing cultural upheaval was necessary. In essence China needed its own renaissance, in which a spirit of assertiveness, rationalism, and individualism would replace the stultifying imprint of Confucian passivity, superstition, and groupism. The commitment to individualism was certainly a qualified one, and a big dose of Confucian paternalism lingered in the New Culture perspective (as will be discussed in chapter two), but still the orientation was toward radical cultural change. Moreover, New Culture advocates believed cultural reform so vital that they assigned it priority over political, social, and economic reform. A solid cultural foundation had to be laid before enduring political changes could occur. The failure of the revolution of 1911 had, it was argued, proved the futility of attempting political reform without the requisite cultural foundation.

New Culture advocates, thus, vowed to refrain from politics and to devote themselves to education and cultural activities. Or to put it another way, as Jerome Grieder has suggested, they endeavored to introduce a new, more limited definition of politics to the Chinese scene.[8] Traditionally, politics and culture had comprised a unified whole, usually labeled the Confucian polity. The cultural orthodoxy was defined by the state, and mastery of its fine points was the smoothest path to success for an aspiring official. Although the Confucian polity was not monolithic, since various schools of thought were tolerated, the boundaries of legitimate diversity were carefully drawn. Variations on the conventional theme were acceptable, but no questioning of fundamental principles was permitted. The Confucian polity was a pervasive presence which shaped the thinking and behavior of all Chinese, from aspiring degree candidates to peasants, by providing a code of proper behavior. Those who deviated from accepted ways were considered rebels. There was no place within the unified Confucian polity for anyone who wished to carve out an independent role as detached critic. In Confucian China the concept of a loyal opposition involved a contradiction in terms. One was either part of the polity or a rebel.

The New Culture ambition was to divide the Confucian polity into the two independent, though interrelated, components of politics and culture. Politics would encompass a narrowly defined range of purely governmental activities. Culture, then, would have an independent identity, with its sphere of activities unrestricted by any governmental orthodoxy. Individuals might safely remain outside government, acting as educators and independent critics to influence cultural values and ultimately influence politics. Thus it would be possible to work from the outside and still be a respectable citizen and not a rebel.

The Dilemmas for New Culture Liberals

The very fact that they felt their basic principles to be a product of rational analysis created some severe challenges to the integrity of New Culture liberals. Because their reform program seemed scientific, liberals were reluctant to abandon it merely because conditions made it temporarily inapplicable. Nor could they join the more activist political reform movements of the times without compromising their intellectual honesty. The combination of inapplicable circumstances and the desire for intellectual consistency created, during the 1920s and 1930s, some agonizing dilemmas for those who held liberal views.

Ironically, New Culture liberals laid the groundwork for their own later difficulties. During the early years of the May Fourth movement (ca. 1915-1919) the New Culture star was ascendant. The New Youth was widely read, Peking University was a beacon of light, and most intellectuals accepted New Culture premises regarding appropriate solutions to China's problems. During this time of relative consensus much was accomplished in bringing Confucian values under scrutiny and in fostering some of the more modern, Westernized attitudes considered so essential. However, the new atmosphere, for which the liberals were largely responsible, sparked the May Fourth incident which proved to be an unhappy watershed. Subsequently, liberals found themselves defending their principles against increasingly strident attacks. The reason was that the apparent success of the incident seemed the product of what most participants, especially students, termed political activities. This conclusion posed a challenge to the liberal scheme of priorities. which subordinated political activism to cultural reform. Indeed, New Culture liberals especially hoped that students would eschew political activities in favor of more cultural and intellectual endeavors. Thenceforth, however, students were less receptive to the liberal vision of reform, preferring speedier, more activist, political alternatives. Adult intellectuals, too, were turning to more comprehensive political programs for change, with Ch'en Tu-hsiu and Li Ta-chao the most noteworthy apostates from the liberal cause.

The liberal commitment to political detachment was also severely tested by the policies of warlord governments in the 1920s. A program of education and intellectual regeneration required a favorable atmosphere for implementation. Yet the warlords curtailed intellectual freedom and crippled education by withholding funds. These circumstances prompted teacher strikes, to recover salaries several months in arrears, and political involvement to the extent of circulating petitions and engaging in political advocacy. On 1 August 1920, several intellectuals issued a "Manifesto of the Struggle for Freedom," which criticized police oppression and urged an atmosphere of free expression. In May, 1922, Ts'ai Yuan-p'ei's name headed a list of signatories to a public statement entitled "Our Political Proposals."

Drafted by Hu Shih and signed by sixteen intellectuals, the statement basically called for a more honest and efficient government. In September, 1922, three of the signatories became members of the cabinet, with the formation of what was optimistically termed the Good Men Government. But, within two months the cabinet was in disarray; and in October, 1923, Ts'ao K'un bribed his way to the presidency in an open display of the powers of corruption. For many this was conclusive proof of the bankruptcy of the liberal posture. Standing aloof from the practical tasks of political organization and relying on the persuasive power of rational argument seemed irrelevant and even irresponsible. Yet liberals viewed the situation in a different light. While others were calling for more political activism, liberals were concerned with having compromised their principles by the limited steps which they had taken. After all, if political activity was justified under certain conditions, what was left of the liberal conviction that intellectual changes must precede political reform?

The 1920s also witnessed the development of a labor movement and growing antiforeign sentiment. Both required a response from the liberals. On 7 February 1923 Wu P'ei-fu forcibly ended the strike of the Peking-Hankow railroad workers, leaving thirty-five dead and many wounded. Students, the Communists, and Sun Yat-sen protested this action by the Peking government. Then and later the pressure was on the liberals to take a stand, as other groups had, with reference to the labor movement. This placed them in an uncomfortable position. The whole idea of class struggle offended the lingering Confucian sensibilities of many liberals. Their hope was to harmonize class differences and instill a sense of community in all China's citizens. Moreover, the labor movement seemed to mean an inevitable resort to extreme measures and violence, and few liberals had the stomach for this kind of direct confrontation. Finally, while liberals certainly desired better conditions for workers, their attitude toward popular movements was always an ambivalent one. The heritage of Confucian paternalism, previously mentioned in relation to liberal advocacy of individualism, also was an important force whenever reference was made to the people. Theoretically, liberals were interested in reaching the people and even "drawing near the people."[9] But the more the liberals learned about the lives of the masses, the more they were appalled by their backwardness and ignorance. As a result liberals were somewhat reluctant to associate with the people, much less empathize with them to the extent that Mao Tse-tung was to do. As with Chinese society in general, the condition of the people or the workers could only be improved by fundamental changes in outlooks and attitudes. Such attitudinal changes must precede economic improvements or the latter would only be ephemeral. Consequently, labor organizations and demonstrations seemed premature to most liberals. They preferred to stress worker education and moral uplift.

Related to and reinforcing the labor movement was the growing antiforeign sentiment. Sparked by the May Fourth incident, it flared into the May 30 Incident of 1925 and the Great Canton and Hong Kong strike which lasted from June, 1925 to September, 1926. In these times of very heated emotions many liberals found themselves caught on the horns of a dilemma. Certainly their sense of nationalism was outraged by the privileges enjoyed by foreigners in China; and they too were enraged by the events of May 30. Yet marching in demonstrations and using passionate rhetoric were generally not their style. Moreover, the expression of extreme antiforeignism conflicted with liberal cosmopolitanism and openness to all ideas regardless of their place of origin. Finally, as always, questions of this sort were judged as premature and pointless according to liberal guidelines on reform. Labor organizations and the expulsion of foreigners might provide fleeting emotional gratifications, but they also diverted limited energies from the more important task of cultural reform. So liberals generally persisted in their belief that no political or social change could endure unless the cultural foundation was solidly grounded, and mostly they contented themselves with perfunctory statements of sympathy with prevailing antiforeign emotions.

In general, then, liberals tried to remain detached from the political and social battles of the 1920s, preferring to work for more long-term reforms. This stance inevitably provoked criticism from many sides, and by 1927 there was no longer any way to avoid the necessity of choice. On 12 April 1927, Chiang Kai-shek implemented his purge of the Chinese Communist party in Shanghai. Liberals had to respond to his action, compelled to choose between the Communists and the Nationalists. The option of aloof neutrality was no longer available to them. Most liberals found Communism anathema because of its dogmatism, economic determinism, emphasis on class conflict, and sanctioning of violence. This fact, plus their hope that the Kuomintang could end internal chaos, served to mute liberal criticism of Chiang's repressive policies against the Communist party. In the final analysis, all were fervent patriots and most sided with Chiang in hopes that he might bring strength and stability to China.

From the beginning of the Nationalist period liberals found the principle of intellectual freedom even more threatened than it had been under the warlords. The Nationalists were more concerned with propaganda and indoctrination than with the objective consideration of ideas. They looked upon education as a tool for inculcating loyalty rather than a process of encouraging inquiry. They narrowed the scope of academic freedom and clamped down on critics of the government. These policies, directly challenging one of the basic tenets of liberalism, aroused vigorous opposition. Liberals created periodicals as outlets for their criticism, and in 1932 the Chinese League for the Protection of Civil Rights was founded. However, as usual, liberals confined themselves to intellectual protest, choosing to be critics rather than politicians.

This distaste for politics was one of the most distinctive features of the ideology of New Culture liberals. Some had been influenced by anarchism in the early part of the twentieth century, and they believed that governments were at the root of most problems. The early anarchist association, the Society for the Promotion of Morality (Chin-te hui), founded in 1912 by Wu Chih-hui, Li Shih-tseng, and Wang Ching-wei, pledged its members to refuse political office. Some found the corruption of politics and the indignities of political maneuvering too degrading. For those who wanted to serve the nation, yet were too fastidious for politics, it was certainly reassuring to believe that intellectual and cultural changes transcended political and economic reforms. Thus, with ideological rationales and ego-fulfilling rationalizations both supporting the same conclusion, liberals rarely ventured farther than social commentary if they were inclined toward political involvement at all. Throughout the period under study liberals addressed themselves, in print, to the main intellectual and social issues of the times.[10] In diverse journals, many founded by liberals, debates flourished over language reform, the new literature, old versus new values, problems versus isms, the role of the family, the emancipation of women, the goal of education, science versus metaphysics, the scientific method, and the place of religion in a modern society. On occasion more political topics were treated, such as the proper balance between government control and individual freedom or which political ideology most suited China. But generally political debates were of a highly abstract and theoretical nature.

Confining themselves to Confucian-like remonstration, and disdaining to mobilize political pressure, the liberals had little success in modifying Kuomintang policies on political dissent and academic freedom. Nor were they, or Western Christian liberals (or gradualists), able to stimulate the KMT toward more dynamic policies of rural reconstruction. Again, liberals, both Chinese and Western, were caught on the horns of a dilemma. They had a genuine sympathy for the plight of China's rural masses, but their ideological vision was too narrow to encompass plausible solutions. The steps required for rural reform--such as the reduction of taxes, rents, and interest rates and ultimately the redistribution of land--seemed too radical to most liberals. An illness requiring revolutionary medicine was beyond the capabilities of the liberal medicine chest. Some intellectuals, like James Yen and T'ao Hsing-chih, went directly to the villages to help provide solutions. But for that very reason both Yen and T'ao fall outside the boundaries of this study. Their activist programs distinguished them from the New Culture liberals, who preferred to stay in the cities and retain their detached perspective.

Moreover, events of the 1930s made many liberals less inclined to question KMT policies, and some even became defensive about the sacred principles of gradualism and education. The cause of self-doubt, and the true touchstone of liberal convictions, was Japanese aggression. Beginning with the Mukden Incident of 1931 and broadening into the movement for an autonomous north China (which prompted the 9 December 1935 demonstrations) Japanese pressure ultimately led to all-out war in July, 1937. Liberals, fervently nationalistic as anyone else, began to question the appropriateness of seeking a gradual, cultural renaissance in the midst of an enemy invasion. Such policies, and even the emphasis on liberal education, seemed to have contributed toward producing a nation vulnerable to Japanese attacks. Perhaps, some thought, KMT educational programs (especially those sponsored by Ch'en Kuo-fu) were right after all. These, in addition to promoting patriotism, were designed to emphasize practical knowledge such as agriculture, engineering, and medicine. The liberal arts and law, as "useless" subjects, were downgraded. Such educational theories struck directly at the fundamental liberal assumption that education was to develop certain habits of mind and lay the foundation for more practical reforms. Yet, in a time of crisis, liberals were forced to choose between conflicting liberal and nationalistic impulses, and many opted for the latter.

Similar arguments impelled liberals to reexamine their beliefs regarding political dissent and civil rights. During the early years of the Nationalist period liberals were the severest critics of government restrictions on discussion and individual freedoms. But conditions of the 1930s seemed to place more of a premium on national unity. As a result, this period saw frequent debates over whether dictatorship or democracy was the best means of producing a strong China. Many liberals began to agree with the KMT that a centralized, and even autocratic, government was justified under the circumstances. Some, notably Hu Shih, resisted this kind of thinking and steadfastly defended democracy.[11] Others tried to hide from the dilemma, burying themselves in their scholarly pursuits. Once again, however, the tempting option of detachment was soon denied to liberals. Increasing Japanese penetration of China compelled a decision from among three unattractive choices: remaining in occupied territory and accepting the humiliation of obeying Japanese commands, joining the Communists in the northwest, or following Chiang's government as it retreated from Nanking to Wuhan and ultimately to Chungking. By this time most had come to an accommodation with the government, as the only hope for resisting Japan. But the decision involved ideological compromises embarrassing to liberals.

2.

Ts'ai Yuan-p'ei, 1898–1919: The Making of a New Culture Liberal

Ts'ai Yuan-p'ei's career effectively illustrates the complex process by which individuals move from questions, to assumptions, to convictions. This chapter seeks to clarify the basic concerns of Ts'ai Yuan-p'ei, to ascertain his definitions of China's needs and problems, and to understand and assess his solutions and their implementation. It focuses on the period from 1898 to 1919 when all the diverse strands of traditional Chinese culture were subjected to their severest challenge. This was a time of continuous political change, including a revolution, two attempts at restoring the monarchy, and the divisive atmosphere of the warlords. But perhaps of greater significance, it was also a time of intellectual inquiry and debate. Defeat in the Sino-Japanese War, failure of the Hundred Days Reform, and the final tragedy of the Boxers convinced all but the most conservative that Chinese civilization was morally, socially, politically, and militarily bankrupt. These twenty years, then, saw Chinese intellectuals scrutinize their own traditions and eagerly absorb knowledge of Western cultures. For all, the basic concern was finding a means to reform and modernize China. The intellectual dialogue was rarely profound, but it was always earnest. The plight of China disturbed everyone. During this period China was an intellectual arena in which the most disparate viewpoints waged battle.

From 1898 Ts'ai was an active participant in the process. He associated with and admired both "reformers" and "revolutionaries." However, as his ideas took shape they

---

A portion of this chapter appeared in an earlier form in "Ts'ai Yuan-p'ei from Confucian Scholar to Chancellor of Peking University, 1898-1923," Asian Forum 2, no. 3 (July-September 1970). Reprinted by permission of Asian Forum.

tended to conform to the gradualist approach, and he remained a New Culture liberal even when it was unfashionable to be one. His devotion to a reformed China existed from the beginning, but only time allowed definition of the kind of reform needed and the means to achieve it. On his deathbed, Ts'ai's last words were: "Science can save the nation, aesthetics can save the nation."[1] Most appropriately, then, his very last words were "save the nation." This end obsessed everyone. But the means were open to question. The final expression of Ts'ai's ideas was a product of his broad background which embraced both Chinese and Western learning.

Fundamental to Ts'ai's evolving system of thought was his childhood in Shaohsing.[2] He pursued the orthodox program of Confucian education, memorizing the classics and writing eight-legged essays. Greatly impressed by the neo-Confucian emphasis on self-examination, he took as his model Liu Tsung-chou, a Shaohsing neo-Confucian official who starved himself to death rather than serve the new Manchu masters whom he considered unworthy.[3] From youth, Confucian attitudes molded Ts'ai's character, and his life exemplified the ideal Confucian pattern. Frequently compared with the duke of Chou, Ts'ai was said to possess the perfect Confucian spirit--gentle, upright, courteous, temperate, and yielding (wen, liang, kung, chien, jang).[4] Numerous witnesses have testified to his complete dedication to his work.[5] Except for an extensive library, his material possessions were extremely scant. In a time of widespread corruption, Ts'ai's estate was so limited that, following his death, financial help from friends and former students was required to educate his children. He was, by all accounts, most accommodating toward others and rarely rejected a request for a letter of reference or preface to a book.[6] In fact, in 1935, he became so overwhelmed that he was forced to call a halt to such activities. Pleading advancing age, he terminated his affiliations with some twenty-five boards of trustees, announced he would accept no further writing assignments (until he had cleared his backlog), and declared he would write no more letters of reference (since, in many instances, numerous applicants for the same job held letters from him, thus completely canceling all his efforts).[7]

While seriously dedicating himself to the hsiu-shen (self-cultivation) aspect of Confucianism, Ts'ai did not neglect the complementary p'ing t'ien-hsia (order the world) obligation. Despite an interest in scholarship, his attention rarely wandered from its central focus on solving China's practical problems.[8] Despite the political atmosphere and the frustrations of working for reform amidst corruption, Ts'ai seemingly never accepted defeat. Like a censor, he fearlessly maintained his own version of the truth regardless of personal consequences. He was fond of citing the ancient lines: "When the weather is stormy, the fowls do not stop their cry" (Feng yü ju hui, ch'i min pu i). That is, even in bad times, good men have the courage to speak out. However, Ts'ai's fighting spirit was tempered by the moderate's ability to compromise.[9] He often remarked that the main strength of Confucianism was its eclectic nature, its facility for blending divisive elements into a harmonious whole. Throughout his career Ts'ai demonstrated the same ability to strike the proper balance between contending positions. He seemed temperamentally inclined toward compromise. On most issues, such as Western versus Chinese traditions, wen-yen versus pai-hua, and individualism versus public welfare, he adopted the moderate stance of compromise.

Needless to say, Ts'ai was not without human foibles. He had, for example, cultivated a taste for Shaohsing wine and insisted on having it served with his afternoon and evening meals.[10] He was also an uncommonly poor orator, speaking in an uninspiring monotone and a Shaohsing accent.[11] Finally, his self-contained manner often verged on aloofness, and despite efforts to appear friendly he apparently had little knack for putting people at their ease.[12]

Ts'ai's Confucian background enabled him to make rapid progress within the traditional bureaucratic structure.[13] He passed the examinations at an unusually early age and quickly established a place for himself within the official world. But his success came at a time of increasing challenge to the orthodox system. The events of the 1890s, especially the Sino-Japanese War, disturbed Ts'ai and prompted him to begin reading translations of Western works. The reform attempt of 1898 evoked his support and sympathy; its failure taught him two lessons.[14] He recognized the futility of working for reform within the Manchu government, and he realized that permanent reform required the understanding of an educated citizenry. Consistent with these beliefs he resigned his official position and returned to Shaohsing. At this time his ideas were still in the formative stage. He vaguely knew the Manchus had to be removed and China had to undergo reform. He had no positive plans for either, except a commitment to broaden China's educational base. Ts'ai's overall approach was still very paternalistic. He thought in terms of creating an atmosphere, through widespread education, more receptive to changes initiated by the qualified few. The masses were to give some undefined support to the changes, but Ts'ai had no immediate intention of instituting a democracy in which the masses participated in the selection of new policies. Ts'ai's views, then, conformed closely to the Confucian ideal of government, whereby an elite ruled but only with the implicit approval of the masses. Moreover, he had no clear idea of exactly what changes should be worked in Chinese society. He had only an awareness of China's weakness and a willingness to investigate Western learning for possible solutions.

At Shaohsing, Ts'ai became supervisor of a school which placed considerable emphasis on Western learning.[15] During the early years of the twentieth century he continued an active role within progressive educational circles.[16] Wherever he taught he attempted to provide a Western orientation to the curriculum, emphasizing independent thinking and lecturing on Western history. These years also saw him involved in revolutionary affairs.[17] He associated with prominent revolutionary figures, was a founder of the Restoration Society, and became a member of the T'ung-meng hui. Ts-ai's journalistic endeavors also were progressive, and he was active on the Su-pao and the Warning Bell News.[18] However, his attitude was more reformist than revolutionary. He advocated the removal of the Manchus because they were a conservative force blocking reform, not as an act of racial vengeance.[19] He also was inclined to see reform as a gradual process of educating and reorientating the viewpoints of society. But he had no precisely formulated schedule of reform in mind. Like so many others, Ts'ai recognized China's obvious weaknesses, but he was still searching for the appropriate direction of reform.

At this time Ts'ai began looking for a way to study in the West. Finally, in 1907, at the age of thirty-nine, he began a four-year stay in Germany.[20] First in Berlin and later at the University of Leipzig Ts'ai pursued a diversified curriculum, including literature, philosophy, comparative history, anthropology, experimental psychology, and aesthetics. In addition, he translated Friedrich Paulsen's Principles of Ethics, produced five textbooks on ethics, and wrote The History of Chinese Ethics. Ts'ai has left no specific comments on his impressions of Europe; however, its influence was undeniably great. As one fleeting indication: on receiving a letter saying his third son had just been born, Ts'ai wrote back directing that he be named Po-lin (Berlin).

In his studies, Ts'ai emphasized anthropology and experimental psychology. He became convinced that man's behavior, both historically and in the present, could be understood by the application of scientific research techniques. From anthropological studies he concluded that social mores, including those connected with religion, had clearly discernible secular origins. Whatever proved practical was gradually accepted by society as morally good, and would soon be strengthened by religious sanctions. Psychological experiments convinced him that human behavior, like that of animals, was largely related to habitual conditioning. Certain stimuli produced predictable responses, and repeated exposure to these stimuli made the established response habitual. In practical terms, what this meant for Ts'ai was that social reform depended upon improving the environment in which people matured and formed their basic attitudes.

His studies and experiences exposed him to two prevailing European strains of thought. First, he encountered the traditional European viewpoints of rationalism and liberalism. He was convinced of the value of rational analysis and the efficacy of the scientific method. All practical problems seemed amenable to reason, and material progress was assured if men could abide by the rule of reason. He also became committed to the environmentalist view that social reform was possible if positive improvements could be worked in the social environment. Human behavior was seen as a product of the conditioning received during the process of maturation. Changes in man's environment would produce predictable changes in man's attitudes. Social reform, then, depended on the long-term effects of environmental reform. The second influential European strain of thought was Neo-Kantianism or neo-idealism, prevalent in the early twentieth century as a reaction against nineteenth century materialism.[21] Neo-Kantianism stressed the Kantian division of the universe into two realms of reality. The phenomenal world was composed of the "phenomena" which one perceived with his senses. However, a deeper, truer reality resided within the noumenal realm, beyond the reach of man's experience. In the twentieth-century context, adherents recognized the validity of science and reason to advance man's knowledge of the phenomenal world. However, they postulated that the most meaningful truths lay within the noumenal world, and progress in this area depended on suprarational techniques associated with the inner resources of the spirit.

Ts'ai found both currents of European thought convincing. He became a consistent advocate of rationalism, urging open-minded analysis of all viewpoints. He pursued this ideal in his own writings, while minister of education, and as chancellor of Peking University. Environmentalist assumptions, which meshed so nicely with certain basic Confucian attitudes, formed the foundation of the reform philosophy which he gradually evolved. The Neo-Kantian noumenal sphere remained an ultimate goal for Ts'ai, although he carefully remembered China's more immediate needs. As with all things, he searched for the proper blend, trying to fit the various separate philosophical strands into a coherent whole.

During his stay in Germany, Ts'ai completed his first major work of scholarship, entitled The History of Chinese Ethics.[22] Careful reading of it reveals Ts'ai's ideas beginning to take shape. One can see the meshing of two outlooks, Chinese and Western, into a coherent whole. The overall tone is one of objective analysis. Nothing in Chinese history was treated as sacred, and all was subjected to critical scrutiny. Classical thinkers were criticized for logical flaws in argument, and they were praised for urging new approaches to new problems. The study, then, was characterized by a basic open-mindedness. So-called truths were to be carefully studied, using the scientific approach. Those withstanding the test of reason were acceptable; the others could be legitimately dismissed. However, despite this iconoclastic attitude, Ts'ai praised certain aspects of Confucianism. He had great respect for its moderation and flexibility, which allowed the eclecticism necessary for survival. He was especially appreciative of Confucian techniques of social control. Rejecting the harsh coercion of Legalism, it utilized moral persuasion which moved people to regulate themselves. The elite, too, was swayed by similar techniques, and an obligation to public service became part of its accepted code of behavior.

By the time Ts'ai's stay in Germany came to a close his ideas had progressed noticeably. He had formed a clear view of the mechanics of social development, and the view seemed based on valid, scientific, evidence. He had developed an orderly schedule of the priorities of reform. Since environmental changes were of preeminent importance, all energies should be concentrated on patiently remaking the fundamental components of Chinese society. However, the exact substance of the new environment was still open to debate. Its creation, according to Ts'ai, should be a product of the critical assessment of Chinese and Western traditions. To Ts'ai's mind, many Confucian values were worth retention but he was eager to subject his views, and all others, to the process of natural selection. The strongest ideas would survive the challenge of rational appraisal. Ts'ai's faith in the scientific approach was characteristic of virtually all the intellectuals of this period, both Chinese and Western.[23] However, always wary of dogmatism, Ts'ai limited his scientific attitude by a parallel commitment to Neo-Kantianism. He recognized that his plans for social reform were only valid with respect to the phenomenal world. The higher noumenal point of view always remained an ideal objective.

One shouldn't form the mistaken conclusion that Ts'ai arrived in Germany with a tabula rasa and returned with a fully developed philosophy of reform. He left China with a background within the Confucian bureaucracy and a deep, though critical, commitment to many Confucian values. He also had formulated a preliminary approach to reform which rested upon faith in the benefits of education. Not surprisingly, the Western ideas Ts'ai found most attractive were those which blended smoothly with the basic viewpoints of his earlier background. The environmental interpretation of reform is not very different from the Neo-Confucian orientation in which Ts'ai matured. The entire Confucian structure rested on the assumption that human nature was naturally good, and man was therefore perfectible. Proper moral cultivation and proper training could produce a good man, even a sage. A fundamental technique of Confucian government was to influence the environment which conditioned everyone, channeling thoughts along morally and socially acceptable paths. A good society, then, was the product of good men; and good men resulted from proper education and proper guidance. Similarly, the Neo-Kantian hypothesis of a higher reality reminds one of such transcendent Confucian concepts as the Tao and the T'ai-chi. Familiar with Neo-Confucian cosmology, and with its Buddhist influences, Ts'ai was receptive to ideas of an ultimate reality beyond that immediately subject to man's perceptions. It is a natural human response to identify new impressions with concepts which are familiar. Faced with a deluge of new ideas, Ts'ai gravitated toward those which tended to support the general assumptions he already held valid.

It is not true, however, that Ts'ai learned nothing new in Germany and that his entire attitude was just traditionalism with a new vocabulary. Certainly he continued to respect specific Confucian virtues, but he did so because he deemed them useful for the reform of China--not because they were Confucian or because they advanced one toward sagehood. The all-embracing Confucian framework, with its unity of morality and politics, no longer retained validity. He freely distinguished between various Confucian elements, denying the traditional assumptions about their integral relation to the Tao. Moreover, while continuing to believe that a better environment would produce better men, and ultimately a better society, Ts'ai felt free to draw upon Western and Chinese ideas to form the components of the environment. With a deep faith in the potential of reason, Ts'ai wanted to analyze all plans and programs, regardless of their sources, which might bring reform to China. His precise vision of reform was no clearer than somehow correcting the many obvious indications of Chinese backwardness and weakness. The reform philosophy which Ts'ai gradually evolved managed to synthesize competing intellectual loyalties which were products of his experiences in two cultures. For Confucians, men might be reformed by exposure to the classics and to superior men imbued with the proper virtues. For Westerners, reform would come if the proper rational, or natural, environment could be provided. Ts'ai accepted the premise that man was a product of his environment, and he critically examined both Chinese and Western ideas in order to formulate the best environment.

In 1911, Ts'ai returned to China to become minister of education, with a chance to implement some of the ideas he had developed.[24] His immediate concern was to shift the spirit of Chinese education toward republican objectives. He updated textbooks to eliminate references to the emperor, introduced coeducation, and broadened the program of adult education. His basic philosophy was fully revealed in the five-theme curriculum of military, utilitarian, ethical, world-view, and aesthetic education. The practical requisites of modern society were recognized within the sphere of military and utilitarian education. Ts'ai wrote knowingly of China's need to become militarily strong and industrially developed. But, of greater importance were the spiritual and intellectal requisites. Ts'ai was attempting to provide China with a new atmosphere through the educational process. Ethical education was essential to instill the proper moral qualities. World-view and aesthetic education were designed to broaden and refine Chinese perspectives. The ultimate goal was the noumenal realm, but Ts'ai's immediate concern was moral and spiritual uplift. His mission was almost evangelical. He wanted to evoke new attitudes of altruism and self-sacrifice among all citizens. Again, one can see a mixture of Western and Chinese viewpoints within Ts'ai's reform framework. He was Western in assigning education a significant role in developing China's military and industrial capacity. Education was no longer viewed solely as a search for self-cultivation, sagehood, and the Tao. But traditional moral and ethical concerns still retained crucial, in fact primary, importance. Chinese reform was dependent upon the creation of a solid environmental base. But the environment was to be composed of Confucian moral values as well as new Western viewpoints.

In 1912, Ts'ai resigned his post as minister of education in protest against Yuan Shih-k'ai's dictatorial policies. He spent the next four years in Europe, mostly in France.[25] There he became involved in the work-study program which enabled numerous Chinese to live and study inexpensively in France.[26] The work-study concept was quite foreign to traditional Chinese attitudes regarding student life, but Ts'ai saw nothing wrong with students working part-time. During this period he also composed a number of ethics textbooks for Chinese workers in France.[27] These reveal Ts'ai's desire to expose the average Chinese to Western history and ideas. But their chief concern was clearly to instill a spirit of responsibility and group orientation. As with so many other Chinese, perhaps beginning with Yen Fu, Ts'ai was trying to work a compromise between conflicting Western and Chinese attitudes toward individualism. Ts'ai struggled continually with his desire to stimulate individual initiative and yet orient the newly awakened individual toward social consciousness. Sometimes he evaded the issue by urging both viewpoints, but more often he leaned heavily toward the side of group responsibility as one of the primary components of a new social environment. He urged individual subordination to the group, then, not because of yearnings for old traditions, but rather because of aspirations for a new society.

In 1917 Ts'ai began his tenure as chancellor of Peking University (Peita). He saw his main task to be eliminating the sterile moral and intellectual atmosphere.[28] He tended to apply at Peita the same reform approach he wished to see implemented throughout all of Chinese society. That is, highest priority was assigned to changing the moral, spiritual, and intellectual environment. Changes in attitudes were all-important. Ts'ai tried to impart a sense of challenge to staff and students, stimulating them with calls for both self-development and service. The Association for the Advancement of Morality was formed, emphasizing the virtues of self-discipline and self-examination.[29] Ts'ai sought to instill a critical approach to learning, urging students to analyze Chinese and Western traditions in search of their basic strengths and weaknesses. He encouraged the broadest spectrum of opinions, sponsoring a climate of intellectual controversy.[30] All viewpoints were expected to contend, the resulting interaction producing a survival of the fittest. In human affairs Ts'ai favored mutual assistance, but in the realm of ideas he felt competition the best policy. Ts'ai succeeded in creating an exciting atmosphere of concerned inquiry among faculty and students. Peita became the focal point for commitment and optimism regarding China's problems. All China's fundamental beliefs were subject to criticism. Weakness and backwardness were no longer passively accepted. Rather, reasons were sought and new policies debated. A spirit of optimism pervaded Peita. All problems were looked upon as resolvable provided the right solutions were adopted. The crucial preoccupation was with finding the correct solutions.

Ts'ai's leadership was a major factor shaping these developments at Peita. His definitions of China's problems and his philosophy of reform came clearly into focus during his early years there. He treated China's political corruption, economic weakness, and social inequities as surface manifestations of a deeper malady. The real problem lay within the deepest recesses of the Chinese spirit. The total society had to undergo a spiritual regeneration, an intellectual renaissance, before political, economic, and social reform could be meaningful. However, it is apparent that the renewal process which Ts'ai envisioned was designed both to awaken certain traditional attitudes long dormant and to introduce new outlooks quite alien to Chinese tradition. The new environment Ts'ai sought was new in the sense that he hoped it would contain dynamic rather than passive attitudes toward problems; a critical, scientific, and open-minded approach to learning; and a controlled element of individualism and initiative. But it was not really new in the sense that he wished for a revitalization of such Confucian outlooks as self-examination, moral cultivation, and a missionary zeal for public service. This is why it is misleading to think of Ts'ai purely in terms of traditionalism and Westernism. He had loyalties to both but his fundamental loyalty was to the Chinese state. He clearly had made the transition in outlook from _t'ien-hsia_ to _kuo-chia_. China had to be changed so it could meet the diverse challenges of modern life, and Ts'ai measured all ideas, whether Chinese or Western, against this standard. He was not specifically looking for a face-saving synthesis, but as he developed his general program of reform, with a strong China as his goal, the final composite naturally included elements from both cultures.

The May Fourth incident provided a fair test of the strength of Ts'ai's convictions. In the atmosphere of political activism gripping the country, it took a courageous man to voice a contrary opinion. But Ts'ai steadfastly rejected political activism, reasserting his own unfashionable view of the priorities of reform.[31] Political upheavals were futile unless preceded by fundamental moral and intellectual changes. Students had a special obligation to contribute to the creation of a new moral climate. Student protesters, then, while praised for their patriotism, were urged to direct their energies in more productive directions. China in its desperate condition could not afford the luxury of political movements. The roots of weakness were set deeply within Chinese society. The need was for further efforts along the lines of the New Culture movement, that is a program directed toward changing attitudes rather than politics. Ts'ai wanted China to go through the rejuvenation that Europe had experienced with its Renaissance.[32] Here he was careless in drawing historical parallels, but essentially what he wanted for China was a new spirit of life-assertion. A new dynamism would replace passivism, new vistas would widen the parochial Confucian viewpoint, and a new rationalism would characterize China's approach to practical problems. If China could just be allowed four decades of tranquility to work the transformation, it could then occupy an equal place among the world's nations.

Here, of course, was the flaw. It was naive to think that China might be granted forty years for quiet intellectual growth. Both domestic and international affairs were too volatile for that. Moreover, few might be expected to have the saintlike patience of Ts'ai, who was prepared to work selflessly for a distant goal beyond the horizon. The young, especially, are not noted for such patience, and many accepted Ts'ai's call to public service but followed their own interpretations of China's needs. For New Culture liberals the May Fourth incident was a watershed. The New Culture consensus collapsed, as more activist and political approaches to China's problems exerted their appeal. For those who maintained New Culture principles it meant some modification in their views as a new liberal posture emerged.

3.

Breakdown of the New Culture Consensus and Emergence of a New Liberal Posture

The May Fourth movement has recently undergone scholarly reassessment, calling into question how much of a watershed it was in modern Chinese history.[1] Studies have suggested that the May Fourth spirit was just an intensification of earlier trends, and that many issues addressed during the May Fourth period have not been resolved even today. Historians are, thus, legitimately asking how pivotal the May Fourth period was. It was, however, pivotal for New Culture liberalism. The May Fourth period, before the incident, produced a consensus which blurred differences of opinion among a most diverse group of individuals. For a short while a broad set of attitudes enjoyed overwhelming support within China's intellectual community. This was the time of New Youth, of Ts'ai Yuan-p'ei's Peking University, of Mr. Science and Mr. Democracy. There was widespread agreement that China needed a new cultural base, a renaissance (which seemed more like the Enlightenment) which would produce a body of rational and progressive citizens. John Dewey's pragmatism was in vogue and Dewey himself arrived just before the May Fourth incident. Intellectuals had faith that rational solutions could be found for China's problems. Education and culture were considered more important than politics as the road to China's salvation. When Hu Shih vowed not to talk politics for twenty years, many people agreed with him.

This consensus collapsed with the May Fourth incident, and even earlier there were signs of divisions. In the fall of 1918 Ch'en Tu-hsiu (founder of New Youth and later one of the founders of the Chinese Communist party), Li Ta-chao (librarian at Peita and another founder of the Chinese Communist party), Kao I-han (political scientist), and Chang Wei-tz'u (political scientist) reached the conclusion that the New Youth was neglecting important political topics. While Hu Shih was in Anhwei for the funeral of his mother they established the Weekly Critic (Mei-chou p'ing-lun) as a forum for the discussion of politics.[2] Hu Shih opposed this development, and at first he contributed only a few poems and translations of short stories to the new journal. However, when Ch'en Tu-hsiu was arrested for distributing handbills, in June, 1919, Hu reluctantly agreed to act as editor. It was then, in the 20 July 1919 issue, that he published "More Study of Problems, Less Talk of Isms." Here he criticized those who were ideologically inclined and who sought a comprehensive panacea for China's problems. He urged the conventional New Culture approach of applying the rational method to specific problems one at a time. Li Ta-chao and others disputed Hu, arguing that some problems were interrelated and required a comprehensive ideological approach. This exchange foreshadowed the split that was soon to become explicit between New Culture liberals and those opting for more activist and political solutions to China's problems.

Temporarily these divisions were papered over. In the fall of 1919, after Ch'en Tu-hsiu's release from prison, unity was seemingly restored.[3] The December issue of New Youth contained a statement, signed by Ch'en, Li Ta-Chao, Hu Shih, et al., reaffirming the New Youth's commitment to the cultural path to reform. However, that winter of 1919-1920 Ch'en moved the journal to Shanghai and began shifting it to the Marxist viewpoint. In December, 1920, invited by Ch'en Chiung-ming to serve as head of the education department in Kwangtung province, he moved again to Canton where his shift to Marxism was completed. The final break between Ch'en and Hu came in the winter of 1920-1921, with an unfriendly exchange of letters over the proper stance of New Youth.

Similar disagreements regarding the propriety of political involvement were occurring within the Young China Association.[4] The Young China Association was founded in June, 1918, by Tseng Ch'i and others. Initially it reflected the conventional New Culture orientation of the times. It had a highly nationalistic fervor, but its emphasis lay with abolishing old customs and substituting modern values. By 1919 strains were developing within the membership over the nonpolitical versus the political approach to creating "Young China." These intensified in 1921 and Li Ta-chao, then a member, urged that the association adopt Marxism as its philosophy, while Tso Shun-sheng defended the conventional New Culture emphasis on cultural change. No reconciliation could be reached, and Li Ta-chao and his followers left to join the Chinese Communist party. Tseng Ch'i and Tso Shun-sheng eventually established the Chinese Youth party, in December, 1923, because of their fear that Russian control of the Chinese

Communist party would undermine Chinese sovereignty. By the early 1920s, then, the pull toward political solutions and political parties engendered passionate conflicts, as the liberal consensus collapsed. Tso Shun-sheng recalled one argument at his house in Shanghai, where his friend Teng Chung-hsia departed with the words: "Well, Shun-sheng, we'll see you on the battlefield!"[5]

Those committed to the nonpolitical position were certainly not unresponsive to the conditions of the times. They were every bit as aware of and distressed by the corruption and repression of the warlords. Yet they sincerely believed that cultural reform was a necessary prerequisite to political reform. Gradually, they established a middle ground, sticking to the world of ideas and culture, but broadening the latter term to include consideration of political questions. Specifically, they began to issue political statements and write for political journals. On 1 August 1920, the Manifesto of the Struggle for Freedom was issued by a group of liberal intellectuals, including Hu Shih, Chiang Meng-lin, Kao I-han, Chang Wei-tz'u, and T'ao Meng-ho (Peita sociologist).[6] It advocated protection of basic civil liberties, honest elections, and tolerance of the constructive criticism necessary for a republican form of government. The manifesto thus implicitly recognized that cultural reform and political conditions were interrelated. A new liberal consensus was emerging, which acknowledged that vital cultural reforms required a receptive political climate. But exactly what liberals might do to help shape this political climate was still a subject of much debate.

In May, 1922, a number of liberals began publishing the Endeavor (Nu-li chou-pao). Over the next two years the pages of Endeavor reflected continuing discussions of this basic liberal dilemma: how far should those committed to cultural reform venture into the political arena? To a large extent the stance of the journal, and of its contributors, remained ambivalent. The first issue, 7 May 1922, reflected this fact. Page one contained a poem by Hu Shih, entitled "Song of Endeavor."[7] The gist was that he and his colleagues must make a big effort or the intolerable warlord conditions would go on interminably. But he was not explicit about what kind of effort he intended: that is, whether he meant continued public criticism, involvement in political parties, or taking up arms. And in the same issue there appeared an essay by him on The Dream of the Red Chamber. A letter to the editor (in issue no. 4) criticized Endeavor for including this article, and for not concentrating exclusively on political questions.[8] Hu replied that the journal was not solely concerned with politics. "In the past," he wrote, "we abstained from discussing political questions to build a solid cultural foundation. Now the times require discussion of political questions, but this does not mean we are abandoning our original advocacy of a new culture." China's basic illness was still rooted in its backward mentality, its superstitions, and its social customs.

What began to emerge from Endeavor was a new consensus, though now held by a smaller group of individuals, of the appropriate new posture for the New Culture liberals. Simply put, the new posture was that of detached, objective, and independent criticism. Distressed by political conditions, but still wedded to the nonpolitical or New Culture approach, a small group of intellectuals tried to prove that the pen was mightier than the sword. They issued manifestoes, wrote for prominent journals, and tried to influence political conditions while remaining detached from them.

The second issue of Endeavor (14 May 1922) contained a statement entitled "Our Political Proposals," with sixteen signatories including Ts'ai Yuan-p'ei, Hu Shih, T'ao Meng-ho, Chang Wei-tz'u, Kao I-han, and Ting Wen-chiang (geologist).[9] Thirteen of the sixteen were from Peking University. This statement basically called for a more honest and efficient government. It listed as China's priorities obtaining good men to participate in government and developing an aroused public opinion to watch for wrongdoing. Other basic concerns were a constitution, more publicity for governmental decisions, and more efficient central planning. Further specific needs included a reconciliation between the northern and southern factions, an effective civil service system with a general reduction in the number of bureaucrats, election reforms, and a balanced budget. The proposal was drafted by Hu Shih and he, in the pages of Endeavor, became the most omnipresent defender of the role of independent critic.

Hu nimbly responded to criticisms from both ends of the political spectrum.[10] Some criticized the liberals for not sticking to their earlier emphasis on cultural reform, reminding them that the revolution of 1911 had failed for lack of a solid foundation of new attitudes among the common people. Others approved the content of the "Proposal," but wished the signatories would go farther. Just calling for good men and relying on political statements was inadequate, they argued. If you merely relied on words, twenty years from now the objectives would still be unattained. Why not organize a National Political Reform Society or a Good Government party? In his replies Hu Shih stressed the importance of unity in a time of national crisis, rather than partisan divisiveness. He pointed out that even American and European political parties put aside partisan objectives in favor of national goals in wartime. No one should forget the divisive behavior of Chinese parties over the last ten years. At present the important task was to popularize the general goal of good government and encourage everyone to struggle against corruption and bad government. Now and in the near future they should occupy the position of mediators, fair men, judges, and supervisors. In the future when politics is on the right track, differences in specific political proposals will perhaps lead to political parties. But that was another question.

To elaborate further, Hu published two short articles in Endeavor (4 June 1922 and 18 June 1922).[11] He recognized that many people were wondering if a political commentator, without joining or organizing a party, could be effective. This was a valid concern, he said, with regard to political critics who were subservient to one party or another. But those critics who could remain above partisan viewpoints could make a valuable contribution. This was especially true if the number of independent critics was substantial, because they could help shape public opinion and bring public pressure to bear on politicians. Gradually a substantial independent electorate might grow, voting for one person or another according to their programs and abilities. This could have an important effect on political conditions.

With regard to those who wished Hu to devote his talents to culture, rather than political questions, he responded:

> As a student about one-third of my time was spent on politics. After studying abroad I returned to China and witnessed Chang Hsün's restoration attempt and the confusion in Chinese education. I realized that the restoration attempt was a natural thing given Chinese conditions. So I vowed not to talk politics for twenty years so as to devote myself to establishing a solid intellectual and cultural foundation for politics. For the next four years I wrote only about thought and culture. When Ch'en Tu-hsiu and Li Ta-chao established the Weekly Critic to discuss politics, I contributed only a short story. When I took over the editorship, after Ch'en's arrest, I felt that I had to talk politics because of conditions under the Anfu clique and because "new" intellectual groups didn't address themselves to concrete political questions. They just engaged in lofty talk about anarchism and Marxism. I couldn't bear this any longer because I am an experimentalist /or a pragmatist, shih-yen chu-i ti hsin-t'u/. So in the Weekly Critic I published my "More Study of Problems, Less Talk of

> Isms." But this was the "introduction" (tao-yen) to my ideas, and I haven't had the chance yet to write the "basic text" (pen-wen). The Weekly Critic closed 30 August 1919, and for the next two years and eight months I was either busy or sick. I couldn't take the time to write about politics or to help shape public opinion. I expected others to do that work. But after two years and eight months I'm distressed to see that "new" intellectual groups only talk of class struggle and Marxism. Political corruption and weakness in foreign affairs are issues which these "new" thinkers don't address. I can't bear it any longer and I must speak out about specific problems. But this is just putting into practice my earlier advice about "more study of problems." It's true that experimentalism is a kind of "ism." But it's only a method of analyzing problems. It's not a grandiose theory, but a means of solving one problem at a time. All my writings have been directed toward getting this attitude of rational analysis adopted in China. I haven't changed my goals or acted inconsistently. At the same time, I won't concentrate exclusively on politics. Philosophy is my profession and literature gives me pleasure. Politics is only a new effort because I cannot bear current conditions. But I only spend one day a week on Endeavor work, and if others who are interested in politics would write more I could devote even more time to philosophy and literature.[12]

Hu Shih was surely the most voluminous in expressing his views on these questions, but he was not alone. Others also tried to resolve the questions of how political to be and what contribution they should make to China. Opinions varied somewhat, reflecting the diversity of views within the liberal camp. Ch'en Heng-che (Sophia H. Chen Zen; Professor of History and first women professor at Peita), for example, contributed an article on Christianity in Europe to Endeavor, and she rejected criticism from those who felt the journal should restrict itself to political issues.[13] Originally, she wrote, Endeavor was modeled after the American periodical the New Republic. This meant taking politics as a central concern, but not excluding other types of articles. It had been thought that China's political corruption was an important source of trouble, but by no means the only source. Subsequently, because of the wishes of its readers, Endeavor had been devoting itself exclusively to politics, but this was not the original intent. Moreover, all "political" questions (such as the elimination of warlordism) were closely related to matters of education, thought, psychology, and so forth. No political problem could be dealt with in an intellectual vacuum.

Kao I-han, too, believed in the close relationship between political and cultural reforms.[14] He maintained that "Our Political Proposals" was not a departure from earlier principles, but rather it was a way of putting into practice what they had long preached. Cultural and educational endeavors would only flourish in a favorable political setting. He wasn't urging that everyone abandon education to involve themselves in politics, but if they wished to preserve their achievements in education they must assure that a good government existed. Chang Wei-tz'u addressed himself to political questions, but in accord with the spirit of Hu Shih's advice. He refrained from broad theorizing and contributed articles on such specific topics as budgets and city government.[15] T'ao Meng-ho, similarly, rejected narrow, one-dimensional panaceas.[16] China's problems were complex, and they required thorough analysis. Moreover, he reaffirmed the basic New Culture belief that arguments over forms of government were futile, given the state of China's masses. The real need was to raise the literacy and awareness levels of China's people.

Chiang Meng-lin had long agonized over these dilemmas, and in the early 1920s his mood was grim.[17] He felt that the good spirit of commitment to cultural reform had been destroyed by the horrible political conditions. Formerly, educators would try to create men of talent to reform a corrupt government. But now, he wrote, government was so chaotic that the educational world was much affected in both economic and psychological terms. Thus the nonpolitical stance of educators had been eroded away. Education needed money for libraries, laboratories, and salaries. In such times as these, when education is crippled by bankruptcy, how can you not talk of politics? Yet all kinds of protests by students and teachers had produced little change in actual political conditions. During the last few years strikes had been used so often that they had lost their utility. Education was floundering in disarray, and educators were at a loss over what to do.

Chiang himself was in a quandary over how intellectuals could alter these conditions. He recognized that both the people and the intellectuals were suffering in China, and that the root of the problem was the political and economic policies of the warlords. He admitted that the warlords would not become enlightened by themselves. To hope for that would be like expecting tigers to give up eating people. However, removing the corrupt politicians and reforming the political structure would only treat the symptoms and ignore the disease. Political problems had their source in the sickness of the total society, and enduring political reform must rest on a solid intellectual and cultural foundation. Yet Chiang hedged on this conventional liberal stance. The question of which had priority, political or cultural reform, was like the old chicken-egg controversy which no one had yet solved. Chiang decided they were interrelated, and both should take place at the same time. With this in mind, he recognized that many people felt that intellectuals should work more actively for this political, as well as cultural and intellectual, reform. But Chiang disagreed. Although intellectuals should not retreat into escapist scholarship, he said, their primary task was analysis and consideration of long-range questions. Thus, the intellectual's political role should be limited to studying relevant social and political problems, in an objective manner, and he should not engage in practical politics. So, Chiang was willing to make only the smallest compromise with his liberal principles. The intellectual, like the chün-tzu, had a special, transcendent role to play. It was his responsibility to "rein in the horse on the edge of a precipice" (hsuan-yai le-ma); but he couldn't stay on the horse and ride it into the safety of the interior. After all, if he did so, who would be left guarding the precipice?

Ting-Wen-chiang had long been convinced of the need to combine intellectual and political reform. He felt that Hu Shih's faith that cultural changes would somehow produce political reform was "a kind of fantasy." Indeed, as early as 1919, Ting was questioning the New Culture dogma that education and new values were the path to China's salvation. In an essay entitled "Eugenics and Genealogy" he laid stress on inherited characteristics, rather than acquired ones, as most dominant in an individual's personality.[18] Biological improvements and genetic planning were the appropriate starting points in creating a new society. This position was consistent with liberal principles in that it advocated a nonpolitical solution. But it evidenced considerable iconoclasm by departing from the fashionable reliance on education and a new cultural climate.

Ting's reasons for turning toward political involvement were explained in a fictitious dialogue, which appeared in Endeavor in 1923.[19] One participant in the dialogue offered all the arguments for refraining from politics. Politics was too corrupt an enterprise, and honest men would be swamped by the corruption and unable to make an impact. It was, therefore, better to concentrate on economic development (as a businessman) and on education to bring about an enlightened political atmosphere. The other participant, who reflected Ting's views, argued that no reforms were possible while the country was run by bandits and warlords. Intellectuals can't take a detached view. They must fight the fire now, where it was. Moreover, Ting argued that history was always influenced by an educated, able, and moral elite.[20] China was no exception, and his greatest fear was that those able few would refuse to participate in political affairs.

Ting's hopes were temporarily fulfilled in the summer of 1922 when three of the signatories to "Our Political Proposals" were appointed to the government by President Li Yuan-hung. These were Wang Ch'ung-hui as prime minister, T'ang Erh-ho as minister of education, and Lo Wen-kan as minister of finance. Within two months internal political conflicts resulted in Lo's arrest on the charge of accepting bribes.[21] The arrest, occuring at 1:00 in the morning, was made by the police without a warrant. In January, 1923, Lo was released for lack of evidence, but he was quickly rearrested, apparently at the instigation of P'eng Yün-i the new minister of education.

The Good Men Government, as it was called, failed because it lacked political sophistication and appropriate connections with the power cliques.[22] The lack of political sophistication was reflected in Lo Wen-kan's Yü-chung jen-yü (Words from Prison), a book he wrote while imprisoned.[23] There he argued that a better electoral system, so as to obtain better members of parliament, was what China needed. He was still thinking in terms of legalistic solutions to China's problems. Hu Shih was perhaps a little less naive about the prospects of the Good Men Government. Upon its formation he wrote in Endeavor of his hopes that Wang Ch'ung-hui, as a signer of "Our Political Proposals," could implement its three main points: a constitution, a more open government, and a comprehensive political plan.[24] In successive editorial comments Hu kept harping on the theme of a plan, and his tone was not optimistic.[25] In fact, from June to October, 1922, a series of tea parties had been held, mostly at Wellington Koo's home, for political discussion.[26] Hu Shih, Ts'ai Yuan-p'ei, Wang Ch'ung-hui, Lo Wen-kan, Ting Wen-chiang, and T'ao Meng-ho, among others, had been present. After the formation of the Good Men Government, the meetings grew tense because of Hu's continued criticism of the government for its lack of a plan. At Ts'ai's suggestion they were discontinued at the end of October. After Lo Wen-kan's arrest, Hu Shih wrote that while no one could question the integrity of Wang Ch'ung-hui and Lo Wen-kan, he was disappointed at their lack of political skills.[27] He was, however, heated in his denunciation of P'eng Yün-i and of the shameless disregard for legal procedures associated with the arrest. Kao I-han, while refusing to judge the merits of Lo Wen-kan's case for lack of information, was similarly outraged at the illegal aspects of the arrest procedure.[28]

The most decisive response came from Ts'ai Yuan-p'ei, who was infuriated by the arbitrary exercise of police power against his good friend.[29] He publicly protested, calling it a violation of civil rights and a cowardly attempt to curry favor with the warlords. Deciding that a more dramatic indication of disapproval was required, he and some of his associates tendered their resignations. Ts'ai's letter of resignation complained of intolerable governmental evils, especially the destruction of judicial independence which had culminated in the illegal arrest of Lo Wen-kan.[30] Shortly afterward, Ts'ai published an elaboration of his views, urging mass resignations as the most effective protest against corruption.[31] Citing the I Ching (Classic of Changes) that "small men know how to advance but not how to retreat," he argued that retreating not only had the negative function of avoiding troubles but could also have a positive effect. The contemporary application of this principle was the policy of noncooperation as implemented through mass resignations. Ts'ai had previously suggested such a policy a number of times.[32] The gist of it was that whenever teachers felt their grievances warranted such a step, they should all tender their resignations to their respective school officials. Nationwide application of this strategy would provide a far more effective bargaining lever than empty protests or merely stopping classes through strikes.

This attitude, permitting faculty resignations, hardly seems consistent with Ts'ai's firm opposition, during the May Fourth period, to student strikes as suicidal. If one of China's primary needs was education, Ts'ai could not consistently sanction either teacher or student abdication of their respective responsibilities. However, Ts'ai presumably felt that as a last resort, when conditions became completely intolerable, some form of dramatic moral assertion was mandatory. One of the most dramatic options available was a public resignation, and Ts'ai had taken this step several times in the past--in 1900 at the Shaohsing East-West School, in 1912 when he was Yuan Shih-k'ai's minister of education, and during the May Fourth incident. He apparently felt that circumstances in the winter of 1922-1923 justified another such resignation of protest. The Lo Wen-kan affair precipitated the act, but Ts'ai's writings make it clear that he had long contemplated the step.[33] Being in Peking had given him a close view of government corruption, and he became increasingly disturbed by the futility of education in such an atmosphere. Given this context, Ts'ai's resignation is more understandable. Ts'ai was a man who still used the rhetoric of hsiao-jen and ta-jen, and moral considerations were of paramount importance. Reform and modernization could only develop, and endure, in China within a new moral atmosphere. If the moral climate was worsening rather than improving, a dramatic attempt to reverse the process was essential.

Ts'ai's moral protest and call for noncooperation evoked only limited popular response. There were some student protests, criticizing the government and asking that Ts'ai return.[34] But the intellectuals, whom Ts'ai hoped to reach, manifested little interest. Ch'en Tu-hsiu thought that mass movements rather than elite protests were needed. Hu Shih, while recognizing Ts'ai's sincerity, argued that Ts'ai was not Gandhi and China was not India.[35] In the shameless China of the time, he pointed out, Ts'ai's appeals to conscience were ineffective. Moreover, it was much easier to arouse anger against a foreign foe, such as the British in India, than against domestic evils. Finally, he cited Ts'ai's own concern for education and his policy of reorganizing Peita so it no longer was dependent on one man. In accord with these ideas, Hu Shih urged educators to express sympathy for Ts'ai, but to make sure that their institutions continued to function. In these circumstances, Ts'ai departed for another trip to Europe, and the period of Ts'ai Yuan-p'ei's Peita came to a close.

In this winter of discontent, 1922-1923, Hu Shih was physically ill as well as distressed by political conditions. In December, 1922, he took a year's leave of absence from Peking University. Rumors circulated that his illness was a ploy and that he was about to flee to the foreign concessions for safety. Hu indignantly denied this, saying he would never flee to the concessions.[36] Those who bore the responsibility for shaping public opinion, through their writing, couldn't worry about the risks. Nonetheless, political conditions worsened through 1923. Utterly depressed, Hu left Peking in May, 1923, and turned _Endeavor_ over to Ting Wen-chiang, T'ao Meng-ho, Kao I-han, and Chang Wei-tz'u. Chang Wei-tz'u tried to put forth a bright face, claiming that it was normal for a nation to endure a period of chaos after a revolution.[37] The French and American revolutions indicated that destruction was easy, but construction difficult. Overthrowing a corrupt government can be done swiftly, but creating a good replacement takes a long time. So one shouldn't lose hope. Kao I-han wrote that he had lost hope in all Peking governments, all cliques, and all parties including the Kuomintang.[38] His final hopes rested with those in educational and commercial circles. Educators and businessmen should form an alliance, as had occurred in Europe at the end of the feudal period, to bring about needed changes in Chinese society. But he provided no specifics concerning how this might occur.

On 5 October 1923 Ts'ao K'un was elected to the presidency of the republic, having spent an estimated Mex. $13,560,000 to secure office. Four days later Hu Shih wrote a letter to his _Endeavor_ associates, suggesting that publication be "temporarily suspended." Lamenting the uselessness of their efforts under current circumstances, he wrote:

> At the present time it is utterly futile to talk politics. If you attack men, you merely add one curse to the nationwide chorus of vilification, and what is the point of that? If you steer clear of personalities and speak instead of problems and proposals, like the parliament, disarmament, or the constitution, then inevitably you incur the misunderstanding of others; while presenting a clear and well-reasoned petition to bandits is not something that we have any desire to do.[39]

Issue number 75 (21 October 1923) of Endeavor printed Hu Shih's formal announcement of a "temporary" halt to publication.[40] He explained his decision by reference to his poor health and his unwillingness to continue imposing on his friends. In the future, he said, he anticipated that an enlarged Endeavor would return on a bimonthly basis. In fact, Endeavor never returned, and the new liberal orientation had temporarily reached a dead end.

4.

The Dilemmas of the Warlord Period

Education, Intellectual Freedom, and the Warlords

Reading through some of the political journals of the warlord period, one occasionally comes upon an expression of optimism. There were a few observers of the scene who felt that the basic aspirations of the New Culture movement were gradually being realized.[1] Mass education was spreading, and China was slowly developing an enlightened public opinion with some influence on governmental policies. The more common view by far, however, was one of unrelieved pessimism. Chang Ching-lu (scholar of the Chinese publishing industry), for one, recalled that in 1926 he went as a tourist to Nanchang.[2] Even though the New Culture movement was seven years old, he searched all the bookstores of Nanchang without finding a single "new" book or magazine. This experience impressed upon him the difficulties of spreading new ideas and effecting cultural reform.

Other reasons for pessimism stemmed from the corruption and fiscal irresponsibility of the warlord governments in Peking and elsewhere.[3] If education was to be the key leavening ingredient in Chinese society, a supportive political and economic climate was necessary. But the warlords spent the bulk of their funds on their military needs, leaving education crippled by bankruptcy. Teacher salaries were frequently in arrears, leading to low morale and frequent teacher strikes. From 4 December 1919 to 12 January 1920, teachers in Peking struck because the Central Bank refused to redeem the paper money used to pay their salaries. From March to July, 1921, professors in all the government colleges and universities in Peking struck because their salaries were three-and-a-half months in arrears. Year after year Chiang Meng-lin (as acting chancellor of Peking University) addressed the students at convocation or commencement ceremonies in the bitterest of tones.[4] He grumbled over the university's shortage of funds and over the embarrassment of having to operate constantly in debt. He even, so he said, had creditors come to his home to collect bills owed by the university. The university needed a new library, a large auditorium, and a dormitory, but all plans were stymied by the government's policies. Again and again he apologized to students for the confusion they experienced while at Peita. At the ceremony celebrating the twenty-fifth anniversary of the founding of the university, in 1923, he asked bitterly what cause there was for a celebration. In 1926 Peking University had its water cut off for failing to pay its bill.[5] In his book Tides From the West Chiang cites with sympathy the remarks an old scholar made to him at the time: "Strikes here, there, and everywhere--strikes yesterday, today, tomorrow and everyday. Mr. Chancellor, what are you going to do about them? When is the thing going to end?"[6]

A variety of plans were offered to guarantee financial independence for education and thus lessen the likelihood of political interference.[7] Wang Shih-chieh, Peita professor and later minister of education under the Nationalists, argued that educators had to take some political action to prevent government interference with education.[8] They must make the educational world strong enough to counter political pressure, and they must obtain independent sources of revenue. However, Wang provided no explicit details on what sort of political activities he recommended, and he stressed that no educator should involve his institution in politics. If he wished to express his political views, it should be as a private individual. Ts'ai Yuan-p'ei offered an elaborate proposal for dividing the country into a number of regions or districts (ch'ü), each having a university.[9] The university would oversee all primary, middle, and adult education in the district. Control of the university and district educational affairs would rest with an educational committee, organized by university professors. The University chancellor would be chosen by the committee, and all the district chancellors would form a council of higher education to formulate educational policy for the nation, along with the minister of education who had to be approved by the council. Funds would come from local taxes, but a poor district could request aid from the central government upon receiving approval from the council of higher education. This complex proposal to remove education from politics was closely modeled after the system operating in France during Ts'ai's stay there.[10] It received little consideration when broached, but in 1927 a related plan, under Ts'ai's direction, was given a brief trial by the Kuomintang.

In addition to shortages of funds for education, New Culture liberals were faced with sporadic warlord repression of intellectual freedoms.[11] Generally, warlord restrictions on freedom of the press were erratic, even quixotic. Opposed to a radical idea like free love, they might confiscate all books with the Chinese character for love (ai) in the title--thus including books with the word amateur (ai-mei-ti) or other equally innocuous words in their titles. All books by Marx transliterated Ma-erh-ko-ssu would be confiscated, but those transliterated Ma-k'o-ssu might be overlooked. Books with the character for society would be prohibited because the character was used for socialism. Beyond such unpredictable measures warlords had few ideological convictions, and they tended to be tolerant of publications unless they felt threatened personally. For example, warlords in Peking would often censure publications with anti-Japanese content to avoid repercussions from the Japanese. On occasion the authorities would withdraw postal privileges from periodicals, so that they could not be mailed to subscribers.[12] But this was usually a temporary measure, and the restrictions would be lifted after the editors promised to behave better in the future.

Some observers, however, perceived matters differently. T'ao Meng-ho wrote that while an individual might express himself freely on matters of religion, he didn't enjoy the same freedom with regard to politics.[13] If an ordinary citizen fell into the garbage in front of your house, you could discuss it with him and criticize his behavior. But not so if he was a government official. If your brother was a wastral and spent money foolishly you could take steps to control him. But if the government wasted the public's money you had no recourse. He recognized the necessity for law and order but he cited Madame Roland's cry regarding liberty ("Oh Liberty! How many crimes are falsely done in thy name?"), and wondered how many excesses occurred in the name of law and order. If a government denied freedom of discussion, he argued, then it was either because it thought itself infallible or because it was not concerned with the best interests of the people. History has shown that governments which obtain law and order solely through repression (such as tsarist Russia and Yuan Shih-k'ai's government) inevitably are overthrown. Only evil governments look on freedom of discussion with hostility. Good governments welcome it. Wang Shih-chieh and Kao I-han expressed similar sentiments.[14] Free societies use the rule of law if abridgements of freedom are deemed necessary in the national interest. In societies that are not free the police can obstruct freedom and interfere in people's business without appropriate judicial procedures. China has been an arbitrary police state from Yuan Shih-k'ai onwards, wrote Wang.

On occasion, warlord repressiveness could be quite

harsh.[15] In April, 1926, Chang Tsung-ch'ang and Chang Hsueh-liang captured Peking and shot two newspaper editors. A friend warned Chiang Meng-lin that his name was on a list of people to be arrested. Chiang fled first to the Hotel des Wagon Lits in the Legation Quarter of Peking, and then to the Legation Quarter in Shanghai. On 6 August 1926, the editor of the Peking newspaper She-hui jih-pao was arrested and summarily executed. But warlord policies in Peking, partly because of pressure from the Japanese, were harsher than elsewhere. In Shanghai, books and journals of all shades of opinion circulated relatively freely, and Chang Ching-lu called the years 1925-1927 the golden age of China's new world of publishing.[16] The dejection so apparent among China's New Culture liberals was not so much based on the repressiveness of the warlords as it was on the futility of the situation. No cultural or educational reforms were possible, and thus the liberal program could make no headway. For many the situation looked hopeless, and they traveled abroad or immersed themselves in scholarship at home. John Dewey recognized this inclination in 1920, writing "It is very easy to see how cultivated people take refuge in art and spirituality when politics are corrupt and the general state of social life is so discouraging."[17]

One rationale for this option was expressed by the historian Ku Chieh-kang.[18] In the mid-1920s Ku wrote an essay entitled "Insomnia" in which he asserted that scholarship was his vocation, and he would not succumb to pressure for practicality or immediate service to society. When Wang Kuo-wei committed suicide in June, 1927, Ku criticized Chinese society for making social demands on its intellectuals beyond their teaching and scholarship. Ku Chieh-kang's reasoning, which was shared by other New Culture liberals, was that the separation of scholarship and politics was necessary for national development. Pure scholarship led to science and progress, as was evidenced by the history of the West. But in China intellectuals had historically been closely associated with the government and with upholding the orthodoxy and the status-quo. Ku believed that scholars could render a larger service to society by independently examining all ideas and striving for long-range contributions rather than being sidetracked into "practical" work which produced immediate but ephemeral dividends.

Political Theory or Political Activism?

Ku's close friend and fellow Peita student, the future historian Fu Ssu-nien, was tormented by a related dilemma during this period. In a letter from America to Ku Chieh-kang, which was published in New Tide (Hsin-ch'ao) in February, 1920, he asks: "Shall I love spontaneity, or shall I love humanity?"[19] In other words should he value self-fulfillment or social service? His intellect told him to opt for humanity, but his emotions inclined him elsewhere. Reminiscing in later years, Fu recalled how lazy and apolitical he was during this time.[20] He kept planning to write essays for Endeavor or a book urging the adoption or new values, but he never got around to it. Another historian, T. F. Tsiang (Chiang T'ing-fu), remembered that in 1925, even though home from abroad for a couple of years, he was completely ignorant about different warlords.[21] He thought they were all the same, all equally bad. So he asked Ting Wen-chiang about them and found that Ting knew the details of age, background, and good and bad points of all of them. Ting believed that some were good men with patriotic sentiments, but lacking the modern education which would have led them to serve the nation. The attitudes of Ku Chieh-kang, Fu Ssu-nien, T. F. Tsiang, and Ting Wen-chiang represent different approaches to the constantly recurring dilemma of what relationship an intellectual should have to society. This was certainly not a problem unique to New Culture liberals, but it caused a special identity crisis for them. Members of the Chinese Communist party, in contrast, knew their proper public role, even if they might sometimes have private conflicts over self-fulfillment versus social service. Romantics like Hsü Chih-mo or Chinese followers of Irving Babbitt's New Humanism had a sure sense of purpose. But New Culture liberals who took their ideology seriously were caught in an agonizing dilemma over their appropriate public role, and how to render the best service to Chinese society.

Generally they temporized in accord with the compromise discussed in chapter three, that is, they wrote about political issues but refrained from active political participation. The pages of Endeavor were filled with discussions of two frequently suggested remedies for China's political disintegration--federalism and a new constitution. Many New Culture liberals were attracted to federalism in the early 1920s as a means of putting an end to warlordism.[22] Their expectation was that more provincial autonomy would produce stability and end constant warlord skirmishes. There also existed some hope that consitutions drafted on a provincial level might guarantee the protection of civil liberties. Hu Shih, for one, argued that the idea of a strong centralized government had been an illusory dream from the time of Ch'in Shih Huang-ti.[23] The lesson of history was that China was too big for one central government. Provincial self-government had, he felt, produced order during the late Ch'ing and early republican periods, until Yuan Shih-k'ai again returned to that illusory dream of national unity. The central government collected all kinds of revenue and then wasted it because of corruption, thus leaving the provincial governments with authority but no resources. Hu argued that provincial governments with both authority and financial resources could provide orderly government and keep the warlords under control. Kao I-han concurred with Hu Shih's conclusions, as did others writing in Endeavor and elsewhere.[24] Kao cited several Western political scientists in support of the argument that sovereignty existed at several different levels of government. Some aspects of government, such as defense, might legitimately be national concerns, but others might better be handled by provincial authorities. Kao I-han was also much concerned with drafting a sound constitution, and he especially hoped it would provide for the election of a president by the people rather than by the National Assembly. This would produce a president responsive to the people rather than merely an instrument of the warlords. Chang Wei-tz'u, too, stressed the importance of a constitution to get China "on the right track."[25] He hoped that political reforms would break the power of the warlords and give the people a supervisory role over the affairs of government. But legalistic solutions to warlord chaos, so frequently suggested by New Culture liberals, were totally impractical. The warlords were too powerful to be restrained by legalistic considerations, as Ts'ao K'un proved when he bribed his way to the presidency in the fall of 1923.

New Culture liberals continued to seek outlets for their political theorizing, however fruitless such efforts appeared to be. In December, 1924, a new journal was established called the Contemporary Review (Hsien-tai p'ing-lun), which was edited by Ch'en Yuan (Ch'en Hsi-ying; professor of English at Peita). The journal's stated purpose was to concentrate on concrete problems in government, economics, law, art, and science.[26] It promised to avoid empty talk. Familiar names from Endeavor, and a few new ones, appeared in its pages. In early issues they discussed China's political conditions in broad terms, or focused more narrowly on such topics as the Aftermath Conference.[27] This conference, announced by Tuan Ch'i-jui in late 1924, prompted much wrangling between Tuan's executive government and Sun Yat-sen's Kuomintang concerning the selection of delegates. When it became clear that it would be controlled by the militarists, the Kuomintang withdrew its support. The conference lasted from 1 February 1925 to 21 April 1925, adopting a number of resolutions concerning governmental reforms. These were enacted by the executive government on 24 April but ignored by the warlords.

In the first months of the Contemporary Review the most extensive critical analysis came from Chou Keng-sheng (S. R. Chow; professor of government at Peita).[28] In a December, 1924, article he argued that a new constitution was not so vital to the nation. What the people wanted were fundamental reforms, and they were not interested in the technicality of restoring constitutional government. The important questions of national objectives and the rights of the people could be settled without a constitution. This did not mean that the government should operate without legal constraints, but these could be obtained by having the government issue a statement guaranteeing it would adhere to certain principles of republican government. By March, 1925, Chou was expressing much dissatisfaction with the Aftermath Conference. Things were in a mess, he wrote, and nothing was being accomplished at the conference because of the makeup of its membership. Failure to have the Kuomintang participate weakened its authority, and control by the warlords minimized the chances for progress. He argued that the greatest failure of Tuan Ch'i-jui's executive government was its inability to weaken the power of the warlords. The urgent objective of the Aftermath Conference (at least as Chou saw it) was that it find ways to control the warlords. But since the warlords dominated the conference, they wouldn't permit meaningful consideration of the question. In conclusion, Chou counseled patience for his colleagues. They must wait for better days and prepare for the future. They must organize the people to recognize their rights and responsibilities in a modern society, so that they could combat the strength of the special interests. A few months later Chou followed up this idea of organizing the people. He said that all the talk by unarmed politicians and political theorists had been mere empty words. On the other hand, it was equally futile to use one militarist to try to overthrow the others. You use *x* to overthrow *y* today, and *y* to overthrow *x* tomorrow. Only organizing the people could put a stop to this endless cycle. And the organization must go beyond the urban middle class with their demonstrations. It must extend to the villages and to occupational or professional groups. China must find local leaders and instill in them a spirit of cooperation and self-government.

Kao I-han went through a similar sequence of attitudes.[29] In January, 1925, he was writing about how little hope he had for the success of the Aftermath Conference. Eighty to 90 percent of the delegates were military men, and even these were not present themselves but sent their subordinates. Given the nature of the delegates selected for the conference there was little hope of accomplishing anything, but prospects were even worse when dealing with delegates of the delegates. By the end of 1925 he was writing of the need for a mass revolution. But by this term he just meant transferring power from the warlords to the people, by means of a constitutional government which could protect freedom of speech and association.

Other New Culture liberals also contributed their thoughts to the Contemporary Review with regard to China's problems. T. F. Tsiang argued that the unification of China, like that of Germany and Italy, would require a combination of military force and skillful political planning.[30] But he specifically repudiated unification by a minority party dictatorship, like Cromwell's England or tsarist Russia. He thought that the combination of internal chaos and external humiliation made China ripe for such a dictatorship, but he hoped it wouldn't come to pass. In the 1930s, by contrast, he would condone dictatorship as necessary for the times.

T'ao Meng-ho contributed a poignant article entitled "The Hope of Us Little People."[31] He lamented that the little people had known nothing but chaos and war for fifteen years. They didn't understand the political significance of a constitution, or communism, or anticommunism. They just wondered why such matters must always lead to fighting. They were afraid of everything--afraid of a National Assembly, or a Senate, or communism, or anticommunism. For them all these meant war. All they wished was to live in peace, with enough income to support themselves. They had no faith that a constitution, or this or that ism, could change things. Making meaningful changes, he wrote elsewhere, was indeed difficult in a society where only a few had any vision and where power rested with those who protected their own vested interests.[32] Creating a new political system was a difficult and painful process when thousands of years of an old, rotten system had to be overturned--and when selfish interests prevailed over public needs. Just as giving birth to a child causes temporary pain to the mother, so giving birth to a new society will cause temporary pain to the people. Such a change will require individuals willing to resist the established order and to risk being branded as rebels. It will also require military force, but it can't rely on the military power of the warlords, who have no concern for the good of society. Enlightened individuals must recognize the fact that it is futile to work with the warlords, and they must put aside partisan interests and work together for political change.

T'ao Meng-ho and others also contributed articles offering some of the tired old bromides of the past. On one occasion T'ao wrote that modern science would overthrow old superstitions.[33] Ch'en Heng-che (Sophia H. Chen Zen) and her husband Jen Hung-chün (H. C. Zen; professor at Southeastern University) reiterated the need for making university education more stimulating.[34] And Hu Shih replayed the familiar refrain that the strength of Western society lay in its emphasis on rationality, science, control of nature, and an assertive spirit.[35]

What emerges from the above synopsis of representative articles in the Contemporary Review is some indication of a more realistic assessment of China's problems. The obstacle to reform posed by the whole warlord system had become crystal clear. There seemed to be a genuine sympathy for the plight of the masses. There is some open admission of the fruitlessness of mere words.

But the New Culture liberals had nothing more practical than words to offer. Their writings still operated within the framework of gradual change through careful planning. They still clung to the frail hope that civil liberties could be protected by paper guarantees. There was some rhetorical head-bobbing in the direction of mass organization, but the New Culture liberals lacked a real commitment to this endeavor. Unlike James Yen and T'ao Hsing-chih, they stayed in the cities, taught in the universities, and wrote for the Contemporary Review and other journals. Unlike the Chinese Communist party, they had no clear ideological basis for rousing the masses and certainly no sympathy for class struggle as a technique. One is left with the impression that New Culture liberals were still at loose ends, still searching for a way to be useful without violating their principles. They were unwilling to participate in politics, unwilling to take up arms, and unwilling to organize the masses themselves. The frustration was almost unbearable, and they watched the progress of Chiang Kai-shek's march northward with eager anticipation.

The Labor Movement and the May 30 Incident

Beyond the personal dilemma of what role they should play in Chinese society, liberals in the warlord period were also faced with taking a stand regarding the growth of labor organizations and of anti-imperialist sentiment. The level of political consciousness was rising in China, a fact which liberals might be expected to approve. Such approval, however, was limited because of the New Culture values which liberals upheld. Labor organizations grew during the 1917-1919 period, and then the May Fourth incident initiated a concerted effort to organize labor on a national level.[36] From January to March, 1922, the Hong Kong seamen's strike immobilized the port of Hong Kong, winning an increase in wages. On 7 January 1923, Wu P'ei-fu massacred the striking Peking-Hankow railroad workers. The May 30 Incident of 1925 sparked the Great Canton and Hong Kong strike which lasted from June, 1925, to September, 1926. On 21 March 1927, a general strike in Shanghai, under the leadership of the Chinese Communist party, incapacitated the city and opened the door for Chiang Kai-shek's entry. Thus, the labor movement was one of the vital issues of the times. What stance did New Culture liberals adopt toward it?

Quite early Ts'ai Yuan-p'ei seemed to express his sympathy for the working man. In a November, 1918 speech, entitled "The Divinity of Labor," he announced his belief that the world of the future would be a "workers' world."[37] That is, a world in which anyone who used his own labor to produce something for others, whether through physical or mental effort, would be considered a "worker." There was in Ts'ai's remarks a utopian spirit which continued in later years. In 1920 he stated that the ideal world would be one which conformed to the principle of "from each according to his abilities, to each according to his needs."[38] But unfortunately, he wrote, China was very far from this ideal. Many social inequities existed, with men working excessive hours and still lacking essential needs. Ts'ai was concerned with social justice and interested in socialism. Chang Kuo-t'ao, in his autobiography, recalled a meeting with Ts'ai in August, 1920.[39] He was in Shanghai for the early stages of planning with Ch'en Tu-hsiu for the founding of the Chinese Communist party. There Chang told Ts'ai of his work with Ch'en and their plans for the Chinese Communist party. Ts'ai replied, according to Chang: "It seems that socialism is the only way for China. From beginning to end, the anarchists have never organized themselves, and that is their weakness. If the Marxists are to achieve anything, they must organize quickly." Chang recognized Ts'ai's innate politeness, but he believed that his remarks were more than mere k'o-ch'i-hua (courtesy words).

Ts'ai certainly possessed considerable sympathy with socialist aspirations in the early 1920s, and probably at that time Marxism and socialism seemed synonymous to him. But he also believed that socialism could only be implemented where the proper conditions existed.[40] Just wanting socialism and stirring up enthusiasm for it wouldn't produce it. Labor must develop a sufficient self-consciousness to begin to organize itself. And that need for heightened consciousness led Ts'ai smoothly into the conventional New Culture emphasis on education and cultural regeneration. Ts'ai's long-term vision might have been of a workers' world, but his immediate approach centered on worker education--through night schools, public lectures, and other forms of continuing education. In January, 1920, night schools were opened for Peita university employees and working people living in the university vicinity.[41] Ts'ai remarked that this was the first time outsiders had been allowed into Peita, although of course the police and military were exceptions. The university furnished rooms and textbooks, but Peita students did the teaching, without pay. Classes met five nights a week with a curriculum of primary- and middle-school material. Even a free meal of soup and Chinese bread was provided, paid for by what the Peita teacher-students could contribute or solicit from outside.

Others writing in the liberal journals of the period offered a variety of perspectives on the labor movement. Hu Shih expressed his opposition to strikes and shutdowns as ephemeral.[42] They might be useful for specific, immediate goals such as those associated with the May Fourth incident. But basic changes in the system, which is what China needed, required organization and long-term planning. Yang Ch'uan (Hsing-fo), who later became secretary of the China League for Civil Rights in the 1930s, took a more sympathetic stance.[43] He argued that a labor movement arose naturally from certain economic conditions, and that strikes were often the only weapons workers had to oppose intolerable conditions. Such developments were not the work of extremists and shouldn't arouse blind fear. People should understand the background and realize that labor organizations and even strikes would inevitably appear as the economy became more developed. The United States and Europe, for example, had more strikes than China, yet no one considered these the work of extremists. Yang's writings were sprinkled with Marxist terminology, and he definitely sympathized with the working class. The way to reduce strikes, he maintained, was to improve working conditions and wages. Kao I-han's language was more restrained, but he too expressed concern for reducing the inequities between classes.[44] He criticized those who believed that China's most important economic need was to increase production, ignoring the parallel need for equal distribution. The West had gone that route, he pointed out, and the result has been much class conflict.

Several articles in the Contemporary Review described the condition of China's working class, painting a bleak picture of exploitation and misery. The social economist Li Ching-han (Franklin C. H. Lee) reported on his year-long study of labor conditions, focusing on the rickshaw drivers.[45] In hard times, he wrote, people had only three choices--the army, banditry, or pulling a rickshaw. Of the three the last was the most honorable choice and involved a contribution to society. Yet few who rode in rickshaws took a sympathetic attitude toward the pullers. These rickshaw men had an extremely difficult time making ends meet, earning about 100 coppers a day in a time of rising prices. Usually their wives and children were forced into the factories or became beggers. And, Li claimed, there were 55,000 rickshaw pullers in Peking--some 7 percent of the total Peking population; but one out of every nine males, and one out of every six males between sixteen and fifty. In another article Li analyzed labor conditions from a broader perspective.[46] He contended that the relative lack of class conflict in China historically would begin to change with the growth of labor organizations. But by learning from the experience of the West, China could minimize the tensions. The three goals of labor have historically been wages, shorter hours, and better working conditions. Chinese workers were still relatively uneducated, and their major concern presently was with wages. Li hoped that good planning and an awareness of mistakes made in the West would allow China to develop a more harmonious relationship between the bourgeoisie and the proletariat.

The stance liberals took regarding the labor movement might well be labeled by someone with more radical values as idealistic. Their hearts were in the right place, their ideals deserved respect, but they lacked a penetrating class analysis. Ts'ai Yuan-p'ei tried to educate the workers. Hu Shih wanted long-term cultural reform. Yang Ch'uan and Kao I'han were concerned with social justice, but as a means to lessen the need for strikes and class conflict. Li Ching-han hoped that good planning would result in a harmonious relationship between the classes. The predominant theme was the search for compromise and harmony. New Culture liberals wanted social justice, but not at the expense of social order. Radical social change and class conflict made them shudder. The attitude of economist Yang Tuan-liu is illustrative. He was quite proud of the Shanghai strikes associated with the May 30 Incident of 1925.[47] A strike of 150,000-160,000 workers lasting more than two months, he wrote in August, was unprecedented not only in China, but also in the whole world. But, he was careful to emphasize, it was important to realize that this was not class warfare, but rather economic warfare by one nation against another. Because of its patriotic character the strike had the support of Chinese capitalists. Some Chinese capitalists doubtless feared that if the strike against the British and Japanese were successful, then labor might next use similar tactics against them. It was important to dispel any impression that Chinese workers harbored thoughts of domestic class warfare, so as to avoid weakening the common stand against the foreigners. Yang's priorities were clear. Nationalism took precedence over class consciousness and internal economic questions. Basically, he was saying, let's not have any radical talk of class struggle in China because we all must stand together against external foes. But judging from the writing of other New Culture liberals, one might well speculate that Yang's disposition regarding class struggle would not have altered even if the external threat had suddenly disappeared. In this, as in some other areas, Chinese liberals expressed views that were common to a more universal liberalism. Their sympathies were with social change, but they could not countenance radical means toward that end.

Another dilemma-laden issue for New Culture liberals was the growing antiforeign movement, symbolized by the May

30 Incident. Even before May 30 the Contemporary Review was publishing some very harsh indictments of foreign activities in China. One account reported that the Shanghai foreign police had searched the Shanghai University bookstore. "Was free speech only for white men and denied to Chinese?" the author asked.[48] Another writer fervently denounced foreigners for their insulting behavior toward Chinese in the treaty ports, especially Shanghai.[49] Particularly outrageous was the way they would treat rickshaw drivers--asking them to run fast, paying a pittance, and beating them half to death if they didn't act humbly enough. It was shameful that China was too weak to protect its citizens from such humiliations. At the same time the Review was objective enough to include articles which placed some of the blame on China. One argued that the slow progress in abolishing opium sales was partly the result of resistance on the part of Chinese merchants making large profits.[50] Another pointed out that the popularity of missionary schools, even though they instilled in Chinese a sense of inferiority toward Westerners, stemmed from the fact that Chinese schools were so disrupted by government policies or student demonstrations that parents preferred the more stable missionary schools.[51] The editor, Ch'en Hsi-ying, even lamented that Chinese readers were so parochial that newspapers included very little foreign news.[52] When the Contemporary Review started to carry some in its Short Items section, he reported, many people requested that it be eliminated. Certainly implicit in Ch'en's lament was the idea that more knowledge of foreign affairs would allow for better relations with foreigners.

The May 30 Incident focused discussion on a specific issue, and one with multiple dimensions. On the most elemental level the response was one of anger. The first issue of the Contemporary Review after the Incident (6 June 1925) contained an angry denunciation of foreign privileges in China which infringed on Chinese sovereignty.[53] The foreign concessions in Shanghai were intolerable, and the power of the foreign police over Chinese was shameful. How much longer can China tolerate such humiliations? In the same issue an article by Wang Shih-chieh compared May 30 with the Amritsar tragedy of 1919 in India.[54] There a British commander, General Reginald Dyer, ordered his troops to fire on unarmed Indians as they peaceably demonstrated against British policies. Now Dyerism had come to China. Wang urged that steps be taken to prevent the recurrence of such an atrocity. First, all taxpayers (including Chinese) in each concession area should elect delegates to a representative body, to replace the Shanghai municipal council; second, the mixed court should be restored; and third, all publishing activities should be free of outside interference. Until these three conditions were accepted he advocated a boycott against English and Japanese goods. And if the foreigners continued to use violence against peaceful Chinese, he wanted the government to send Chinese police into the concession area to protect Chinese lives. The next two issues of the *Review* contained angry articles by Chou Keng-sheng.[55] He was particularly furious at the British, the most powerful nation in the Shanghai concession. Other nations, especially the Japanese, bore a share of the blame, but the British bore the largest responsibility. "How could the British let students be killed?" he asked. Chou also directed some of his fury toward his own government, which he criticized for its pallid response to the shootings. All they had done was to investigate and lodge a formal protest. Because of the government's indecisiveness, all the sacrifices of the people had thus far been wasted. Other writers contributed further outcries to the *Review*, concerning foreign mistreatment of Chinese and how to deal with it.[56] There was extensive discussion, and much disagreement, over how effective a boycott of England would be in altering British policies toward China.

Cooler heads also offered their opinions. Yen Shu-ch'ang, professor of law at Peking University, advised that only careful planning would yield productive results.[57] Wasted effort and overreaction must be avoided. He urged that China work toward the specific goal of restitution for injuries associated with May 30, and guarantees that would prevent future recurrences. Some colleagues wished to seek such broad goals as the abolition of unequal treaties, extraterritoriality, and the foreign concessions. But these were complex issues, involving important interests for many nations. If China opened up these questions, it would incur resistance from all nations and lessen the chances of settling the more limited grievances against the British and Japanese over May 30. The tactic he suggested was a boycott and general strike against the British and the Japanese. China was too weak to take military action against the foreigners, and it would be suicidal to institute a total boycott directed against all foreign countries, as some misguided patriots suggested. But a boycott directed against Britain and Japan would, he believed, be as successful as the 1922 Hong Kong seamen's strike. T'ao Meng-ho's reaction was even more dispassionate.[58] He recognized that an emotional impulse to avenge foreign insults was natural, but it prevented a logical analysis of the problem and it produced ephemeral enthusiasm rather than sustained policies. The pressure of British imperialism, which had existed from the Opium War, was not going to be reduced by a short-lived emotional outburst. The Boxer Rebellion had proved that. Chinese should intensify their determination, but also calmly analyze the nature of British oppression, how many people were involved, and what special rights the British enjoyed. Then their protest could be based on facts and understanding. Without facts and understanding, China would repeat the failure of the Boxers.

Some other New Culture liberals, from whom one would expect the voice of moderation, were abroad at the time of the May 30 Incident. As Chinese abroad defending the homeland, their responses tended to be more passionate than had they been at home and surrounded by others whose emotions were hot. Ts'ai Yuan-p'ei, for example, was in Europe at the time. He was much affected by news of the event and sent a statement to newspapers in France, England, and Germany--entitled "A Proclamation to the Whole World on the Shanghai Incident."[59] There he tried to explain to the West the resentment which China felt toward foreigners because of the humiliations associated with unequal treaties and special privileges. He pointed out the bad working conditions and low wages of Chinese workers in Japanese factories. He was very critical of the British policy for firing so soon on the students and workers gathered in demonstration. He recommended that the Japanese establish an eight-hour day and fair wages, and he demanded that compensation be paid for those Chinese killed or wounded. For the future he called for the negotiation of new treaties on the basis of equality. Ts'ai's former student at Peking University, Lo Chia-lun, was in England when he heard of the May 30 Incident. He was quite indignant, and he even appealed to the British Labour party in hopes of getting Parliament to correct the behavior of the Shanghai British police.[60] He printed and circulated five thousand copies of a telegram, written by Ting Wen-chiang, which stated China's grievances.

The initial emotional impact of the May 30 Incident was undeniably substantial. The fact was that Chinese workers, protesting conditions in a Japanese factory, were fired on by British police. It all seemed to epitomize the lowly place of Chinese within their own country. Even the normally nonpolitical literati of the Association of Literary Studies were moved by patriotic sentiments.[61] However, another way of looking at the Incident, and one which grew in prominence with time, was to see it as another student demonstration and to assess it within that context. In fact, shortly before the Incident the issue of student demonstrations was brought to people's attention. The Peking government had issued an order prohibiting demonstrations commemorating the May 4 and May 7 protests. One writer in the *Contemporary Review* said he could understand the government's stance regarding May 4, since that was a protest against policies of Chinese officials and the issue was long-since closed.[62] But the May 7 protests were directed against pressures from abroad in the form of Japan's Twenty-one Demands.

He thought it was important to keep such nationalist sentiments alive. T'ao Meng-ho agreed with this viewpoint.[63] He emphasized that the May 7 demonstration was patriotic, and that it was a good idea to remind the Chinese people periodically of the lesson that national weakness invites outside pressure. He thought it unfortunate that the government didn't see it that way. One can, of course, understand why the Peking government saw things differently, wishing to avoid antagonizing the Japanese. Chou Keng-sheng argued that in a developing country, in a transitional period, a lively patriotic student movement wasn't a bad thing.[64] Especially because in a backward country the students represented a progressive segment of society, with an awareness of political questions. Also, because they were organized they could assume a leadership role in social affairs. However, he qualified his remarks by stressing that students should primarily use their time to study. Only in special circumstances, for specific political purposes, was their leadership called for.

The May 30 demonstrations crystallized this issue. And, after time had cooled the passions, T'ao Meng-ho and Hu Shih enunciated the conventional New Culture viewpoint. Writing in August, T'ao Meng-ho said that students were so incensed by insults to the nation that they left their classrooms out of a sense of responsibility to the nation.[65] But they had been so engaged for two and a half months, and from the standpoint of education this was time lost. He admitted that the May 30 tragedy might yield some long-term benefits--the strike would enhance the status of labor, the boycott of foreign goods would encourage domestic production, students would get some practical political experience, and student proclamations would spread patriotic sentiments among the people. But the boycott only involved workers and merchants in certain areas, while the student movement was nationwide. Some 300,000-400,000 students had missed their studies, and no nation could sacrifice education and survive. Indeed, China's present vulnerability to foreigners stemmed largely from its shortage of skilled people. The West came in and used its superior knowledge to exploit China's resources and build factories. Foreigners didn't fear slogans such as Patriotism or Anti-Imperialism. They feared a strong, self-reliant country. Patriotism had been present in China for twenty or thirty years, yet China still hadn't become a strong, independent country. It takes more than patriotism. It takes learning and planning. He had respect for patriotic students, T'ao wrote, but he also respected those who used their knowledge and ability to help the nation.

Writing the next month, Hu Shih expressed similar views.[66] He recalled that after the May 7 demonstrations (held despite the government's prohibition) a mass meeting was held of Peking University students. Some 1,100 attended and more than 800 voted against a strike. It looked like a new day for the student movement, with education as the uppermost concern. But the May 30 Incident occurred and student restraint couldn't continue. This was understandable given the fact that even old men were talking of declaring war. One couldn't expect young students to show restraint under such circumstances, and one should respect their patriotic motives. But that patriotic fervor had ebbed very quickly, and those students who wrote big character posters on the walls in front of Peita were now just sitting around or sleeping all day. He then repeated the familiar litany of how saving the nation required education and long-range contributions rather than brief emotional displays. Trying to fortify the wills of students being taunted by friends to leave their studies for demonstrations, he cited the example of Goethe and other Europeans who produced enduring intellectual work in the midst of political turmoil.

Liberal reaction to the May 30 Incident, and to later demonstrations such as the March 18 Incident of 1926, illustrated the ambivalence of most liberals toward the whole question of antiforeignism. They were as patriotic as any group in China, and they resented foreign encroachments on Chinese sovereignty, but their outlook was complicated by other considerations. They wanted to achieve tariff autonomy, and eliminate extraterritoriality and other kinds of special privileges, but they wanted to do so through gradual, legal means. They recognized that China's long-term growth required cooperation with the international community and thus China couldn't afford a belligerent posture. Moreover, Western privileges in China had developed in the nineteenth century out of large historical forces, and so it was wrong to direct one's anger at the people of those Western countries today or to expect overnight changes. Many liberals also resisted the tendency to distort nationalism into xenophobia. They were generally too cosmopolitan and too catholic in their interests for that. They recognized the strong points of Western culture, and they felt it was a self-delusion to shift all the blame for China's problems onto foreign imperialism. They could be critical of foreign values, and of the behavior of foreigners in China, but they tried to maintain a larger perspective on the question.

Fu Ssu-nien

Chiang Meng-lin

Chiang T'ing-fu

Hu Shih

Liang Shih-ch'iu

Lo Chia-lun

Ts'ai Yuan-p'ei

5.

The Early Nationalist Period, 1927–1933

Political confusion and uncertain educational funding made the warlord period a particularly frustrating time for liberals. So they watched the progress of the Northern Expedition with much anticipation. Articles in the Contemporary Review conveyed the impression that warlords had made a total wreck of Chinese affairs, and authority was inexorably shifting southward to the Kuomintang (KMT). One article, in November, 1926, expressed surprise that the United States had failed to recognize this reality and was still dealing with the Peking government instead of the Nationalists in Kwangtung.[1] The Review represented the Nationalists as dedicated reformers while simultaneously downplaying the influence and questioning the intentions of the Communists. Yang Tuanliu, professor of economics at Wuhan University, in reporting on his visit to Canton focused on what he considered the key question in everyone's mind--how much Bolshevik influence was there on the Nationalists?[2] Yang concluded from firsthand observation that the Russians in Kwangtung were just advisors. The Chinese were in complete control of political and military affairs. Another writer stressed that the Kuomintang and the Chinese Communist party (CCP) shared a common concern for the success of the Northern Expedition.[3] But he left no doubt that in the long run the Communists stood for policies inimical to China's interests. They wanted China to be part of the worldwide revolutionary movement and would thus follow orders from the Comintern; and they urged class struggle and sought to bring benefits to only one class, the proletariat.

This generally negative attitude regarding the Chinese Communists affected reactions to the Shanghai massacre of April, 1927, which consolidated the Nationalist victory. A vigorous debate occurred in the pages of the

Contemporary Review, but the prevailing theme was that the Nationalist victory and the destruction of Communist influence were in the best interests of China.[4] The Communists were portrayed as unprincipled opportunists, scheming to take control of the Kuomintang through any means at their disposal. Clearly the Kuomintang could not tolerate this rebellious conduct. The Kuomintang was presented as a party which favored social revolution, but within the framework of the Three People's Principles. Thus it would avoid the violence and extremism of the Communists, and would bring benefits to all people rather than to one special class. Its revolution would rest on class harmony rather than class struggle. Moreover, the Kuomintang would bring about a revolution for the sake of China, under Chinese control, rather than involving China as an instrument of world revolution under the direction of outsiders.

The Review did print some very angry letters to the editor which expressed a different point of view. One writer argued that the Communists had been very progressive in their behavior, never working against the Chinese revolution.[5] He charged that the Nanking clique (that is, Chiang Kai-shek's Nanking government) were false Kuomintangers, who were merely perpetrating a new type of warlordism. In some ways they were even worse than the old warlords in their killing of workers, peasants, and students. And like the old warlords they cooperated with the imperialists to oust revolutionary elements. How could this be considered revolutionary activity? It was the Hankow government which represented the true, the revolutionary Kuomintang. Another letter writer was critical of Chiang Kai-shek, accusing him of thinking only of his own glory.[6] Chiang paid lip service to the Three People's Principles, but these were just empty words. He continued to collaborate with the warlords and the imperialists, as evidenced by the way he arranged the April 12 massacre. The Communists had no immediate plans to rebel against the Kuomintang, and Chiang's actions were taken to win favor with the bourgeoisie. So how could one hope that he would accomplish the goals of eliminating the warlords and the unequal treaties? Under the Kuomintang, China would have a "democracy" which was enjoyed only by the bourgeoisie. The Review printed such dissenting opinions, but followed them with responses which disputed their point of view. The Chinese Communists were rebels against the ideas of Sun Yat-sen and were under Russian control. The KMT was genuinely concerned with reform, and it offered the best hope for bringing peace and order to China. Were this not the case, the party would not enjoy the support of such honorable men as Ts'ai Yuan-p'ei, Li Shih-tseng, and Wu Chih-hui.

Ts'ai Yuan-p'ei, and other New Culture liberals, did indeed express optimism regarding the prospects of the newly victorious Kuomintang. Writing shortly after April, 1927, Ts'ai voiced his admiration for the speed of the Northern Expedition.[7] He reviewed the recent history of the Kuomintang and the dire circumstances in which Sun Yat-sen found himself in the early 1920s. Those compelled Sun to open the party to the Communists, with all their secret schemes and their policy of violent revolution. Ts'ai recalled that Borodin had recently told him that China needed to kill 5 million people to assure the success of the revolution. Borodin's plan, said Ts'ai, was to sacrifice China for the sake of revolution. Fortunately, Chiang Kai-shek recognized CCP intentions and acted decisively. Fu Ssu-nien and Chu Chia-hua (vice-chairman of the Board of Trustees of Chung-shan University, and later minister of education under the Nationalists) viewed the Kuomintang as the best-organized party in China, with the best chance to introduce reforms and make China strong enough to regain its sovereignty.[8] It needed a well-conceived strategy to assure the long-term support of the peasants and workers, and it needed to create a union of the world's weak powers to resist imperialist pressures. But the Kuomintang was China's best hope for success in these areas. T'ao Meng-ho expressed similar views.[9] He was generally supportive, but stressed that enduring popular support could come only from the ultimate implementation of well-designed programs for social progress. The first priority was to convene a conference of experts to analyze current Chinese conditions and make proposals for improvements.

New Culture Liberals and the Kuomintang

After the establishment of the Nationalist government, New Culture liberals were faced with deciding whether to associate with the new administration. Their philosophy stipulated cultural reform as a prerequisite for political reform. Hu Shih had vowed not to talk politics for twenty years. As preceding chapters have shown, neither Hu nor other liberals adhered to this strict proscription. Still, in the post-May Fourth years most restricted themselves to the role of educators and political critics, trying to effect a new cultural environment. But now that a new government was established, and one that promised to be more reform minded than its warlord predecessors in Peking, the liberal position was subject to reevaluation.

Ts'ai Yuan-p'ei, for one, was associated closely with Chiang Kai-shek (his fellow Chekiangese) and his faction of the Kuomintang from 1926 on. He directed underground work in Kiangsu and Chekiang during the Northern Expedition, became a member of the Central Supervisory Committee, and participated in all the important conferences which established the Nationalist government. Indeed, he along with Li Shih-tseng, Wu Chih-hui, and Chang Ching-chiang (Jen-chieh) were called the "four elder statesmen of the Kuomintang."[10] Chang Ching-chiang, a powerful behind the scenes supporter of Chiang Kai-shek, was Ts'ai's old friend, and it is likely that he played a key role in winning Ts'ai over to the KMT side.[11] At the time of the April, 1927 massacre and the subsequent conflict between the Nanking and Wuhan governments, Ts'ai sided with Chiang Kai-shek. In fact, at Chiang's December, 1927, marriage to Soong Mei-ling, Ts'ai officiated at the public ceremony in the ballroom of the Majestic Hotel.[12]

We should not forget, however, that Ts'ai later became disillusioned with the Kuomintang, retreating from politics to involve himself in the creation and development of the Academia Sinica, of which he was the first president. One of the causes of his disillusionment was his losing battle to free education from political interference.[13] In 1927-1928 Ts'ai's university council plan was given a brief trial. This proposal, first suggested by Ts'ai during the warlord period, called for dividing the country into university districts. Each district would have independent sources of revenue, and all educational affairs would be directed by the president of the national university located in that district. When implemented in 1927-1928 its effects were limited, partly because Kuomintang authority encompassed only a few provinces. But, beyond this, Ts'ai's goal of educational independence conflicted with an alternate view that education should serve the needs of the party. This meant that the party should control finances, have influence over the curriculum, and manage the student movement as an instrument of party policy. By the summer of 1928 it was clear that this latter viewpoint had prevailed within the Kuomintang, and on August 17 Ts'ai resigned all his government posts except that of president of Academia Sinica. In fact, however, he didn't sever all ties with the Kuomintang, and Ts'ai served as elder statesman and mediator on a number of occasions in subsequent years. But his relations with the KMT and Chiang Kai-shek were never again so cordial.

Chiang Meng-lin, too, expressed early support for the Nationalists by becoming involved in the administration of Chekiang Province after the Nationalist occupation in February, 1927. In July, 1927, after implementation of the university council plan, Chiang became chancellor of the Third Sun Yat-sen University (later National Chekiang-Kiangsu University) and in control of all education in Chekiang and Kiangsu Provinces. With the abolition of the university council plan and the restoration of the ministry of education, Chiang was named the first minister of education in the new Nationalist government. Chiang experienced the same conflicts as Ts'ai Yuan-p'ei regarding the Kuomintang's efforts to exercise tight control over education.[14] He was even required to betray his commitment to academic freedom, when instructed to stifle Hu Shih's criticism of the Kuomintang. Obeying orders, he revoked the registration of the China College of Shanghai, of which Hu Shih was president. Chiang Meng-lin's behavior helps clarify the liberal dilemma of the time. He desired national unity and a strong nation, and the Kuomintang offered the best hope for realizing those goals. Yet he disagreed with the KMT's educational policies, which emphasized state control, and he contemplated withholding his services on principle. His sense of responsibility to the nation proved the stronger impulse for a time, but in December, 1930 quarrels based on principles and personalities forced his resignation as minister of education.[15] He accepted the position of chancellor of Peking University, like Ts'ai returning to the classic liberal posture of nonpolitical service.

Lo Chia-lun, a Peking University student leader in the May Fourth period, also became an enthusiastic supporter of the KMT. He headed Chiang Kai-shek's editorial committee during the Northern Expedition and in 1927 became Tai Chi-t'ao's assistant at the Central Party Affairs Institute.[16] Given authority over hiring, Lo tried to fashion a Chinese replica of the London School of Economics. When he was appointed president of Tsinghua University in 1928, his close ties with the KMT aroused strong protests from students and alumni. Lo's inaugural address was entitled "Educational Independence and the New Tsinghua."[17] He explained that by changing Tsinghua into National Tsinghua University it could serve a more national purpose than just educating students for the United States. He claimed it could serve a more independent function. He also enunciated some fairly progressive, though conventional New Culture, ideas about accepting women students on an equal basis, encouraging research, and emphasizing graduate schools. Unfortunately for Lo, Tsinghua students and alumni didn't share his vision of the university's function. His appointment sparked widespread protests over his inexperience and his association with the Kuomintang.[18] The fear was that Tsinghua's true independence (based on its $8 million endowment) would be undermined and it would become a political football. He served two years, but alumni protests finally forced his resignation in May, 1930.

Tuan Hsi-p'eng, like Lo Chia-lun, absorbed the New Culture mood of Ts'ai Yuan-p'ei's Peita.[19] He then studied at Columbia University and in Europe, with the intention of returning to China to teach and to spread modern ideas. But upon his return in 1925 he abandoned this conventional liberal ambition for an active role in the Kuomintang. Support for national unity, as well as concern over the threat of communism, underlay Tuan's decision. He became a fervent member of the anti-Bolshevik faction of the KMT and was identified with the CC (Ch'en brothers) clique. By way of contrast Fu Ssu-nien, another May Fourth student leader and close friend of Lo and Tuan, remained detached from politics--serving as head of the Institute of History and Philology at the newly created Academia Sinica. Chang Po-ling (president of Nankai University) similarly resisted pressure to accept a political position, including mayor of Tientsin, because of his commitment to education.[20] Hu Shih was abroad from July, 1926, until the spring of 1927. In November, 1926, he gave a talk at Chatham House in London, admitting that he might have erred in opposing "political" solutions to China's problems.[21] But back in China he remained outside the government, assuming (along with several other New Culture liberals) the familiar role of political critic.

Political critics were no more welcome to the Nationalists than they had been to the warlords, but the restrictions on their activities were probably better enforced. Unlike the warlords, the Nationalists had an identifiable ideology and the desire to spread it nationally. Dissenters were not welcomed. Even during the Northern Expedition, the Kuomintang, as it advanced, closed schools and magazines associated with the Chinese Youth party.[22] The Awakening Lion Weekly, a Chinese Youth party periodical, was forced to move to Tokyo, and the party was banned as illegal for ten years. Teng Yen-ta, founder of the so-called Third party, was executed as a traitor in 1931. Indeed, Hu Shih maintained that virtually everyone with even innovative ideas was purged from the Kuomintang within a couple of years of its achievement of power.[23]

In December, 1930, a new publication law gave the Kuomintang considerable powers of censorship. Publications could be prohibited by the government in "times of necessity." Yet, studies seem to indicate that Nationalist policies of censorship were a patchwork quilt characterized by much confusion.[24] The Nanking government's authority didn't reach very effectively into north China, and newspapers and periodicals in Peking and Tientsin criticized the Kuomintang with relative impunity. The foreign concessions in Shanghai and elsewhere also offered some sanctuary from government interference. Often news printed in English language newspapers would be permitted, but then censored from the Chinese language press. Postal privileges were sporadically withdrawn from a number of publications, but usually they were quickly restored. Anti-Kuomintang, and even communist, literature circulated widely through ploys such as frequently changing the titles of journals or publishing a false title on the outside cover. Perhaps reflective of the Kuomintang's limited success with repression is the fact that it also attempted to buy off journalists with lucrative offers of favors or official positions.[25]

Despite deficiencies in enforcement, the Kuomintang's attempt to censor the press and restrict the scope of discussion struck at the fundamental liberal principle of free speech. This situation produced the first major confrontation between New Culture liberals and the Nationalist government. Writing in Crescent Moon (Hsin-yueh) liberals subjected the government to strongly worded attacks for its repression of freedom. Hu Shih led the onslaught, recounting numerous incidents of governmental interference with free speech.[26] Arguing that China needed the rule of law rather than the arbitrary whims of party officials, he urged the drafting of a constitution with a bill of rights. On 20 April 1929 the government had issued a statement announcing the protection of the rights of the people. Hu dismissed this as vague and limited to infringements of rights by individuals and groups. It provided no protection against the real threat, interference with rights by the party or the government. In a nation governed by law, the ordinary citizen and the leader were equally constrained by the laws of the land. This was not the case in China.

Hu also criticized Sun Yat-sen for not trusting the people's ability to govern themselves, thus insisting on a period of political tutelage. He suggested that those most in need of a period of tutelage were the government and the party, which needed the tutelage of living under the legal constraints of a constitution. Hu took the position that the ability to participate in government didn't require genius or expertise, just experience. So participating in a constitutional government was the best form of political tutelage. But political tutelage without a constitution and bill of rights was just autocracy and thus could never prepare the people for democratic government. Hu also took issue with Sun Yat-sen's adage that "Action is easy, but knowing is difficult." He argued that the division was artificial, that you learned from doing, and then you put your ideas into practice. Hu was acting in accordance with the liberal principle that the broadest diversity of opinion should be encouraged, and that public opinion would be edified and the best programs would emerge from unfettered public debate of the issues. The New Culture movement, he wrote, tried to liberate thought and to create an atmosphere of questioning and doubt. But currently it was a waste of money to buy a newspaper. There was no genuine news and no responsible criticism. The Kuomintang once was quite progressive in its thinking, but since the reorganization of 1924 it had become reactionary. Hu's sharply critical writings went too far for the KMT, and he was subjected to public rebukes and private pressures. However, he suffered no physical harm or arrest, perhaps because of his national reputation or because of the intervention of men such as Ts'ai Yuan-p'ei, Chiang Meng-lin, and Wang Ch'ung-hui (president of the Judicial Yuan).[27]

Liang Shih-ch'iu (literary critic) and Lo Lung-chi (editor of Crescent Moon and political scientist at Kuang-hua University in Shanghai) were also very much involved in the Crescent Moon defense of free thought. Liang argued that while some things should be under centralized control, such as the army and finances, ideas best prospered without any attempt to unify them.[28] There was no divinely ordained "truth" which was the monopoly of one individual or government, and society progressed because courageous individuals had the independence of mind to doubt and question. A republic needed freethinking citizens, and the government should not try to produce passive, indoctrinated robots. Individuals must resist efforts to restrict their freedom of expression, just as Sun Yat-sen did in opposition to the Manchu government. During the May Fourth period China had enjoyed an era of intellectual freedom, but this unfortunately was over.

Lo Lung-chi penned a series of articles criticizing the Kuomintang, especially its repression of human rights and its policy of party dictatorship.[29] Human rights were defined by Lo to include the right to life (including the right to food, clothing, shelter, and work), security, and the pursuit of happiness as long as that pursuit did not injure the welfare of the larger society. Echoing the ideas of Locke, Lo argued that the state's function was to protect these human rights, and when the state ceased to fulfill its function then individuals no longer were obliged to obey it. The rule of law, an independent judiciary, and freedom of thought were also components of a society enjoying its legitimate human rights. But China, far from being such a society, was instead a one-party dictatorship. And the Kuomintang's one-party dictatorship, he argued, had exceeded even the party dictatorships of Russia and Italy in its authoritarianism. Moreover, the party dictator in China (that is, Chiang) was far less able than Mussolini and so not even the Italian rationale of efficient management could be applied to China. Sun Yat-sen, wrote Lo, was a strong advocate of free speech, so anyone who repressed it was violating the teachings of Sun Yat-sen. Sun took the scientific attitude of considering all points of view before forming an opinion. In analyzing a problem he was always willing to have his views challenged by others if their ideas were valid. This is the way a great man operates, observed Lo, and somewhat sarcastically he pointed out that he was only following the Kuomintang's advice of studying party principles.

Lo Lung-chi's remarks led to his arrest on 4 November 1930, although after a few hours of questioning he was released on the good offices of Ts'ai Yuan-p'ei and T. V. Soong.[30] Apparently not a bit cowed, Lo afterward published a long article describing his arrest and his reactions to it.[31] Lo wrote that at 1:00 in the afternoon the police came to Wu-sung where he was teaching. They took him to the local police station and very politely told him how much they respected him and how very sorry they were to arrest him. They refused to allow him any phone calls, quite frankly admitting they intended to search his home and didn't want him tipping anyone off. He was taken to Shanghai at 5:30 p.m., where he was presented with a warrant stating that a Kuomintang official had accused him of reactionary writing and insulting the Tsung-li. He then was allowed to leave and returned to his house by 6:15. Lo observed that his experience indicated that any petty KMT member could accuse someone of reactionary acts, and the KMT district office could have the police arrest him. As a political scientist he was familiar with the basic responsibilities of a government to protect people's rights. The Kuomintang's arrest of individuals without proper legal procedures was a national disgrace. It was barbarism! It was crucial for the nation that schools be allowed free discussion. Once the police start arresting teachers, it is the end of education for the whole nation. In addition to such rhetoric, Lo offered the perceptive argument that such illegal arrests were very harmful to China's efforts to persuade Western nations to yield extraterritorial rights. It was unlikely that foreign nations would believe China's claim that its legal system was modern and able to protect the rights of foreigners when China treated its own citizens in such a high-handed way.

In the early 1930s the Kuomintang increasingly resorted to the arrest and execution of its critics and political opponents.[32] On 17 January 1931 five Communists were arrested, including the writer Ting Ling's husband, Hu Yeh-p'in. On 7 February these five and eighteen other alleged Communists were executed, despite the efforts of the writer Shen Ts'ung-wen who asked Ts'ai Yuan-p'ei and Hu Shih to intervene with the Kuomintang. In November, 1931, Teng Yen-ta of the so-called Third party was executed for treason. In July, 1932, Liu Yü-sheng, editor of the Chiang-sheng jih-pao of Chinkiang, was arrested by the government of Kiangsu.[33] The Control Yuan investigated and recommended that General Ku Chu-t'ung, chairman of the Kiangsu Provincial Government, be impeached. But this recommendation was announced on 23 January 1933, and Liu had been executed the previous day. General Ku (whom the China Forum characterized as an "appointee and henchman of Chiang Kai-shek") claimed that Liu had been a Communist who incited class struggle. Liu had published articles describing the suffering of the poor and criticizing the government for its corruption and its profiteering through opium sales in Kiangsu. In October, 1932, Ch'en Tu-hsiu was imprisoned, and in December, 1932, two Peking professors were arrested for an alleged association with the Communists.

The growing atmosphere of party dictatorship and repression distressed liberals, and many others. Even the supposedly "safe" delegates who attended the national emergency conference, at Loyang in April, 1932, adopted resolutions calling for a national representative congress and the protection of civil liberties.[34] This was despite the fact that the government, fearing criticism of its one-party role, had specifically limited the agenda to the three topics of foreign aggression, famine and flood relief, and suppression of the Communists. This restriction had led many non-Kuomintang delegates to boycott the conference in protest. Liberals were certainly angered by the trends of the time, but their mood might best be described as one of frustration. They were disgusted by the party's policies, yet they could see no alternative to the Kuomintang. T. F. Tsiang perhaps put it best when he complained that anyone who contemplated the policies of the party got a headache.[35] Yet Tsiang admitted that although the government was not very good, there was no alternative available.[36] Fu Ssu-nien expressed similar views.[37] Many urged the Kuomintang to distribute political power, he said, but to whom? There was no one who could assume power, and the collapse of the Kuomintang would add ten times over to China's problems. Yet, this situation stemmed from the weakness of others rather than from any Kuomintang strength. So, rather than feeling self-satisfied, the Kuomintang should be mindful of its deficiencies. Ting Wen-chiang similarly warned that a party dictatorship which refused to permit free discussion would produce a revolution, however much it wished to avoid one.[38] To truly avoid revolution, the government must accord those with different political views a means of peaceful expression. Even the Communist party, as long as it didn't break the law or stir up internal disorder, should enjoy the right of free speech.

Liberal Attitudes toward the Communists

As indicated above, in connection with the April, 1927

massacre, many New Culture liberals were highly critical of the Chinese Communists for their extremist methods, intolerance of dissent, and apparent subservience to Russian direction. Certainly some who enjoyed successful careers in Taiwan after 1949 frequently uttered hindsight rhetoric which echoed this early line of thought. Fu Ssu-nien, for example, wrote in the 1950s that "throughout history people have been subjected to many swindles, but the Communist party has devised the most thorough, scientific, and applied plan of swindling."[39] The Marxist dogma of class struggle sounded convincing as a comprehensive explanation of social development, he stated. But historical analysis shows the invalidity of a single predictable pattern of historical development. Communism appealed to poor peasants and to frustrated intellectuals, but the Communists just used these people to gain power for their own benefit. Chiang Meng-lin, also looking back from Taiwan, explained Communist success as the result of seducing the young into abandoning their sense of ethics.[40] The Communists disregarded right and wrong and adopted the policy that the end justified the means. But the times were bad, there was much corruption and disorder, and the Communist message sounded appealing. The young felt that existing governmental programs were inadequate, and the Communist slogans won many converts who were deceived by their promises.

However, in the early 1930s, the attitude of some liberals toward communism was a good deal more sophisticated and undogmatic. The arrest of Ch'en Tu-hsiu prompted a response from Fu Ssu-nien in the liberal journal, the Independent Critic.[41] Fu wrote that he hoped Ch'en would receive a fair trial, with the judgment based on law. He pointed out that Ch'en had been expelled from the Communist party earlier. He also urged that Ch'en's whole career be viewed in its proper perspective when rendering a verdict. He had made a major revolutionary contribution to China in the early years of the republic. Moreover, the Kuomintang itself had been interested in the labor movement for many years before the Communist party's interest. Thus Ch'en's turning to socialism could be interpreted as progressive for its time, rather than as reactionary (as Ch'en was then labeled by the Kuomintang).

In 1930 Lo Lung-chi wrote a series of articles offering his thoughts on communism.[42] In a critical vein, he argued that the ideal of a stateless and classless society was impossible. Even if the Chinese state was eliminated, England, France, America, and Japan would continue to exist. China would need some instrument to deal with them or it would likely be conquered and parcelled out. Regarding classlessness, he said that even if a proletarian society could be created, it would immediately begin breaking down into classes. The slogans Workers of the World Unite and From Each according to Ability; To Each according to Need were naive and unrealistic. Lo was willing to give qualified support to the Marxist idea of dialectical materialism as a theory of history. Economic factors and class conflict were significant causative factors. But it was too simplistic to think of them as deterministic. He pointed out that just as Marx and Engels could transcend their own bourgeois, material conditions to become leaders of the proletariat, so could others.

Despite his critical tone regarding its theory, Lo was quite realistic about the chances of communism gaining power in China. He ridiculed those who said there was no need to talk about communism (kung-ch'an chu-i), citing the old saying that China "had no goods to share" (wu-ch'an k'o-kung). Even if China was poor, there was still wealth and land which could provide communism a basis for development. In other words, it was foolish to dismiss communism with a flippant quip. Moreover, communism had more chance of success in a poor country than in a wealthy one where there was much wealth to distribute. Russia, for example, was poor yet this posed no obstacle to communist success there. While in America the people were well enough off and there was no large gap between rich and poor. But in China the government protected the special interests of a minority, there was much corruption, and there were large economic inequities. All these factors were grist for the communist mill, and the Chinese Communists had a real opportunity in China. Their success, he maintained, would depend largely on the quality of their leadership and on international developments. The Kuomintang lacked a great leader, and if the Chinese Communist party developed such a leader it might be the decisive factor. Presently, the Chinese Communists were just youths who knew how to shout slogans and throw bombs. But what would they be like later? Communism in China would also be affected by how successful communists were elsewhere in the world and by the behavior of foreign capitalists in China. All this, written in 1930, shows remarkable vision.

Lo also offered some sensible suggestions concerning how the government might combat communism in China. It should foster the development of an ideology to counter it, as occurred in Britain with the growth of Fabian Socialism. As the popularity of Fabianism rose the attraction of Marxism waned. So, instead of rigidly trying to "unify thought" and politicize education, the Kuomintang should encourage diverse parties and points of view. As things stood then, Lo stated, all the nonparty individuals who opposed communism had no way to work positively toward their goals. If they organized themselves, they were accused of being rebels. Thus, the existing one-party dictatorship alienated many non-Communists and prevented the development of something like Fabian Socialism in China, which could provide an alternative to communism and thus weaken its appeal.

As Communist strength grew in Kiangsi, Chiang Kai-shek mounted his five Extermination Campaigns, which by 1934 forced the Communists to undertake the Long March. New Culture liberals were anti-Communist and supported Chiang's efforts, but they clearly recognized the crucial political dimension to the struggle with the Communists in Kiangsi. Ts'ai Yuan-p'ei, for instance, agreed with the need for the military defeat of the Communists.[43] Their tactics of beguilement and secret organization made them a grave threat. But even if you have killed a snake, its poison is still dangerous. In the case of the Communists their poison was their propaganda, which had insinuated itself deep within the minds of the people. This poisonous propaganda must be drawn out, but to do so required a recognition and rectification of the horrible conditions which had allowed the propaganda to penetrate in the first place. The Kuomintang needed to introduce reforms which would prevent the area from again being controlled by corrupt officials and gentry. The Three People's Principles must be faithfully implemented to eliminate inequities and offer hope. Reforms were required to produce a more equal sharing of wealth, a fairer tax and rent structure, and broader opportunities for education.

T. F. Tsiang, too, objectively assessed Communist success in Kiangsi and the failure of early extermination campaigns.[44] The Communists had answered the people's needs, he wrote, and if the Kuomintang hoped to win the confidence of the peasants it must assure that its troops not abuse the people nor its officials cheat them. The Communist land distribution policies had greatly benefited the peasants, and the Kuomintang must convince the peasants that it will not overturn the land distribution program once the Communists are removed. It must persuade them that the KMT wants to eliminate the Communists because they are rebels, not because it plans to restore the special privileges of the gentry and the landlords. For one thing, he argued, you couldn't restore the past because all the old deeds were destroyed. But, more importantly, Communist propaganda emphasized the idea of class stuggle. If the government gave the impression of trying to restore the old landlords, it would lend credibility to that propaganda. The first task in defeating the Communists was to break the peasants' faith in them, and so it was crucial to avoid confirming the Communist charge that the Kuomintang represented the interests of the landlords.

Tsiang hoped that a program of land distribution in the recaptured territories would spread into a genuine national program of rural reform. The rural economy was the lifeblood of the nation. If it failed, China would collapse even if no external threat from Japan were present. Moreover, giving land to the tiller was originally a Kuomintang idea which had been preempted by the Communists. The Russian Revolution showed that the peasants were most concerned with land and would side with whatever party promised to eliminate the landlords and give them land. Some excesses were bound to occur in a land reform program. But the Kuomintang had no real choice. It could either implement a land distribution program now and undercut Communist success, or it could do it later, after the Communists had gotten the jump, and accompanied by much bloodshed. Tsiang argued that it was more sensible to "remove fuel from the pot" (fu-ti ch'ou-hsin), that is, to weaken the Communist appeal by making land distribution part of government policy.

Ting Wen-chiang used even blunter language to warn that Chiang Kai-shek and Wang Ching-wei had better wake up to reality and recognize the basis of Communist strength in Kiangsi.[45] The Communists weren't "bandits," but rather they were political opponents. As such, it would require more than military might to defeat them. The Communists had organization, ideology, and weapons. Their movement had grown because of China's internal chaos and governmental ineffectiveness. He was opposed to communism, but he wanted a more sensible effort to defeat it by political and social programs which eliminated the conditions from which it grew. Ting also made an effort to evaluate communist theories objectively. He recognized that Marx had made a contribution to economic thought by pointing out the inequities in the capitalist system. The poor were caught in a vicious circle, with their fate in the hands of the rich and little chance to escape. But it was too simplistic to take a deterministic viewpoint which ignored changes which had or could occur in the capitalist system. Besides, Russia hadn't yet created an equitable society, though he found the experiment there quite intriguing. On balance, Ting found communism an interesting theory, worthy of respectful attention. With regard to the prospects of the Chinese Communist party his attitude was more skeptical. First, he was troubled by the extent of Russian control over the party. Revolution was a complex matter, and he doubted if it could be directed by foreigners with little knowledge of Chinese conditions. Second, he questioned the quality of leadership available within the party. Lenin and Trotsky were intelligent and capable. They were able to seize the opportunity to make a revolution and to build a postrevolutionary society. He said that he had read the writings of the current Chinese Communist party leaders. They struck him as shallow and lacking historical perspective.

What is apparent from a review of liberal writings on communism is that they reflected the classic commitment to examine all ideas objectively. The Kuomintang, by way of comparison, adopted a dogmatic hostility to communism, and indeed they viewed almost any dissent as threatening. The result was the series of repressive acts discussed earlier, culminating with the arrest of Ch'en Tu-hsiu. These circumstances led to the formation of the Chinese League for the Protection of Civil Rights, in December, 1932. The chairman was Madame Soong Ch'ing-ling and Ts'ai Yuan-p'ei was vice-chairman, with other well-known members including writers Lu Hsün and Lin Yutang, Chiang Meng-lin, Li Chi (archeologist), and Hu Shih (until his expulsion after quarreling with the majority over conditions in China's prisons).

Chinese League for the Protection of Civil Rights

After Ch'en Tu-hsiu's arrest, Soong Ch'ing-ling issued a statement critical of the stance which many of China's newspapers had adopted on the issue.[46] They defended Ch'en, she said, because he had previously broken with the Communists. Madame Sun believed this was insufficient, and she defended him because his arrest was yet one more example of Kuomintang terrorism against working people, intellectuals, and students. And she announced her intention to establish an association to protect civil rights. Lin Yutang, who later was to join, initially expressed doubts about the idea in his column "The Little Critic."[47] He pointed out that the Crescent Moon had tried to defend freedom of expression, and the result was that Hu Shih moved from Shanghai to Peking and Lo Lung-chi was expelled from the university with which he was associated. And Lo Wen-kan, arrested without due process in 1922 while minister of finance, had expressed similar views to no avail. Nonetheless, the league was established in December, 1932, and Soong Ch'ing-ling stated that its three main goals were: (1) to try to liberate political prisoners; (2) to publicize prison conditions and illegal arrests and thereby arouse public opinion; and (3) to help in the struggle for freedom of the press, speech, organization, and assembly.[48]

Soong Ch'ing-ling, as the wife of Sun Yat-sen, was always a revered member of the Kuomintang, at least on paper.[49] Beginning in 1926 she was elected to the Central Executive Committee at every meeting of the party National Congress. But, in reality, she identified herself with the Left-Kuomintang as closer to the teachings of her husband, and she was sympathetic to the Communists. She sided with the Wuhan government against Chiang Kai-shek's Nanking government in 1927. After the Wuhan government purged itself of Communists and moved to rejoin Chiang, she issued a statement of protest. In August, 1927, she went to Russia, issuing statements critical of the Kuomintang for betraying Sun Yat-sen's ideas. Returning to China in May, 1929, for the state burial of Sun Yat-sen in Nanking, she made it clear that her presence should not be interpreted as support for Chiang Kai-shek. Shortly thereafter she left for a tour of Europe in 1930-1931, returning afterward to China where she lived in Shanghai from 1932 to 1937.

In creating the League for the Protection of Civil Rights, Soong stressed that it was not a political organization, even though its goals were political. In this sense the league was well within the liberal tradition, and it is no surprise to see so many New Culture liberals associated with it. However, in her statements concerning the league's goals, Soong enunciated a position that must have been uncomfortably radical for many liberals. "To those who accuse the league of defending terrorist rebels, we can answer that terrorist activities are common in repressive times. Even Wang Ching-wei felt forced to resort to them in his younger years."[50] Thus, implicitly, Soong was comparing Kuomintang repressiveness to that of the Ch'ing (on occasion she compared it to that of Hitler), and she was justifying rebellious activity. She dismissed the government's guarantees of civil rights, with their qualifying phrase "in accordance with the law," as worthless.[51] She stressed the need for a successful revolution in China. The capitalist nations were united, and China and other colonial peoples were weak. China needed a revolution if it was to avoid being conquered and divided up by the imperialist nations. She left little doubt that she felt the Kuomintang unqualified for this task.

The activities of the League for the Protection of Civil Rights were closely covered by Harold Isaacs's periodical, the China Forum. Isaacs and Agnes Smedley were the only two non-Chinese members.[52] Reappearing in February, 1933, after "more than five months' involuntary suspension" during which it had been denied postal privileges, the China Forum supported the league and its slogan For the Unconditional Liberation of All Political Prisoners.[53] It was not, however, initially very optimistic about the commitment of the league's members or their chances for success--fearing that it would be only a temporary enthusiasm for "high-class" Chinese, and that it would be suppressed by the Kuomintang. Nonetheless, the Forum provided considerable coverage of the league's efforts, particularly with regard to political prisoners and prison conditions. It printed statements from the league and letters from political prisoners concerning conditions in Kuomintang prisons.[54] All manner of tortures were described in vivid detail. These letters from prisoners became a bone of contention between Hu Shih and other members of the league.[55] Hu charged that they were forgeries, and this was the overt issue which led to Hu's disassociation from the league, in February, 1933. But the quarrel had deeper roots since Hu distrusted the methods of some of the more radical members of the league, such as Soong Ch'ing-ling and the secretary, Yang Ch'uan (Hsing-fo). Hu was much more willing to accept the government's right to prevent subversive activities and much more insistent than they that dissenters operate within the established legal framework. After Hu's disassociation, Soong Ch'ing-ling called him a false friend, and the China Forum wrote: "The Chinese masses can afford to lose intellectual aristocrats who would only be missed by foreign academies and ladies' tea clubs in Keokuk, Iowa."[56] The Forum rejected the argument that legal means could be used to remedy Kuomintang abuses. "It is futile--and more, it is reactionary--to speak of 'legalities' in connection with a struggle for civil rights when the present legal system in China is itself precisely designed to prevent the Chinese people from exercising their civil rights and is executing them and torturing them if they try to do so!"[57]

Following the episode with Hu Shih, the league continued to work on behalf of political prisoners. They visited prisons and tried to publicize the plight of those imprisoned for political reasons. The China Forum reported on league activites, effectively dramatizing the moral issues involved. Considerable attention was devoted to the case of the young and handsome Lo Tuan-hsien, leader of the Hong Kong strike in 1925 and secretary of the Seamen's Union.[58] The Forum made one feel the poignancy of a young man, with such prospects, wasting away in prison because he dared to act in accordance with his beliefs. The league protested the sentence imposed on Ch'en Tu-hsiu--thirteen years imprisonment and fifteen years deprivation of civil rights.[59] It also protested the imprisonment of two university professors based on their lecture notes. On 14 May 1933, a cause celebre occurred with the kidnapping of the writer Ting Ling. The Forum managed to obtain and print an eyewitness account of the abduction, which everyone believed was the work of Kuomintang agents.[60] Such an overt act was characteristic of the times. Indeed, Soong Ch'ing-ling and the league's secretary, Yang Ch'uan, received frequent threats on their lives. Soong, and presumably men such as Ts'ai Yuan-p'ei and Lu Hsün, were too revered by the public to be harmed. Yang Ch'uan, however, was not so protected, and on 18 June 1933 he was gunned down while taking his son for their regular Sunday morning drive.[61] The China Weekly Review reported that Yang's car was riddled with bullets from four or five gunmen who had been waiting in front of the Academia Sinica. Both his son and the chauffeur were wounded. The Review speculated that Yang's death was in retribution for the alleged murder of a Kuomintang agent by the Communists, which itself was an act of vengeance for his (the agent's) kidnapping of Ting Ling. Others believed that Yang was killed because he had information concerning Ting Ling's case.

The assassination shocked league members and liberals. Yang had been closely associated with Ts'ai Yuan-p'ei and was serving as secretary-general of the Academia Sinica, of which Ts'ai was president. Ts'ai was growing increasingly distressed by Kuomintang authoritarianism, and in 1935 he resigned from all administrative positions to concentrate fully on his work at Academia Sinica.[62] The liberal periodical, the Independent Critic, expressed its outrage at the assassination in a somewhat impersonal statement by T. F. Tsiang. As an item in the This Week section, without mentioning Yang Ch'uan by name, Tsiang issued a very strong denunciation of assassination as a political weapon--"Assassination is not politics, it is not party competition, it is murder, the lowest and vilest murder."[63] Use of assassination, he wrote, announces to the world that the ruling party is too impoverished in ideas to maintain the support of the people. Such a party can never win the trust of the people. This focus on the issue rather than the individual is not surprising given the fact that the Independent Critic was edited by Hu Shih, who had earlier had his disagreements with Yang Ch'uan.

Soong Ch'ing-ling's angry response was more personal.[64] She wrote that Yang had recently come to see her, showing her the threatening letters he had been receiving. Some of them also made threats against Soong, and Yang wanted to warn her. She replied that she had received similar letters, often in the most vulgar language, and she warned him to be careful. That was the last time she saw him alive. Soong vowed that Yang's death would not intimidate her or the league, but would just make them more determined. "The human dregs who carry out these crimes by order of their highly placed superiors are like beasts unchained . . . . When mad dogs run wild, everyone knows what has to be done to put an end to them."[65] But despite these strong words, the assassination accomplished what was probably one of its main objectives. The league was never a meaningful force afterward.

Yang Ch'uan's assassination points up an important consideration in assessing the actions of Chinese liberals. Despite the KMT's reputation for ineptness in its attempts to become a tightly disciplined dictatorship, its efforts did occasionally meet with success. Yang Ch'uan was killed; Ch'en Tu-hsiu was arrested and sentenced to thirteen years imprisonment; Ting Ling was kidnapped; labor leaders, journalists, and students were sporadically arrested and many died in prison. In other words, the Kuomintang--however inept--was still an authoritarian party, and it required courage to risk incurring its wrath. It is true that Chinese liberals never took any practical steps to threaten KMT authority, limiting themselves to the roles of educators and political critics. But such activities, often putting them in conflict with the authorities, carried risks ranging from government harassment and arrest all the way to death. That reality should be kept in mind when reviewing the most characteristic activity of liberals during the Nationalist period, that of creating and writing for literary and political journals.

6.

Liberal Periodicals during the Nationalist Period, 1928–1937

One of the most characteristic activities of New Culture liberals was that of establishing and writing for political journals. From Ch'en Tu-hsiu's New Youth to countless ephemeral local publications, the New Culture movement spawned a veritable avalanche of periodicals. During the warlord period the key liberal periodicals were the Weekly Critic, Endeavor, and the Contemporary Review. This chapter will examine some major liberal periodicals of the Nationalist period, paying special attention to the shifts in attitude which occurred with changing events.

First, a word is necessary about the context for this characteristic liberal activity. The underlying rationale was the long-standing liberal concern for influencing and educating society without active involvement in politics. This self-imposed caveat against politics made the role of political commentator, along with that of educator, a logical one for New Culture liberals.[1] Many Chinese with more radical proclivities criticized liberal political critics as dilettantes or reactionaries. Yet within their self-defined framework of principles, liberals could not have chosen a more activist stance and still been consistent with their beliefs. Indeed, as was discussed in earlier chapters, even the decision to talk or write about political questions involved much agonizing for some liberals. Another aspect of the context which bears repeating is the fact that political criticism in liberal journals, however dilettantish it appeared to some, carried real risks to one's personal safety. The Kuomintang might be laughingly inept at times, but one could never be sure when they would succeed. As mentioned earlier Yang Ch'uan was assassinated, Lo Lung-chi was arrested, and Ting Ling was kidnapped. In later years journalists Chang Chi-luan (editor of Ta kung pao) and Tsou T'ao-fen (editor of Life Weekly) were both arrested. One shouldn't forget that it took courage to be an independent critic in Nationalist China. Finally, it's important to appreciate that the ever-intensifying Japanese threat put considerable pressure on the liberals' conviction that they should be objectively critical of the government. Deeply patriotic, they could not remain unaffected by threats to the nation. And most felt that the Kuomintang, whatever its deficiencies, offered the only hope for unity and national resistance. So there was an understandable inclination to pull one's punches and support the government in a time of national crisis. Some even believed the national crisis so severe that they felt obligated to join the government, to make whatever contribution they could. In short, there was a noticeable gravitation of political critics toward the government as the years passed and the Japanese threat intensified.

The Crescent Moon

The Crescent Moon (Hsin-yueh yuen-k'an), mentioned earlier in connection with liberal resistance to KMT thought-repression, was founded in March, 1928, by poets Hsu Chih-mo and Wen I-to, Hu Shih, Lo Lung-chi, Liang Shih-ch'iu, among others.[2] It was initially a literary journal, created to counter the alleged decadence, pornography, and polemics of literature then being published in China. Taking as its slogan Dignity and Health, it wanted to show man as a whole being and evoke positive and pure emotions.[3] The journal represented the so-called Anglo-American group (that is, those educated abroad in England or America), and many American and English writers were introduced in its pages. Epitomizing the liberal spirit, it maintained the position that cultural reform was the first prerequisite of human change. Just as the "crescent moon" foreshadowed the glorious full moon to come, so did the encouragement of purer emotions and the liberation of human energy today give promise of a brighter day tomorrow.

Crescent Moon adhered to this philosophy during its first year of publication. There were poems, short stories, Hu Shih on Hung-lou meng, Wen I-to on the pre-Raphaelites, translations of Elizabeth Barrett Browning, and so forth. But beginning with the 10 April 1929 issue (volume 2, number 2) the journal regularly included one or two articles on contemporary political questions. A later special announcement explained the change, saying that many of the Crescent Moon group felt conscience-bound to speak out against the intolerable conditions in China.[4] Thus, an editorial decision was made that each issue include one or two articles dealing with contemporary affairs. Such articles were individual expressions of opinion, not the statement of a party or clique, and they were within the spirit of constructive and detached criticism characteristic of modern Chinese liberals. Most of the political articles were written by Hu Shih, Lo Lung-chi, and Liang Shih-ch'iu, and one of the major themes was KMT restrictions on human freedoms as discussed in chapter five.

In addition, Lo Lung-chi contributed some penetrating observations on China's political needs.[5] He argued that ideology was subordinate in importance to efficient administration. Ideological hair-splitting was thus implicitly a waste of time, since good administrators could make any system work. Lo wanted to replace the militarists and political hacks with a government of experts selected by competitive examinations. Indeed, he advocated a civil service system after the American model, with job protection to eliminate political pressure. He also urged schools to train public administrators. In eighteenth- and nineteenth-century Europe, he wrote, the ideal was laissez-faire. But presently people expected the government to assume much greater responsibilities, and managing a complex industrial state required special expertise.

Along with his plan for a government by experts, Lo also urged that China's one-party dictatorship be replaced by a constitutional democracy, with elections in which all parties might compete equally for votes. This violated his earlier advice against ideological debates, but he judged it necessary. He strongly objected to all personal, party, or class dictatorships because none protected the people's rights. Only the people, through a system of representative government, could protect their own rights. He also opposed temporary dictatorships and tutelage periods, especially when the temporary dictatorship was incapable of tutoring or providing a model from which the people might learn. He called for the immediate convening of a constituent assembly to devise a government that would combine entrusted power and expert service. In Lo's mind a country might be compared to a business. Just as a business ran smoothly with its directors and its expert managers, so a country would have its broad policies decided by its "directors" (that is, the people through their representatives in the legislature), and these would be implemented by its expert civil servants. Lo said he was aware of those who felt reforming people's minds was more important than political reforms. But he responded that even if people were bad, a good political system gave them less chance to do evil. Thus, Lo Lung-chi, in several articles in Crescent Moon, presented a statement of views that was more specific and systematic than the usual vague liberal exhortations.

Hu Shih, by way of contrast, rehashed some shopworn liberal cliches in several of his Crescent Moon articles. In "Which Road Do We Travel?" he reviewed the background to China's problems and reiterated his familiar homily that the scientific method, applied to China's problems one by one, offered the best prospects for the future.[6] When criticized by Liang Sou-ming for not placing enough blame for China's troubles on foreign imperialism and the warlords, Hu responded that the problems of poverty and internal chaos had existed prior to both of these factors. In another essay, his well-known "Introducing My Own Thought" which was reprinted in Crescent Moon, Hu wrote that the two men who had most influenced him were Huxley and Dewey.[7] Huxley had taught him to debate, and Dewey had taught him the experimental method. The gist was a restatement of his problems versus isms position that social issues were very complex and no dogma could encompass them all. The scientific method, applied on a one-problem-at-a-time basis, was the best approach. While Lo Lung-chi's Crescent Moon essays were pursuing new lines of thought, those by Hu Shih reflected a more conventional liberal faith in the potential of political commentary. He even took to sending a copy of Crescent Moon to Ch'en Pu-lei, Chiang Kai-shek's personal secretary, in hopes of promoting mutual understanding.[8]

The Independent Critic

Beginning with volume four, number 2 (September, 1932) Crescent Moon reverted to its old format as a purely literary magazine, and its final issue was dated 1 June 1933. But in the meantime the far more politically oriented Independent Critic (Tu-li p'ing-lun) had been developed. According to T. F. Tsiang, this journal had evolved from discussions among intellectuals about how they might help the nation after the Mukden Incident of 1931.[9] The discussants, in addition to T. F. Tsiang, included Ting Wen-chiang, H. C. Zen, Hu Shih, Fu Ssu-nien, Ch'en Heng-che, T'ao Meng-ho, and Weng Wen-hao. In a standard liberal conclusion, the majority decided that in addition to teaching they might create a new journal.

The proper role for intellectuals in a time of national crisis was a recurring concern which grew more pressing as the Japanese threat intensified. Several New Culture liberals addressed the topic in essays in the Independent Critic. Ch'en Heng-che wrote that she could recall her days as a student in the West, in the late 1910s and early 1920s.[10] At that time everyone was certain they would never accept a government position, they would avoid like the plague any connection with the government. Students in that period were very idealistic and wanted to serve their country, she observed, but the political system was so corrupt that it didn't appeal to them.

Moreover, students then deeply believed that the basis for saving the country lay with science, education, industrialization, and scholarship. They thought these more significant than politics. But in the last ten years it had become clear that because politics were not on the right track, industry hadn't developed, education was more decadent and less worthwhile, and scholarship could make no progress. The shortsightedness of the past had become apparent, and unless politics could be reformed there would be no basis for education, industry, and scholarship. Now men of talent were reconsidering their position and were willing to accept official positions. However, Ch'en wasn't advocating that all scholars become politicians. She cited the example of Weng Wen-hao who was nominated by the government, and served briefly, as minister of education. Many people thought he could provide more service to the nation by remaining as director of the National Geological Survey, and Ch'en tended to share this view.

Weng Wen-hao, in fact, also addressed this question of what role he should play in society.[11] He wrote that he had always wished to do some job which gave him satisfaction and caused no harm to society. He had never had any particular interest in big philosophical, social, or political questions. But the urgency of national issues since the Japanese invasion had forced him to come to grips with such larger matters. People were asking him to join various organizations and sign various statements. Also, many students were confused and were asking for his advice. So he concluded that he must formulate his views on political and social questions and state them publicly, even if they were beyond his area of expertise and consequently not very sophisticated. Weng therefore conveyed the impression that scholars could no longer enjoy the luxury of disinterest in political questions. They must inform themselves on these matters and be willing to express their views. But he was not a joiner of organizations or a signer of statements. Nor did he feel everyone must join the army or the government to contribute to the national welfare. He felt his job was important, and he intended to do it to the best of his ability. The fact remains, however, that Weng along with T. F. Tsiang would join the government in December, 1935.

The question of the proper role of intellectuals in a time of national crisis was most thoroughly analyzed by T. F. Tsiang.[12] "What Can We Say Now?" Tsiang asked in an Independent Critic article. We literary men lack the qualifications to criticize the military. We have no military training and so can't go onto the battlefield. What can we say in the midst of the Japanese invasion and student demonstrations? First of all, Tsiang urged intellectuals not to feel the whole burden of saving the nation was on their shoulders. In earlier times the main goal of Chinese intellectuals was to become officials, and many still looked to China's current intellectuals to assume special governmental responsibilities. Many, including the intellectuals themselves, asked why China's intelligentsia couldn't play the same vital role as their French and Russian counterparts had after their revolutions. And after Mukden the expectations regarding China's intellectuals grew even greater. But Tsiang strongly argued that Chinese conditions placed limits on the potential influence of intellectuals. The educational level among the masses was low and so the calls of the intellectuals reached only a limited number of ears. Chinese conditions of poverty meant that most people of necessity concerned themselves with their own affairs and couldn't be stirred to think in larger national terms. So saving the nation required the cooperation of all segments of Chinese society, and couldn't be the exclusive task of the intellectual.

Having said all this, however, Tsiang was honest enough to recognize that some of the blame for China's problems did rest with the intellectuals. He criticized them for naively, and sometimes opportunistically, consorting with one warlord after another over the last twenty years. They refused to learn the lesson that their idealistic plans had no chance of implementation under any warlord regime. Moreover, too often they had been guilty of formulating high-blown reformist programs based on abstract Western political theories rather than on a realistic assessment of Chinese conditions. Vague, long-range programs had no relevance to the immediate needs of the Chinese people. Finally, Tsiang offered his suggestions for proper behavior on the part of China's intellectuals, and his views (written in May, 1933) were widely shared by liberals very much aware of the Japanese threat to their nation. First, he urged intellectuals to work toward a more unified Chinese society, with a more effective central government. Only such a government could create a strong country and a modern economy. The central government was in the spotlight so its errors were very visible, but intellectuals should not withdraw their support. If it made mistakes, intellectuals should try to correct them legally while continuing to give the government their support. Even if the central government did not satisfy the needs of all the people (that is, even if it was not the reformist government liberals wished to see), it was still far better than a fragmented society. Second, he urged that intellectuals be modern men, by which he meant rational, active, and community-spirited. Chinese intellectuals were still too bookish and detached from the real world. Those inexperienced in foreign affairs were telling the government to declare war; first-year students were telling university presidents how to run the university; those who had never been in a factory were offering solutions to the labor question. Tsiang wanted intellectuals to move away from their books and into the real world.

Variations on this last theme were played by several writers in subsequent issues of the Independent Critic. Wu Ching-ch'ao lamented over how few intellectuals were willing to take their knowledge to the countryside.[13] Wu claimed he asked one of his classes how many planned to go to the countryside after graduation. Only one of thirty raised his hand. He understood the reasons why so many preferred the cities, with their professional opportunities and amenities. Also, there were family pressures which discouraged university graduates from living in the villages and thus missing opportunities for professional advancement. Even those who studied agronomy preferred to stay in the cities, at universities or as government bureaucrats. Wu understood the situation, but he regretted that it was so.

Yen Shu-ch'ang (professor of law at Wuhan University), on the other hand, indirectly defended the reluctance of intellectuals to venture into the countryside.[14] He did so by strenuously criticizing James Yen's efforts in Tinghsien. Yen Shu-ch'ang, who was from Tinghsien, maintained that the people there were very distrustful of James Yen as an outsider. They wondered why he didn't carry out his experiments in Szechwan, where he was born. They felt that his mass education society had been all symbol and no substance, and that it had brought no benefits to them. Yen said that such criticism would not be found in the official report, but that was how the people of Tinghsien actually felt. This writer clearly believed that a massive influx of intellectuals into the countryside would do more harm than good. T. F. Tsiang felt called upon to respond, adding an epilogue to Yen's essay.[15] He argued that China's rural problems were immense. While he didn't like to use the term "revolution" because of its connotation of violence, the rural areas did need revolutionary changes (though without violence) to deal with poverty and backwardness. He said that Yen Shu-ch'ang's comments on the hostility of Tinghsien to outsiders did not surprise him. Certainly many intellectuals who went to the countryside had misconceptions about rural matters and made foolish blunders. But this was no reason to terminate projects such as that at Tinghsien. On the contrary, it was all the more reason to work harder to understand the problems and modernize the countryside. In fact the difficulty wasn't the overzealousness of intellectual reformers, but rather the failure of people to appreciate the seriousness of rural problems. Fortunately a few individuals were willing to go to the countryside to implement experimental programs. Inevitably they would make mistakes, but they deserved all possible support for their efforts. Tsiang's response to Yen was written despite his admission that he had never been to Tinghsien. Some months later after a visit there, Tsiang wrote a highly favorable assessment of James Yen and his mass education program.[16] The villagers were beginning to read and to understand new ideas. This made them much more receptive to change and much less suspicious of outsiders. He was especially impressed by the high spirit and motivation of the peasants who were getting the chance for an education. If university graduates could have the same spirit, China's salvation would be assured.

The Independent Critic lived up to its name during 1934 and 1935. The New Life movement was treated in less than complimentary fashion by Hu Shih.[17] There were frequent articles about the suffering of the peasants, and the need for an effective rural policy. Wu Ching-ch'ao criticized the government's actions in Kiangsi after the successful campaigns against the Communists.[18] He pointed out that the Communists had made such inroads there because of their land distribution policies, and land to the tiller was still one of China's most fundamental needs. There also appeared the familiar liberal criticism of Kuomintang policies of thought repression. In the 12 May 1935 issue, articles by Chang Hsi-jo and Hu Shih reasserted the belief that a strong, healthy nation consisted of strong, healthy individuals.[19] Chang pointed out that Europe had recognized the importance of the individual during its Renaissance, which led to the liberation of thought and then to the scientific revolution. China began this process during the May 4 Period, but unfortunately it had been curtailed by the Kuomintang's policies of thought unification. Chang admitted that individualism and free thought had some drawbacks, but on balance these were outweighed by the advantages. One of the special advantages was that an individual with freedom of expression and freedom to criticize the government would know that his opinion meant something. Consequently, he would develop an active interest in his government and support for those policies which he helped shape. Clearly Chang felt this preferable to the passive citizens of a party dictatorship. Hu Shih agreed with Chang that the sincere, brave, free-thinking individual was the best foundation for social progress. Such individuals should be nurtured because a modern society would be made up of men who loved freedom, not by slaves.

Hu Shih also restated his oft-repeated arguments about the need to end one-party rule and implement a constitutional government.[20] He argued that the corruption and inefficiency of the present administration was largely due to the monopoly of power by the KMT. The best way to rectify this was to allow one or more opposition parties to act as a check on Kuomintang abuses. Ch'en Chih-mai disagreed, saying that the abolition of one-party government would cause confusion and make it harder to deal with the nation's problems.[21] Chinese conditions were not suitable for an expansion of political rights to the people. As a compromise he suggested that the Kuomintang allow different factions within the party to publicly express their different views. Lo Lung-chi strongly reiterated his preference for an end to the period of political tutelage, citing three reasons.[22] First, it was important to preserve faith in the government. The period of tutelage was supposed to be for a limited time. In 1929 the government said it would end in six years, which meant 1935. Since the New Life movement listed trust as one of the eight virtues, it was crucial that the government set a good example. Second, involving the whole nation in the political process would produce a more unified national spirit. Finally, he argued that ending political tutelage would enhance executive efficiency. The present system mixed dictatorial characteristics with democratic characteristics (such as the five Yuan and separation of powers). Trying to blend mutually contradictory elements was causing confusion. China needed a fundamental reorganization of its political system.

The characteristic tone of the Independent Critic in the years preceding the Sian Incident was indeed one of objective criticism. On the fourth anniversary of the journal's establishment, in May, 1936, Hu Shih expressed his pleasure that circulation had risen to 13,000 and that the journal had maintained its independent stance.[23] However, these years also witnessed a growing acceptance of the viewpoint that the national crisis compelled a more sympathetic attitude toward the government. It was clearly reflected in T. F. Tsiang's "What Can We Say Now?" and again in another of his articles published in November, 1935--one month before he accepted Chiang Kai-shek's invitation to join the government.[24] The Kuomintang had been in power for almost ten years, he wrote, and its enemies claimed that its only "accomplishments" were economic bankruptcy and submission to Japan. But Tsiang urged that readers sift through the propaganda and avoid oversimplifying complex issues. Although there were many ways in which the Kuomintang had failed to satisfy the wishes of the people, the blame for "submission to Japan" shouldn't be placed on its shoulders. He then cited a Japanese general who had said that the KMT was firmly resisting imperialism and trying to abrogate the unequal treaties. The issue of economic development was also complex, he maintained, relating more closely to large factors such as Chinese traditions than to one individual or party. Also the internal divisions, begun during the warlord period, and the worldwide economic depression had much impact on China's economic condition. And these could not be blamed on the party. So China's problems were grounded in broad forces, and political changes such as ending the period of tutelage would have little effect.

The China Critic

The general liberal perspective, and its modification with time, are nicely reflected in the pages of another liberal journal of the Nationalist period, the China Critic. This English language periodical, founded on 31 May 1928, was indirectly connected with the New Culture liberals surveyed in this study. Hu Shih was listed as a contributing editor and the calligraphy for the Chinese title was written by Ts'ai Yuan-p'ei. The staff was composed mostly of Tsinghua University alumni, and a familiar Anglo-American and New Culture character was definitely present. The first editor, Chang Hsin-hai (H. H. Chang), was born in Chekiang in 1898, went to the United States on a Tsinghua scholarship, studied literature at Harvard, completed a Ph.D. dissertation on Matthew Arnold, and in 1923 became a professor at Peita and Tsinghua.

During the early Nationalist period the China Critic adopted positions similar to those of the New Culture liberals analyzed thus far. It echoed Ts'ai Yuan-p'ei's argument that student involvement in politics, while previously justified, was no longer appropriate.[25] It also wanted to keep education free of politics, with the corollary that educators and politicians should stick to their own baliwicks.[26] It expressed the conventional view that the Communists were a grave threat to peace and order. In June, 1929, the Critic applauded Chang Hsueh-liang's raid on the Soviet consulate in Harbin, which captured documents and broke up a secret meeting of forty-one Communists.[27] The Communist threat justified overriding the normal immunity of foreign consulates. In December, 1930, it praised Chiang Kai-shek's efforts to "eradicate the red bandit menace" in the south. According to the Critic the seriousness of that menace was demonstrated a few months earlier when " . . . the reds suddenly pounced upon the city of Changsha and visited communistic terrorism upon the innocent people."[28] But by the spring of 1932 it was taking a more realistic, though equally hostile, look at the Communists in Kiangsi.[29] It recognized that they were winning the support of the peasants by eliminating landlords, reducing taxes, and redistributing the land. So, to defeat them the government would have to learn a lesson from the Communists and provide for the needs of the people. The use of force alone would never get at the root of Communist support. It would merely increase government expenses and thereby the tax burden on the people, and as such would be counterproductive.

The Mukden Incident and the Japanese threat received thorough coverage in the China Critic, which adopted a very anti-Japanese stance. A 3 December 1931 editorial, entitled "Courageous Youth," had high praise for the thousands of students who went to Nanking, waiting twenty-eight hours in front of a government building until Chiang Kai-shek came out and pledged to go north to recover the lost territory.[30] It even went so far as to urge the government to attack the Japanese without a declaration of war. The enemy was so deceitful that the normal rules of international conduct should be waived. In January, 1932, the Critic again defended student demonstrations calling for resistance to the Japanese-- " . . . this is a republic, and in a republic when the government is not meeting a critical situation in such a way as the public opinion demands, the people have the right to take a hand in directing that policy."[31] The students would respect governmental authority, it wrote, when there was true authority which deserved respect.

Despite its criticism of government inaction regarding the Japanese, it was apparent that the Critic was feeling the pull of patriotism. Coverage of the national emergency conference, in April, 1932, is a case in point. As discussed in chapter five, many non-Kuomintang members boycotted the conference, and New Culture liberals criticized it, because the agenda was restricted to resisting foreign aggression, famine and flood relief, and suppression of the Communists. This restriction was imposed because the government wished to avoid discussion of its one-party rule. Yet even this supposedly safe conference passed resolutions critical of government policies. The China Critic, however, supported the carefully tailored agenda, although it recognized the sincerity of those who sought to discuss an end to party dictatorship.[32] In a time of crisis, it editorialized, the country must concentrate on the three issues raised. The problem of party dictatorship was not crucial at that time. The people were willing to accept any form of government so long as it could function effectively. It was action that counted, not political formalities. The Critic's patriotism also affected its stance on the question of freedom of the press. While supporting freedom of the press in principle, the Critic on several occasions expressed approval of governmental restrictions against journalists whom it felt were maliciously hostile to China. George E. Sokolsky, of the North China Daily News, and Hallett Abend, of the New York Times, were placed in that category. It supported the deportation of Sokolsky, whom it accused of trying to undermine Chinese morale. Stressing that even the American government suppressed the socialist press and imprisoned Eugene Debs during World War I, the China Critic stated: "We need not point out the difference between slander and criticism."[33]

Although the Critic might at times pull its punches if circumstances warranted, it did not wholly abdicate its responsibility for criticism. It did, in general, protest government violations of civil rights and call for a Bill of Rights.[34] It did basically champion freedom of the press, particularly for itself. After one public assurance by the government that freedom of the press would be guaranteed, the Critic wrote that it would test the government's sincerity by publishing editorials and articles of a "constructively critical nature" to see if they were tolerated.[35] Despite its previously mentioned comments on the April, 1932 national emergency conference, in July it editorialized that China needed a constitution to provide a legitimate means for opposition parties to contend for influence.[36] When the Chinese League for the Protection of Civil Rights was formed, in December, 1932, the Critic expressed its support. Conservatives would doubtless be upset, wrote the Critic, but they overlooked the fact that " . . . the best way to deal with the so-called dangerous elements in society is not by suppressing them, or locking them up in gaol."[37] While cautioning that liberty did not mean license, it argued that the national crisis did not mean that civil rights should be sacrificed for the sake of state unity.

Despite this rhetoric, the Critic's reaction to Yang Ch'uan's assassination in June, 1933 was cautious, one might even say timid. It warned that Madame Sun's charges were only allegations and yet to be proved. It criticized the league for previous extremist statements and for displaying China's dirty linen for the whole world to see. It argued that a call for civil liberties was futile until the masses understood them, and it urged the league to devote itself to educating the people gradually about such matters. It concluded that if the government was indeed involved, " . . . we, as staunch supporters of the national government as the only one qualified to speak for China at this critical period of her history, would feel this incident all the more keenly."[38] A few months later an assassination attempt was made on Lo Lung-chi, who was then editor of the independent-minded I-shih pao in Tientsin. On this occasion the Critic admitted that many saw the government's hand in recent unsavory acts. However, it refused to believe that " . . . our political leaders are capable of such base tactics."[39]

It is reasonable to infer that some degree of prudent discretion was involved in the Critic's apparent deference toward the government. Yet it is also true that both external and internal threats to the nation were intensifying, and the Critic felt duty-bound to demonstrate its loyalty to the government in power. The Fukien rebellion, in November, 1933, was angrily denounced by the China Critic. It argued that whatever grievances the rebels had against the national government, they were minor compared with China's grievances against Japan. Everyone must help the country pull together in this time of crisis, and " . . . any Chinese who ignores that duty and contributes to the difficulty of its fulfillment is guilty of downright treason."[40]

By late 1933 the China Critic had gravitated into a position of loyal support for Chiang Kai-shek and the Kuomintang. The New Life movement and the restoration of ceremonies honoring Confucius prompted much enthusiasm. The New Life movement, which "promises to become presently the craze of the country," was portrayed as offering solutions to China's moral and physical degradation.[41] The Critic gave quite thorough coverage to the democracy versus dictatorship debate which began in late 1933, printing articles on both sides. But special prominence was given to the views of T. S. Tsao (former president of Tsinghua University), who felt a dictatorship was necessary to eliminate the waste of time and resources resulting from recurrent civil wars. He saw such a dictatorship evolving in China at that time, and he welcomed it. Dictatorships were not necessarily desirable in the long run, but they were vital for solving pressing immediate problems. As he put it, " . . . some twenty odd nations today have accepted dictatorships so that they may better meet the political exigencies of the moment."[42]

As the Japanese threat intensified, the pull of patriotism grew stronger. The December 9 student demonstrations received cautious approval at first, but soon the Critic was parroting the government line and urging "constraint and caution." Students should study and prepare themselves until called upon "to make the supreme sacrifice."[43] The Critic voiced little criticism regarding the arrest of the seven intellectuals of the All China National Salvation Association, in November, 1936, despite its implicit admission that the arrests were politically motivated.[44] The Critic merely said that legal proceedings should progress quickly to see if the defendents had broken any laws. If the arrests proved politically motivated, it hoped the government would be lenient. By late 1936 the China Critic was almost fawning on the government and Chiang Kai-shek. The Sian Incident horrified the Critic, although it took some consolation in the orderly way the government functioned in Chiang's absence. Chang Hsueh-liang was branded a traitor, whose behavior was "treachery against a patriot and leader who deserves the gratitude of all Chinese." Chang's rationalization, that the government was refusing to resist the Japanese, was rejected categorically by the Critic. Never before had the government taken a firmer stand against Japan in its negotiations, it argued. It advocated "swift and sure punishment to the rebels and traitors."[45]

The China Critic began in 1928 with a characteristic liberal stance. As the years passed, and the Japanese threat became more frightening, the Critic felt the ever-increasing pull of patriotism. In the end it gravitated into orbit around the government. The same force operated upon all New Culture liberals, and few could resist it. Japanese aggression made the dilemma of modern Chinese liberalism, already painful, still more difficult to resolve.

7.

The Japanese Threat and Gravitation toward the Government

Japanese aggression, beginning with the Mukden Incident of 18 September 1931, posed a final series of dilemmas for New Culture liberals. Well informed about world affairs, they were highly sensitive to the Japanese threat in Manchuria. As early as 1927 Chang Po-ling, president of Nankai University in Tientsin, was troubled enough to make a personal investigation.[1] Afterward he organized a Northeast Study Society, with ten members, to analyze and report publicly on the population, economy, agricultural prospects, and other matters in the area. He wanted to heighten public awareness of the potential of Manchuria and of the need to pay more attention to developments there. But balancing this patriotic concern over Japanese aspirations were the conventional liberal faith in rationality and the antipathy to violence. For quite some time China's New Culture liberals viewed Japanese actions with the remarkable patience that comes from a conviction of the sweet reasonableness of their fellow man. There were exceptions, but generally liberals upheld the position that war against the Japanese would be ill-advised (especially given the state of China's preparedness), and that an accommodation could be reached through good faith on both sides. Yet the unrelenting pressure from Japan made this position increasingly untenable.

Many in China, especially the students, couldn't view Japanese actions with calm detachment. On 15 December 1931, a group of students demonstrated in Nanking in protest against the government's lack of resistance to Japanese aggression. The Kuomintang's Central Executive Committee was meeting, and it designated Ts'ai Yuan-p'ei and Ch'en Ming-shu (acting chairman) to talk with the shouting students.[2] Going into the crowd, they were surrounded and roughed up a bit. Ts'ai suffered a head injury. Afterward, in an interview with the press, he expressed sadness over his treatment after having devoted so many years to educating the students.[3] Politely, he took the blame upon himself and explained the demonstrations as the work of "reactionary elements" (meaning the Communists). The students had the highest patriotic intentions, he said, but they were being used and they were misusing their time. They should be preparing themselves for a long-term contribution to the nation. Ts'ai was as patriotic as anyone. Indeed, Lo Chia-lun wrote that once while pleading with Wang Ching-wei to be less friendly with the Japanese, Ts'ai felt so deeply about the matter that tears dropped down his face into his soup.[4] But he felt that China was too weak in defense capabilities and economic resources, and it was wiser to concentrate on preparedness.

Hu Shih's position was similar. He was outraged at the creation of the "false state" of Manchukuo. But the basic cause of Japanese aggression was Chinese weakness, and you couldn't "cure a seven-year illness with a three-year medicine."[5] The source of China's weakness lay in all the bad habits and customs which had evolved over thousands of years. These couldn't be done away with overnight. Progress, industrial development, and national strength came from cumulative efforts. They couldn't come by fits and starts. Moreover, Hu sincerely dreaded the devastation of war. He kept hoping that the force of world opinion would restrain Japanese aggression, and he reacted hopefully to the League of Nations' Lytton Report in the fall of 1932. "If this kind of serious restraint exercised by world opinion still cannot, even at the moment of gravest crisis, make a drunken people sober up a bit, then our country and the whole civilized world must prepare to live through ten years of hell."[6]

T. F. Tsiang, too, seemed generally approving of the Lytton Report, particularly for its emphasis on the potential benefits of economic cooperation between China and Japan.[7] Tsiang felt that such cooperation, in Manchuria and elsewhere, was the best way for China to develop itself. And it was China's economic and military weakness which had invited Japanese aggression. So China needed to be strong to discourage similar threats in the future. For the present he, like Hu Shih, recognized that China's fate was dependent on the winds of world events, but he weighed China's prospects here quite realistically. He took pains to disabuse those who expected Russia to intervene on China's behalf.[8] Some thought that Lenin's theory of opposing imperialism would lead Russia to help China resist Japan. Tsiang responded that not only was Russia unable at that time to aid China, but that actually it hoped Japan would invade China and get bogged down there. This would lessen the threat to the Soviet East. With regard to the United States, he was troubled by the results of the 1932 presidential election.[9] He worried that Roosevelt and the Democrats might not be so well disposed toward China as Hoover and the Republicans. He had the impression that the Democrats favored independence for the Philippines, and thus less American involvement in the Far East. He recalled that a Democratic president, Woodrow Wilson, had betrayed the Chinese at Versailles. Finally, he understood that as long as the United States refused to cooperate with the League of Nations, the league would be ineffectual in Asia. As a result neither the league nor such international agreements as the Nine Power Pact or the Kellogg-Briand Pact could offer much hope to China.

The dilemma posed by Japanese pressure was perceived in more personal terms by some New Culture liberals. Weng Wen-hao (geologist and educator) urged everyone to assume his appropriate responsibilities in defending the nation.[10] But he had grave reservations about joining the various anti-Japanese organizations urged on him by friends. He found their programs too overstated and open-ended. He didn't wish to sign any document declaring his hostility to Japan unless it was precisely limited to the current circumstances. A middle-aged man such as he might expect to live thirty or forty more years, he said, and in that time international relations would surely change many times. He didn't want to be locked into a position which might prove embarrassing in the future. Ch'en Heng-che offered advice to a young female student who wanted to fight against the Japanese.[11] Ch'en suggested that such a course of action based on momentary emotions, however understandable and praiseworthy, would not be as important to the nation as more long-term contributions. It would be tragic for someone with such potential to be killed because of excessive patriotism. The external threats to the nation were less important than the internal disorder, the backwardness, the scourge of opium, the poverty. The best way to save China was to work for the long-range health of the nation. This was a position which Ch'en Heng-che had articulated before, and it was the course which she followed in her own career. Lo Chia-lun (chancellor of National Central University in Nanking during the period) wrote that he was in a very difficult position during the 1930s.[12] He knew of government plans for "preparing" to resist Japan, but at the same time he was in daily contact with fervent youths who wanted immediate resistance. It was a painful situation for him, as he could only counsel patience and direct the singing of patriotic songs and the organization of military training.

The question of what scholars could do was on many people's minds. After the Mukden Incident a meeting of

Peking University faculty was convened.[13] Much discussion ensued regarding how scholars could serve the nation. One conclusion reached was that they could put together a comprehensive history of China, to foster nationalism, and the history department took this as its special responsibility. One member of Peita's history department, Fu Ssu-nien, actually ventured beyond his area of academic expertise to publish An Outline of Manchurian History.[14] His purpose, as he explained in the Introduction, was to show how Manchuria had been a part of China and to refute Japanese claims to the contrary. Japan had made the claim that Manchuria and Mongolia were not historically a part of China, and used it as a rationale for invading the northeast. Chinese historians, thus, could serve the nation while remaining historians--by taking up this kind of historical topic. Fu even had the book translated into English to reach Western audiences, sending a copy to the League of Nations. This was how one liberal sought to reconcile his patriotic impulses with his liberal principles. The book was written in haste, however, and other scholars were not willing to suspend their critical judgment for patriotic reasons. They criticized the work on scholarly grounds, and Fu dropped the idea of future volumes.

Fu Ssu-nien also published several articles on Japanese aggression in the Independent Critic, whose creation in May, 1932, resulted from a group of intellectuals seeking another way to make a contribution to the nation. An extended analysis appeared on the first anniversary of the Mukden Incident, where he described his feelings one year after Mukden.[15] First, he regretted that the Incident hadn't unified the Chinese people. He had expected that after Mukden everyone would pull together against the common enemy. Unfortunately, this hadn't occurred and governmental factions were as strong as ever. Few people had any faith that fragmentation and regionalism would respond to government exhortation. Second, he was disappointed that China was still living in a dream world of unreality. There was still no apparent determination to face the crisis. People of the northeast purchased Japanese goods as always, thus continuing to strengthen Japan. The middle class was still concerned with its own small comforts and hadn't perceived that its fate was linked with the fate of the nation. Third, he was distressed by the ineffective reaction of the world community. Neither individual nations, like the United States or Britain, nor the league had made any meaningful response to Japanese aggression. He was especially disappointed with England for its failure to recognize that Japanese ambitions clearly threatened British interests worldwide.

Another cause of distress for Fu was the bankruptcy of

KMT policy regarding Japan. Yet he saw no alternative to the party. One wouldn't wish to hand power over to the Peiyang, Anfu, or political science cliques. Nor did he believe that the Chinese Communists offered any constructive solutions. However, despite all these negative observations, Fu maintained that there was no cause for despair. China had great staying power, as indicated by her three thousand years of history. Things often looked bad in the past, but they eventually improved. The northeast was inhabited by Chinese, and no amount of Japanese control could change that fact. He cited Taiwan as an example of how Japanese control could not destroy the essential Chineseness of an area. In essence, he was relying on the old adage that China always absorbed or expelled barbarians, and he indicated his belief that eventually a rebellion would drive the Japanese out of Manchuria. It was also possible that international forces would soon be more positive. Thus far the international response had been disappointing, but he expected that to change. The British would have to protect their interests in the Liaotung Peninsula. The United States would have to recognize its moral commitment stemming from the Washington conference, and its strategic interest based on its involvement in the Philippines. If China could hold out a little while, international events would shift in its favor. The great strength of China, like that of the Jews, was its ability to endure hard times and to survive.

Fu's optimism was based on the long term. For the short run he was not so sanguine, and he was definitely not cheered by the publication of the Lytton report in October, 1932.[16] He felt the ambiguous tone would lessen the likelihood of international action and encourage further Japanese aggression. In this expectation he was absolutely right. From Japan's point of view, the Lytton report was neither sympathetic enough nor threatening enough to justify restraint. Japan decided to consolidate its strategic position in Manchuria by incorporating Jehol into its area of control. Liberal reaction to this step was one of disappointment, but the liberals continued to argue that China's best hope for security lay in some form of international response. It was futile, said T. F. Tsiang, for China to think of recovering Jehol by military means if it acted alone.[17] China could only cooperate fully with the League of Nations, even if temporarily the league's actions were minimal. The league provided the best chance for China to get its message to the world and enlist public opinion to restrain Japan. At the same time China had to reform itself internally, ending corruption and political squabbles, and build its military strength for a future attempt at recovering lost territory--when the international climate was right.

Tsiang's position, urging patience, coincided in spirit with that of the Kuomintang, though certainly not from any calculation of self-interest on his part. The same may be said of Hu Shih, whose general stance and specific reaction to the seizure of Jehol paralleled that of Tsiang.[18] Hu, in April, 1933, reiterated his opinion that China's best chance, in the long run, for regaining lost territories was by working with other nations and the league.[19] This would take time, but he was prepared to wait. In 1914 Belgium had been occupied by Germany; in 1871 France lost two provinces to Prussia. Both countries eventually had matters restored to their proper place, and so China would eventually regain its lost territory. It took four years for Belgium and forty-eight years for France, and China should be prepared to wait fifty years if necessary. But in a country with a history of thousands of years, what were fifty years or so? Hu was simply unwilling to yield to any emotional impulse for war. He expressed his respect for those who were willing to make the ultimate sacrifice for the nation, but his conscience wouldn't permit him to use his pen to urge that course on others.[20] And he was very scornful of those who issued emotional calls for war when they really had no intention personally of doing any of the fighting. War was not just a word, he said, it was an extremely complicated undertaking requiring immense resources and planning. It was not something you entered upon on the spur of the moment.

In May, 1933, hostilities in north China were suspended by the Tangku truce, which created a demilitarized zone in eastern Hopei Province. Both Japanese and Chinese troops were evacuated from a zone north and east of the Tientsin-Peking area. But the exclusion of Chinese troops from a natural defensive position in front of these cities could only be interpreted as another Japanese victory. Nevertheless, Hu Shih defended the Tangku truce as a means of buying time. Fu Ssu-nien was so enraged by Hu's position that he wanted to dissolve the Independent Critic Society, of which they were both members.[21] Hu was very hurt by this criticism from a former student, and he had Ting Wen-chiang urge a more conciliatory attitude on Fu Ssu-nien. At Ting's request, Fu eventually agreed to drop his idea of dissolving the society, but he refused to soften his hard line against the Japanese. T. F. Tsiang's position, as before, coincided with that of Hu Shih.[22] China had to prepare for the right moment, strengthening itself militarily. The Tangku truce was a national humiliation, and everyone knew it. But it was just like the humiliation suffered by the French in 1871 and Germany at Versailles. Such wrongs couldn't be redressed by a haphazard, one-day act. It required political, economic, and military preparation --applied at just the right moment. Meanwhile, China should use the time granted effectively to protect north China against further Japanese advances. It was a dog-eat-dog world in which national strength was all that mattered. But a nation's strength was also related to the health of its political, economic, and social institutions--all of which were badly in need of reform.

Gradually, as the months passed without any softening of Japan's antagonistic posture, there was a perceptible hardening of attitudes among those writing for the Independent Critic. One can maintain faith in the sweet reasonableness of mankind for only so long. The so-called Amau Statement, a Japanese "Monroe Doctrine" for Asia which was issued in April, 1934, disturbed both Hu Shih and T. F. Tsiang. Hu called it the most critical challenge to China since 1931, perhaps a more severe threat to Chinese sovereignty than the Twenty-one Demands.[23] Tsiang was infuriated, and he hoped that the seriousness of the threat would finally unify China so that it could totally dedicate itself to the task of preparing to resist Japan.[24] Fu Ssu-nien, already quite firm in his opposition to the Japanese, urged no further accommodation with the enemy.[25] If China yielded any further, still more would be demanded in the future. Today we talk about defending the Great Wall; tomorrow it might be the Yellow River. Yet, despite this slow transition in liberal attitudes, the familiar optimism of the past would also appear in the pages of the Independent Critic. T'ang Erh-ho (former president of Peking Medical College and member of the Good Men Government in 1922) returned from a trip to Japan and reported that Japanese moderates were likely to have a restraining influence on the irrational behavior of the militarists.[26] He still thought there was cause for hope that rationality would prevail.

Steadily the Japanese intensified pressure on north China, eventually reaching the point of proposing the creation of an Autonomous North Chinaland (which would, of course, have been a Japanese puppet). The liberals, particularly those within the Peking educational community, were outspoken in their opposition to this pressure. In the winter of 1935 a meeting was called by the mayor of Peking, doubtless at the urging of the Japanese, to conciliate members of Peking's educational community.[27] The hope was that they could be convinced to support an autonomous north China, or that they could at least be persuaded to remain quiet. At this meeting both Hu Shih and Fu Ssu-nien stood up and firmly denounced the plan for an autonomous north China. Indeed, Fu's patriotic fervor was so intense by this time that when his son was born he named him Jen-kuei, after a T'ang dynasty general who defeated Japanese troops fighting in Korea.[28]

In June, 1935, the Ho-Umetsu Agreement was signed which meant the withdrawal of all Chinese troops from Hopei and Chahar. Articles in the Independent Critic grew more pessimistic and more critical of the government's policy of appeasement. Chang Hsi-jo (professor of political philosophy at Peking University and Tsinghua University) wrote perceptively that he thought Japan would pursue its plans to swallow up China.[29] This would bring about World War II, Japan would be defeated, and China would regain its freedom. He felt that Japanese agressiveness had been fueled by the tradition of Chinese submissiveness and by Chinese weakness. If only China had solved its internal problems, strengthened itself, and resisted external encroachments earlier. Then China, Japan, and the world wouldn't be faced with such grim future prospects. If only China and Japan could have cooperated to help China modernize, all of East Asia would have benefited. Now it was too late, and China could only attempt to fight so as to reduce the extent of the disaster and improve its chances for independence after the war was over. Hu Shih and Fu Ssu-nien wrote articles in the Independent Critic urging that the government stand firm and not surrender to Japan.[30] China should not be like Russia, which yielded to Germany at Brest Litovsk because Lenin wanted to concentrate on domestic needs. North China was China's Ural Mountains, and it couldn't be given away. Fu Ssu-nien also offered an analysis of the Abyssinian question and its relationship to China.[31] The world was slowly learning, he wrote, that moral force would not suffice to uphold the principles of the League of Nations. Sanctions had to be employed and adhered to uniformly by all nations against the sanctioned country. So Fu hoped that China would participate in whatever sanctions the league imposed on Italy, regardless of what difficulties that might pose for China. If China supported the league then, it would be more likely to work on China's behalf later.

By the fall of 1935, the Japanese pressure for an autonomous North Chinaland was intense, soon to result in the December 9 and December 16 student demonstrations. On November 24 the presidents of the universities in Peking issued a statement firmly opposing any division of China into separate units. Hu Shih, Fu Ssu-nien, and Weng Wen-hao all wrote articles in the Independent Critic denying that the people of north China wanted to be autonomous and stressing the richness of north China's cultural traditions and natural resources.[32] No nation could survive if it began to fragment into separate pieces. A threat to one part of the nation must be viewed as a threat to the whole.

The Japanese directed special pressure at Chiang Meng-lin, then chancellor of Peking University. Many rather heavy-handed attempts were made to persuade Chiang and other members of the Peita community to be more friendly toward the Japanese. On one occasion he was even called before General Kawabe of the Japanese garrison in the Legation Quarter.[33] There, in a locked room with an armed guard present, he was asked why he was so anti-Japanese and why he opposed the Autonomous North China-land movement. Chiang replied that the manner in which China was governed was an internal matter and had no relation to any anti-Japanese movement. When asked whether he was a friend of Japan, he responded that he was a friend of the Japanese people but an opponent of Japanese militarism. His interrogator then said that a car was waiting to take him to Dairen for further questioning, but Chiang refused to go. He said that they could take him there by force, but this would cause the Japanese terrible embarrassment when the whole world learned what had been done to the chancellor of Peking University. This seemed to unnerve the Japanese, and Chiang calmly smoked his cigarette (as Chiang tells it). Suddenly a phone rang in the room, presumably from superiors listening to the conversation, and Chiang was allow to leave. The next day an aide from Sung Che-yuan urged Chiang to leave Peking because Sung feared he could no longer protect him. But Chiang refused to be intimidated and stayed on at Peking University.

On 9 and 16 December the students of Peking demonstrated in the streets against Japanese aggression and against the government's failure to offer resistance. The Japanese suspected Hu Shih and Chiang Meng-lin as key instigators of this December 9 Movement, but this was far from the truth.[34] Both, as New Culture liberals, had a long history of opposition to student activism and especially student strikes. Indeed, in the debates in Peking University faculty meetings over whether to support the December 9 student demonstrations, Hu and Chiang maneuvered things so as to prevent a formal faculty stand. According to Ma Hsü-lun, Peita professor of philosophy, only senior faculty were allowed to participate in the meetings because the younger faculty were more likely to favor supporting the students.[35] In the meetings, Ma urged the faculty to demonstrate their opposition to the Japanese. Hu Shih disagreed, arguing that the government should deal with that question. In the end, the decision was to send Hu as a delegate to a conference in Nanking to discuss resistance to the Japanese. Ma, furious at this temporizing, walked out of the meeting.

Hu Shih's public reaction to the December 9 Movement was expressed in two articles in the Independent Critic.[36] He recalled that fifteen years earlier (that is, after the May 4 Incident) he had said that in nations without an instrument for reform, such as a representative assembly, movements of a political character were likely to emanate from the students. Then, and in the present, older people were less willing to take the risk of involving themselves, but students felt deeply and were willing to act on their beliefs. In times of national difficulties a nation needed a fearless, independent public opinion, and he respected the students for expressing their views. However, he didn't approve of students stopping classes as a means of protest. Since May 4 the student strike had been so overused that it had lost its ability to elicit sympathy from society. Moveover, as he had said so often, the students' primary responsibility was to study and to prepare for the future. In fact, he even urged the students to request a cancellation of the winter vacation to make up for classes missed and exams not given. Needless to say, many of the students--as they went out into the countryside to try to arouse the masses--rejected Hu's liberal gradualism.[37] Some saw him as irrelevant; others accused him of selling out to the government. But more penetrating is Jerome Grieder's interpretation that Hu Shih's position throughout this period of Japanese aggression reflected: " . . . the confusion of a mind which shunned violence in a violent age and clung in a time of duplicity to a naive faith in goodwill, and which stubbornly prized reasonableness above all else in a deranged world."[38]

Hu Shih's firmness of conviction might indicate loyalty to principle or foolish stubbornness. Probably it was some of both. But certainly it should not be taken to indicate aloofness from the events of the time. No one who took his own principles seriously could ignore the agonizing dilemma posed by the Japanese threat. It forced everyone to clarify his priorities, his political philosophy, and his own personal responsibilities to the nation. It dramatically altered the context in which one considered China's political and social needs. Liberals in particular found many of their principles severely called into question by the Japanese invasion. Two issues--educational policy and the democracy versus dictatorship debate--help clarify the kinds of questions liberals were forced to confront and the variety of responses they made, resulting finally in an accommodation.

Educational Policy

Since assuming power, the Kuomintang's view of education differed substantially from that of the liberals.[39] Both saw it as a tool to serve the nation, but the Kuomintang looked for much more immediate and tangible results. It wished the curriculum to stress practical subjects, while also inculcating loyalty to the nation and the party. At times there was talk of organizing the students for political ends to prevent them from going to the Communists by default. Liberal educators, especially Ts'ai Yuan-p'ei and Chiang Meng-lin, resisted this politicization of education. Ts'ai argued that earlier, before the successful Northern Expedition, student activism was necessary.[40] The temporary sacrifice of educational work was justified because the party was weak and the country torn apart by warlords. But later circumstances were different. In a time of reconstruction rather than revolution student activism would be harmful to the national interest. If anyone called for students to sacrifice their studies when it was not necessary, it would be like "groaning without being sick." Regarding curriculum, the conventional liberal view rejected the Kuomintang's emphasis on political indoctrination and narrow specialization on practical subjects. Most liberals, with their Anglo-American backgrounds, favored the broad liberal arts approach. Pure science and the liberal arts would stimulate students and provide the most benefits to the nation in the long run.

The trouble was that the Japanese invasion aroused concern for the more immediate needs of the nation. Many thoughtful Chinese, within and outside of the party, began to wonder whether future-oriented education on the Anglo-American model hadn't left China vulnerable to attack.[41] Many became receptive to a Kuomintang program, articulated by Ch'en Kuo-fu (one of the Ch'en brothers of the CC clique), which called for an emphasis on such practical subjects as engineering, medicine, and agriculture. In its most extreme formulation, Ch'en's proposal even considered closing all departments of liberal arts, law, and the fine arts as useless. Liberals were forced to respond to this challenge to their educational principles. One liberal who supported a more practical definition of educational objectives was Fu Ssu-nien, whose deep patriotic concern has been remarked upon previously.[42] Fu expressed the view that Chinese education remained too elitist, with too many remnants of the old feudal shih-tai-fu (gentry) tradition. China had been burdened throughout its history, and continued to be so, with the separation of hand- and mind-workers. Education was still too bookish, with insufficient emphasis on integrating book knowledge with practical skills. Fu was also distressed at the duplication of effort characteristic of Chinese education, and he was supportive of the more rationally organized educational system which was also part of Ch'en Kuo-fu's proposals. He was not, however, willing to accept an authoritarian system similar to that of Prussia. He wanted a certain degree of local autonomy in policy making and financing. Moreover, Fu's position departed in other respects from Ch'en Kuo-fu's ideal. First, he envisioned a distinctive role for higher education, one quite consonant with conventional liberal values.[43] While primary and secondary education should foster discipline and impart practical knowledge, university education should stimulate a spirit of inquiry and provide the tools for further learning. He did not see the university as the place for acquiring practical, specialized skills. Instead, he wanted it to open students' minds and teach them to work creatively and independently. Second, despite his emphasis on practical education at the secondary level, he was not willing to banish history (his own discipline) from the middle-school curriculum.[44] History could broaden perspectives, help students understand human nature, and develop patriotic citizens. In short, the values of a liberal education were still important to Fu, however much he might preach the utility of practical education.

T. F. Tsiang wrote that when he first read Ch'en Kuo-fu's plan to de-emphasize the arts and sciences in favor of agriculture, engineering, and medicine he couldn't believe it.[45] He thought Ch'en was being misquoted by the newspaper. But he soon came to realize that Ch'en's point of view was held by many, and as such it deserved to be considered. Tsiang maintained that just because you trained someone in a special skill was no guarantee that he would benefit the nation. You had to train the whole person, to make sure that he would apply his skills with the right spirit. To neglect the intellectual and attitudinal facets of China's problems, while focusing solely on its material and physical needs, was to repeat the errors of the nineteenth century _t'i-yung_ reformers. Tsiang rejected Ch'en's argument that the liberal arts, law, and the fine arts were actually harmful because they wasted money and produced students with no respect for authority. He argued that such fields of study yielded essential guidance to the nation on political, social, economic, and artistic questions. Without people trained in such areas the nation would be in chaos. However, Tsiang like Fu Ssu-nien was willing to grant qualified support to some of the Kuomintang's point of view. Like Fu, Tsiang was critical of the _shih-tai-fu_ mentality which lingered on in many students--such as the scholarly affectations, distaste for physical work, splitting of scholastic hairs, bookishness. Some progress had been made, but many bad habits persisted. He also recognized that China needed more systematic surveys of its national needs and resources. One should analyze how many engineers, and what specific types, China would need over the next five or ten years. With such information, perhaps a serious plan could be devised. But that plan needed to operate within the framework of the true purpose of education, which was to educate the whole person.

H. C. Zen argued that "politicizing education" was a contradiction in terms.[46] Education was involved with developing the whole being, politicization only in making a narrow disciple; education stressed the individual, while politicization stressed the organization; education encouraged free inquiry, but politicization couldn't permit this because it might weaken the absolute faith in the party. So the two couldn't coexist. If you wanted education you couldn't have politicization. And Zen left no doubt that he wanted education, both for its intrinsic value and for the traditional liberal reason that a healthy nation was made up of well-educated citizens. Weng Wen-hao was equally convinced of the intrinsic value of an education, but he also was aware of the reality that many college graduates were unemployed.[47] He expressed some sympathy for the need for practical skills and for matching fields studied with social needs. However, he seemed to feel that this should develop through student initiative, rather than being imposed by the government. In sum, New Culture liberals were sensitive to the pressures for more practical and politicized education, but they resisted the pull away from their basic educational philosophy. Education as a leavening agent was an essential ingredient in the liberal vision of reform, and they were understandably reluctant to abandon it.

Democracy versus Dictatorship

While the Japanese threat prompted only reluctant modifications in educational philosophy, the impact of that threat on liberals was considerable. One indication was the tolerance, and even advocacy, of a more "statist" political philosophy. Threats to the nation made some liberals less willing to criticize Chiang Kai-shek and the KMT for fear of weakening the government's capacity to deal with the Japanese. Similarly, some were willing to accept the argument that the perilous circumstances justified some sacrifice of individual liberties and democratic procedures in the interest of a strongly centralized government. Yet while liberals justified the compromise of their principles because it would assist the government in resisting the Japanese, the government showed no signs of undertaking that resistance. Moreover, the individuals whose freedoms were most affected by government restrictions (which liberals were now more likely to tolerate) were those journalists, educators, and students calling upon the government to act more decisively against the Japanese.

The dimensions of this intellectual conflict were clearly drawn in the debate over democracy versus dictatorship waged in the Independent Critic and other journals beginning in late 1933.[48] Hu Shih was the most prestigious defender of democracy, but he did so with the somewhat eccentric argument that China's very backwardness was the best reason why democracy was most suited to its needs.[49] According to Hu, democracy was a simple or "kindergarten" system of government which just required common sense (which the masses had), whereas dictatorship was a complicated form of government requiring men with outstanding talents. Perhaps after China had experienced thirty or fifty years of training in democracy, it might then be ready for an enlightened dictatorship. This line of argument outraged other defenders of democracy because it took the position that dictatorship was a more advanced and sophisticated form of government. A more orthodox defense of democracy, and one of the more persuasive, was offered by Chuan-hua Lowe (contributing editor of China Critic).[50] He pointed out that China had, from the time of Shih Huang-ti, had many dictators, and their accomplishments were not worthy of emulation. Moreover, China then had a dictatorship under Chiang Kai-shek, with a very heavy concentration of power in the hands of a few individuals, and yet there was no sign of an effective handling of problems. China was just too big and complex to be governed by a dictatorship. In the long run, he maintained, the best solution to China's problems would come from a better-educated citizenry. Enlightened citizen participation in political life and voluntary cooperative efforts, rather than orders from above, offered the best hope for China.

Other New Culture liberals offering defenses of democracy were Chang Hsi-jo and T'ao Meng-ho.[51] Chang disputed Hu Shih's claim that democracy was a kindergarten form of government. Based on the consent of the governed, a democracy functioned through persuasion and discussion rather than force. It needed citizens who were knowledgeable enough to participate in the affairs of the nation, thus requiring an effective educational system. It utilized a parliamentary system, which was not simple to create. All this was proof that democracy was actually a very advanced form of government. T'ao Meng-ho was less euphoric, claiming only that democracy was less imperfect than other forms of government available. Democracy was flexible, allowing for peaceful and gradual change. Democracy started with a basic concern for the worth of the individual, unlike dictatorship. Democracy in its advanced form--in Britain, America, and France--offered clear examples of its potential; whereas the South American states revealed the consequences of dictatorship in undeveloped countries. China needed to develop on a solid basis, and there was no shortcut through dictatorship.

In effect, the liberal defense of democracy was rather half-hearted and uninspired. A number of New Culture liberals had reluctantly reached the conclusion that

China's urgent problems demanded a more authoritarian approach. The political scientist Ch'ien Tuan-sheng had in 1930 expressed his "limitless hopes for democracy."[52] But by 1934 he had decided that a "totalitarian state" was necessary for China's salvation, though he hoped it would be enlightened and concerned with the welfare of the people. National affairs were just so complex that central planning was needed to make the best use of China's resources. Ting Wen-chiang similarly argued for the efficiency of an enlightened dictatorship, though he was not convinced that Chiang Kai-shek and the Kuomintang were suited to the task.[53] In China's circumstances a dictatorship was unavoidable. Even the American president had assumed extraordinary powers in a time of crisis, and China's crisis was ten times worse than America's. But Ting hoped for a "newstyle" dictatorship--interested in the national welfare, determined to modernize the country, and able to inspire the best people to serve the nation. Such a dictatorship was not feasible in China at present, but the first step toward such a "new-style" dictatorship was to stop advocating democracy.

Wu Ching-ch'ao and Ch'en Chih-mai (both Tsinghua University professors) emphasized the need for more centralized planning to make the best use of China's resources. While both personally preferred a democracy, with its freedoms, the fact was that conditions in China did not allow for a democracy. Only the next decade or several decades would reveal whether China would ever have the necessary conditions for democracy. Wu stressed that a unified central government could centralize tax collection and eliminate all the abuses of petty warlords.[54] A stronger central authority would result in better rural conditions (because the peasants would not be bled by local warlords), broader educational opportunities, and more efficient utilization of natural resources. Ch'en wrote that China had to abandon idealistic democratic ideas in favor of a strong, efficient centralized authority.[55] But while he wanted a strong government, it shouldn't be oppressive. Abandoning democracy did not mean abandoning freedom, and China's government should have the support of the people. Moreover, there should be provisions for the peaceful resolution of political disputes and the legal transfer of authority. One of the deficiencies of dictatorships was their failure to include such provisions. Ch'en's ideal was a government with the efficiency of a dictatorship, yet one which retained some of the good points of a democracy.

The spokesman most clearly identified with the dictatorship side was T. F. Tsiang.[56] In fact, his article in the 10 December 1933 Independent Critic initiated the debate. Tsiang's position was that while representative government was the ideal, it was not best for China at that time. The people didn't understand the principles of representative government, and those representatives elected didn't represent the people. China needed to establish one strong dictatorship to replace all the petty dictatorships throughout the country, which were only concerned with their own self-interest. England had its Tudor dictatorship, France its Bourbons, and Russia its Romanovs. But China had never experienced such a dictatorship, which developed a sense of nationhood and prepared the ground for real national construction. Historical analogies were usually instruments of convenience in Chinese intellectual debates. They were meant to clarify the advocate's vision for China rather than persuade by historical example. Such was the case with Tsiang, who wished to articulate his preference for a strong dictator. His contemporary model, however, was not Mussolini or Hitler so much as it was Kemal Atatürk of Turkey. He wanted someone who could inspire the people, arouse a spirit of nationalism, and modernize the country quickly. In the long run, Tsiang favored democratic government based on an educated public opinion, but for the short run he opted for dictatorship.

Despite all the qualifications about the long run or preferring democracy later but something else now, there was still an undeniable pull toward dictatorship for many New Culture liberals. Despite doubts about the Kuomintang's competance and compassion, there was still an undeniable pull toward the idea of working with the party and trying to enlighten it. As the historian T'ao Hsi-sheng put it, all the theoretical debates were a waste of time.[57] In practical terms, China had a party dictatorship under the Kuomintang. Many New Culture liberals began to look favorably on the idea of working within the party to steer it in the right direction. Soon after the democracy versus dictatorship debate, T. F. Tsiang, Weng Wen-hao, and Wu Ching-ch'ao joined the government. As the national crisis intensified, liberals gravitated toward the government.

The Ultimate Accommodation

In December, 1935, T. F. Tsiang and Weng Wen-hao accepted Chiang Kai-shek's invitation to join the government.[58] Weng became secretary-general of the executive Yuan and Tsiang director of its political department. Tsiang had attracted Chiang's attention by his articles which urged that the nation build up its strength before fighting the Japanese. The two had met on several occasions, and Tsiang had earlier agreed to go as a private individual to Russia to ascertain the likelihood of Russian support for China against the Japanese. Tsiang recognized the threats to personal integrity which were involved in government service, but on balance he believed that such concerns should be laid aside in times of national need. Others with liberal backgrounds had reached this conclusion earlier, such as Tuan Hsi-p'eng, Lo Chia-lun, and Chu Chia-hua.

On the other hand, some liberals--equally loyal to the nation--persisted in their more conventional liberal attitudes. Ting Wen-chiang, for example, accepted the position of secretary-general of the Academia Sinica in 1934.[59] Ting was impressed by the New Deal in the United States and by the efficiency of economic planning in Russia. His hope was to develop a core of experts and a body of scientific research, and to coordinate them efficiently to serve the nation. Ts'ai Yuan-p'ei, Fu Ssu-nien, and T'ao Meng-ho also remained at Academia Sinica. Chiang Meng-lin continued as chancellor of Peita and Chang Po-ling as chancellor of Nankai University. Hu Shih and Lo Lung-chi continued as educators and political critics--Hu in the Independent Critic and Lo in Ch'en Pao and I-shih pao. Two other notably independent critics were Chang Chi-luan, editor of Ta kung pao, and Tsou T'ao-fen, editor of Life Weekly (Sheng-huo chou-k'an). Both suffered arrest, Chang in September, 1936, and Tsou in November, 1936. Nonetheless, even those who stood outside the government and retained their critical stance could not be unmoved by the perilous state of the nation. Liberals writing in the Independent Critic were very much opposed to the brief Liang-Kuang rebellion in June, 1930.[60] Whatever the Kuomintang's shortcomings, no "heresy" could be allowed to threaten national unity.

The gravitation toward the government was accelerated by the Sian Incident. Liberals rallied around Chiang, showing no inclination to see Chang Hsueh-liang's motives in a sympathetic light. Fu Ssu-nien wrote that Chiang Kai-shek was indispensable to the welfare of the country.[61] If he was lost, only the traitors and the Communists would benefit. He advocated firmness on the government's part, to convince the Young Marshal that his cause was hopeless. Lo Chia-lun was equally critical of Chang Hsueh-liang, asking how he could justify his action on the grounds of saving the country when he was, in fact, jeopardizing the country's safety.[62] As president of National Central University, Lo joined with two other Nanking university presidents in sending a telegram of rebuke to the Young Marshal. He was, however, more conciliatory than Fu, suggesting that the Young Marshal escort Chiang Kai-shek to safety, and then he could present his views. Hu Shih wrote a Sunday editorial for Ta kung pao on 20 December with the title "The Treason of Chang Hsueh-liang."[63] In it he was very supportive of Chiang Kai-shek, stressing his crucial role in unifying the nation. He denounced the United Front idea because the Communists, as part of an international movement, could not be genuinely patriotic. Their talk of opposing the Japanese was just a ploy. The editor of Ta kung pao, Chang Chi-luan, issued an open letter and had copies dropped from an airplane over Sian. The letter stated: "Please listen! Both the culprit and his accomplices are wrong, so wrong that it may cause the extinction of the country and yourselves."[64] Chiang's safe return generated a vast feeling of relief. But the experience had made everyone even more aware of just how fragile Chinese national unity was, and how apparently vital Chiang Kai-shek was to its preservation. Fu Ssu-nien suggested that authority in the central government be distributed more broadly, so that one man didn't become so indispensable.[65] But he clearly wanted the central government to be as strong as possible in the face of foreign threats. He was unsympathetic to the United Front with the Communists, which he called the "garbage front."[66] And he seemed little concerned with the question of moving from political tutelage to constitutional government. The national crisis clarified priorities for him.

The Independent Critic was absent from the scene during this period. The 29 November 1936 issue had included an article by Chang Hsi-jo which argued that north China should not be made an autonomous region. This prompted Sung Che-yuan, ever sensitive to Japanese feelings to order the suspension of publication. The next issue did not appear until 18 April 1937. But, indicative of the muting of criticism is the fact that the Independent Critic resumed publication with scarcely a word of protest over its suspension. An "Editor's Postscript" announced simply that publication had been stopped for a while and thanked all those who had inquired why.[67] No explanation was given, and the editor merely said that the "Critic was still independent" and urged its friends to continue to give their support. Articles in the Independent Critic, in the spring and early summer of 1937, were only rarely even mildly critical of the government. Hu Shih continued to urge a constitutional government and to argue that democracy was a "kindergarten" form of government.[68] So China should end its period of tutelage and initiate democratic government in an elementary form. Later it could progress to a higher stage of democracy. Chang Hsi-jo took strong exception to Hu's method of defending democracy as a kindergarten government.[69] That approach only served to provide ammunition to those who opposed democracy. Chang, in fact, wanted a democracy in China because it was the highest form of government ever devised by man. But China could, and should, begin at an elementary level and work gradually to a higher level. Yet historian T'ao Hsi-sheng maintained that China's internal and external problems necessitated a strong party government, and he didn't wish to see an end to one-party dictatorship.[70] Moreover, even if the KMT lifted its ban against parties, it would not be easy to establish any meaningful new party. And in fact such was not necessary because the independent, nonparty point of view had various means of expression and of influencing policy. H. C. Zen, too, placed stress on national unity as the "foundation of progress."[71]

The gravitation toward the government was rendered complete with the Marco Polo Bridge Incident of 7 July 1937. With the prospect of all-out war, the Independent Critic editorialized that everyone must be willing to accept the commands of the central government.[72] Virtually all the New Culture liberals discussed in this study acceded to this viewpoint and reached an accommodation with the government. They responded to Chiang Kai-shek's request to attend planning conferences, retreated westward with the government, and served in the advisory People's Political Council which was formed in 1938. Hu Shih, who had consistently maintained his critical distance through the 1930s, accepted membership in the People's Political Council and served as ambassador to Washington from 1938-1942.[73] Chang Po-ling, after his beloved Nankai University was damaged by Japanese bombs, was reportedly much moved by Chiang Kai-shek's assurance that "As long as there is a China there will be a Nankai."[74] He agreed to serve as deputy speaker of the People's Political Council. Other members of the People's Political Council included Ch'ien Tuan-sheng, Fu Ssu-nien, Liang Shih-ch'iu, Lo Lung-chi, T'ao Hsi-sheng, T'ao Meng-ho, and H. C. Zen. Lo Chia-lun and Chu Chia-hua, long associated with the Kuomintang, served in many capacities during the war. Chiang Meng-lin participated in the joint administration of National Southwest Associated University, as well as holding positions in the Chinese Red Cross and other nonpolitical organizations. Ch'en Chih-mai became councillor of the executive Yuan in 1938. Weng Wen-hao was minister of economic affairs from 1938 on, and Wu Ching-ch'ao was a senior secretary in the same ministry. T. F. Tsiang was director of the political affairs department of the executive Yuan throughout the war. There were, however, a few exceptions. Ts'ai Yuan-p'ei, partly for reasons of health and partly from opposition to Kuomintang policies, went to Hong Kong instead of following the government westward. He died in 1940. Ch'en Heng-che spent most of the war in Kunming or Chungking. Her husband, H. C. Zen, was a member of the People's Political Council and was associated with various cultural organizations in Chungking. But she could never reconcile herself to the corruption and mismanagement of the government. Ting Wen-chiang was spared the necessity for choice for he had died in 1936.

During the war years the threat to the nation subsumed all other questions in the minds of patriotic Chinese. But with the war's end in 1945, all the old issues and dilemmas resurfaced.[75] The Kuomintang was still dictatorial, repressive, and unable to deal with China's problems. Raging inflation, with its devastating effect on middle-class Chinese including intellectuals, made the situation all the more intolerable. The Communists, while impressing some by their effective government of certain areas during the war, still carried the stigma of violence, intolerance of dissent, and control by foreigners. The civil war years offered few attractive choices to New Culture liberals, and the Third Force was never a viable option. The final choice in 1949, like so many others faced by New Culture liberals during their lives, could only be between the lesser of two evils.

8.

Modern Chinese Liberalism in Comparative Perspective

Much has been written about the naivete of modern Chinese liberals and of the futility of their ideas, given Chinese conditions.[1] Reviewing the working definition of New Culture liberalism, stated at the outset, supports this assessment. Liberals wanted political freedom and institutional checks on authoritarianism at a time when the central government was more concerned with the inadequacy of its authority than with the possible abuses of excess power. No liberal arguments about constitutional government or one-party dictatorships could constrain those determined to extend their power to the limits of their ability. And even some liberals grew more acquiescent toward strong authority as the threat from Japan intensified. Liberal support for civil liberties and vigorous dissent similarly received a cold welcome from governments intent on consolidating their tenuous position. They certainly were unwilling to encourage criticism which might undermine such efforts. The optimistic liberal faith in gradual, peaceful, and rational reform seems particularly unsuited to the chaos of the warlords, the desperate condition of China's peasants, the violence of Japanese aggression, or the nature of Kuomintang politics.

Liberal preoccupations with certain questions may seem foolish in the light of later developments. How could liberals hope to influence indifferent authorities by writing in intellectual journals? How could they misjudge Japanese intentions so seriously? How could they fail to see the need for organizing the masses? Yet, history has a way of making the losing side appear more foolish than the facts warrant. At the time, a Communist victory hardly seemed inevitable, and even within the Chinese Communist ranks there was no agreement on the proper program. Future events will doubtless play the same tricks on many who argue passionately about certain issues in our own time--for example, on questions of economic growth, population control, nuclear energy, disarmament. Future historians will look back and wonder how anyone could have failed to recognize the obvious. But only time makes certain positions obvious. In an earlier period the outcome is less clear, and one should be cautious in making charges of irrelevance or naivete.

Liberals, given the fact that they took their ideas seriously, found their options narrowing as the pace of events quickened. They could take some small comfort in remaining consistent to their principles while regretting their meager influence on national affairs. Individuals such as Chang Po-ling, Ch'en Heng-che, Chiang Meng-lin, Hu Shih, Liang Shih-ch'iu, Lo Lung-chi, T'ao Meng-ho, and Ts'ai Yuan-p'ei chose this course. They could join the government, justifying their actions by reference to the national emergency. Some followed this path at different stages of the Nationalist period, but this choice carried a heavy emotional price for those who were genuine liberal ideologues. Where else could liberals have turned? They were unanimous in their rejection of Communism as a dogma involving violence and class warfare. Mao Tse-tung's vision of social revolution and the potential of the peasants was totally beyond the ken of most liberals. Non-Communist programs for rural reform, such as those sponsored by T'ao Hsing-chih and James Yen, inspired no passionate migration of liberals to the countryside. They were too elitist, able to sympathize with the masses but unwilling to identify with them. The option of organizing a political party, to exert pressure on the Kuomintang, was foreclosed to liberals because of their ideological principles. But even had this constraint not existed, the experience of the Chinese Youth party, the so-called Third party, and the National Socialists does not suggest that another party would have had much impact.[2] The fact is that liberals, given their principles and the circumstances of the time, were boxed in. Even hindsight, with its perfect vision, reveals no solution to the liberal dilemma in republican China.

Comparative Perspective: Republican China as a Modernizing Society

As inhospitable as this period was for the liberal vision, it was certainly not a unique time. Republican China displayed many of the characteristics of an underdeveloped country searching for ways to modernize. Many of the dilemmas for Chinese liberals--such as the role of education, the extent to which dissent should be tolerated, the balance between individual freedom and social control, and the pull of loyalty in a time of national crisis--were the products of one of the most persistent tensions present in modernizing societies. I am referring to the question of how compatible liberal-democratic values are with the pressing political, economic, and social needs of such societies. The Chinese case study enhances our understanding of this tension, and reflection on the problems of modernization provides another framework for assessing the experience of New Culture liberals in republican China.

There was a time, in a more confident age, when scholars of the modernization process assumed that all developing nations followed a common pattern which culminated in democratic institutions.[3] Such developments as urbanization, industrialization, secularization, the spread of education, and democratization seemed to occur in some regular pattern as a nation progressed toward modernization. Democratic institutions and liberal values gradually, but inevitably, appeared as the traditional culture was replaced by modern ways. This early paradigm of modernization has undergone considerable revision since it first took shape in the 1950s. Sharp distinctions between tradition and modernity have been blurred, as some modern values have been called into question and some traditional customs have been judged useful to the modernization process. The model of inevitable stages of development, with reasonably parallel developments in various social, economic, and political categories, has not been upheld by the available evidence. Most relevant to this present inquiry, doubts have arisen about the conventional assumption that democracy is the natural and inevitable culmination of modernization. Most scholars of modernization still believe democracy to be the best available form of government, and they lament the fact that few developing nations are able to achieve it.[4] But they are more cognizant of the special circumstances in which liberal-democratic institutions evolved in the West, more aware of the absence of most of these conditions in the Third World, and more understanding of the attractions of authoritarian routes to modernization.

Democracy emerged in countries such as England and the United States in a measured way, and with the industrial revolution well under way. While experimenting with broader political participation, these countries were spared the added burden of having to produce a rapid industrial transformation. They enjoyed a high level of technology and entrepreneurial skills. Safety valves for excess population existed in the American frontier and in the British colonies abroad. Both countries had stable and flexible social systems, with a broad consensus regarding social values. Social mobility was possible, ascriptive status was diminishing, and a circulation of elites occurred. A tradition of limited government had evolved, certain human rights were considered inalienable, the concept of a loyal opposition was established, and dissenting opinions were tolerated. The levels of education and literacy were adequate. A sizable, urban, middle class existed, with a reasonably equitable distribution of wealth.

Most nations in the early stages of modernization, including republican China, exhibit few of the conditions listed above.[5] They have little industrial development and few entrepreneurial skills. They face worsening problems of overpopulation, with few or no safety valves. Often their social systems are unstable, and their sense of national identity is very fragile. These societies are usually hierarchical, with an entrenched privileged class very resistant to changes in the status quo. The political system is authoritarian, lacking traditions of human rights, toleration of dissent, and a loyal opposition. Education is limited to a tiny segment of society. No substantial middle class exists and disparities in wealth are large. Despite these unfavorable conditions, many developing nations try to adopt democratic institutions in one fell swoop, contrary to the fact that democracy grew very gradually in the West. The British House of Lords, for example, was important until 1911; and United States senators were elected by state legislatures for 125 years.

Given the absence of so many preconditions for democracy, some modernization scholars have concluded that other problems might deserve higher priority, and that they might be solved through more authoritarian procedures. Gunnar Myrdal, for example, wrote: "National independence, national consolidation, changes in institutions and attitudes, equalization, rise of productivity, rise and redirection of consumption, and, more generally, planning for development can be attained by an authoritarian regime bent on their realization."[6] Myrdal in his analysis, primarily of South Asia, stresses the need for developing countries to eliminate the characteristics of a "soft state."[7] These would include the lack of social discipline, the disinclination of officials to abide by the law, corruption, collusion, the inability to defer gratification, and the absence of any sense of national cohesion. Myrdal points out that such soft-state characteristics can and do exist in totalitarian regimes, and sufficient social discipline <u>can</u> develop in a democratic setting. But he leaves a strong impression that some form of compulsion, some toughness, will be required if developing nations are to deal with the broad range of problems facing them.

Moreover, Myrdal argues for the necessity of "radical reforms" to lessen the great, and growing, social and economic stratification that exists in underdeveloped societies.[8] Established privileges need to be broken down and a fairer distribution of wealth achieved. Yet, when the underprivileged are weak and inarticulate, such reforms will have to be undertaken by coercive direction from the top. In such circumstances how much free speech and participatory democracy can be tolerated, when those speaking and participating would be the individuals whose privileges need to be redistributed?

Others have suggested additional potential advantages of an authoritarian approach to modernization, without necessarily endorsing that approach.[9] It has been argued that capital accumulation and the rational allocation of resources can best be implemented by an authoritarian government. Some maintain that national unity, especially in a country with strong ethnic or local loyalties, requires a strong central authority. Popular participation, in this situation, will only give expression to those fissiparous forces which weaken national unity. Indeed, the necessity for political order, in the midst of wide-ranging intellectual, social, and economic changes, is one of the attractions of authoritarian governments to members of developing societies and to outside observers.

Even someone as committed to humane values as Michael Harrington admitted that the "Stalinist temptation . . . haunted me from time to time" during a visit to India.[10] After three weeks of travel he concluded that many of India's cultural values and traditions had to be "smashed" if India was to begin to deal with its many problems. Elsewhere Harrington wrote of the increasingly oppressive burdens of modernization in these more complex times. The costs of technology and creating the required infrastructure were beyond the means of most Third World nations. Traditional social values were often obstacles to entrepreneurship and economic growth. However, in the end Harrington rejects the Stalinist temptation. Any such approach, while it might bring desirable material improvements, would bring them at the terrible cost of more inhumanity, further inequities, the stifling of creativity, and the creation of a new bureaucratic elite. The necessary changes should be implemented in a gradual, democratic way.

Others commenting on these issues have also questioned the costs, as well as the supposed effectiveness, of authoritarian governments.[11] Popular participation and liberal values, it is argued, increase communication and make for more informed policy makers. Besides the inefficiency and errors inherent in an authoritarian regime, there is also the problem of officials being unwilling to take responsibility for fear of the consequences of failure. So more decisions are "pushed upstairs" to an increasingly isolated and misinformed elite. In response to the argument of fragile national unity, the point is made that popular participation can be a means of fostering national identity and of legitimizing an otherwise tenuous administration. There is also a response to the charge that democracy would allow the privileged to prevent the necessary redistribution of wealth. Some have suggested that the most effective social reform comes through broadening the political process to include the lower classes.[12] Building political consciousness among the poor enables them to put pressure on local elites and gradually effect fundamental social reforms. In sum, democracy and liberal institutions can be a means to political legitimacy, national unity, social justice, and efficient decision-making.

These conflicting arguments indicate the lack of consensus regarding the proper place of liberal-democratic values in the modernization process.[13] Authoritarian regimes generally pose serious threats to human rights and human dignity. Moreover, they run the risk of bureaucratism, intellectual stagnation, and isolation from reality. At their worst, they can turn into brutal dictatorships, destructive of the national interest and impossible to remove. At the same time, democracy runs the risk of becoming a sham if it is dominated by a privileged class which is opposed to meaningful social reforms. Under such circumstances the necessary redistribution of wealth, which translates into land reform in most developing countries, might best be implemented by a revolutionary elite in an authoritarian manner. Moreover, the process of capital accumulation and resource allocation, the nurturing of patriotic sentiments, and the spread of a broad group of desirable modern attitudes can probably best be accomplished under centralized direction. Yet centralized direction need not mean a one-party state in which no dissent is tolerated. And authoritarian means, when they are used, must be scrutinized to see that they are not merely being used to suppress embarrassing criticism or eliminate potential rivals.

Comparative Perspective: British Liberalism

Probably the model for classical liberalism was nineteenth-century England, particularly the Victorian period. Touchstone liberal worthies such as Bentham, Mill and Gladstone lived and labored during the period. Liberalism changed considerably during this century, with the gradual transition from a laissez-faire approach to the more "constructive" philosophy of the New Liberalism. But certain principles remained fundamental and consistent. The traditional liberal goal of enlarging individual freedom persisted. Liberals continued their opposition to arbitrary authority and privileges which obstructed the fullest development of individual potential. The defense of civil liberties remained a high priority. Broadening popular participation in government continued as an important concern, though some began to have second thoughts as the century progressed. Finally, liberals maintained an enduring confidence that reform could be rational, gradual, and harmonious. They were particularly anxious to avoid stimulating class antagonisms which might fragment England into competing interest groups. They searched for ways to bring benefits to the whole society, rather than to one group at the expense of another. They feared that the loss of social cohesion would involve dangerous consequences for the welfare of all English citizens.

Looking at Victorian and Edwardian England for comparative purposes yields some interesting insights. First, many liberal advocates were not as liberal as one might expect. Second, much liberal progress resulted from a mixture of motives and historical forces, many of which were quite unrelated to liberal ideological principles. Third, the goal of reform without jeopardizing social harmony, also an important concern for Chinese liberals, proved to be an unattainable ideal.

Jeremy Bentham had a certain sympathy for the people as he tried to bring about "the greatest good for the greatest number." He wanted to open up the closed, aristocratic society of eighteenth-century England and give people broader opportunities for greater happiness. He wanted to clarify the law so that it could be an instrument of justice and human happiness rather than a tool in the hands of the privileged. Yet Bentham was no advocate of unconstrained individualism. "Natural rights is nonsense," he wrote, " . . . inalienable and imprescriptable rights is merely nonsense on stilts."[14] He was very disturbed by the excesses, as he saw them, associated with the American and French revolutions. Excessive liberty seemed to him an invitation to anarchy. Only laws could assure rights, and only limits on the rights of some through laws could provide rights for others. He expected that a good government, through prescriptive laws and legislation, would interfere with the antiutilitarian behavior of some to produce the utilitarian goal of "the greatest good for the greatest number." On the other hand, in the best laissez-faire tradition Bentham opposed any governmental interference for the intended purpose of improving people's lives, as opposed to preventing others from causing harm to people. He believed that individuals knew far better than the government what was best for themselves. His advice was that the "watchword of government, on these occasions, ought to be--Be quiet."[15] Obviously, there can be no question about Jeremy Bentham's liberal credentials for membership in the classic laissez-faire school of liberalism, but one shouldn't ignore the limits of his liberalism. He was distrustful of excessive liberties and quite willing to use the government's coercive power to prevent certain forms of undesirable behavior.

John Stuart Mill is another distinguished member of the liberal pantheon, and deservedly so. Yet it is important to appreciate the limits on his liberalism. In the early 1830s Mill was less enthusiastic than his father (James Mill) and others about the advantages of more democracy as represented in the Reform Bill of 1832. Indeed, there was a constant tension in Mill's mind between an elitist government by the fittest and the desire for democratic participation in government. In his writings in the 1830s he leaned toward representative government with the chosen representatives acting according to their own conception of the best interest of the people who selected them. If they lost the confidence of the people they would then be voted out of office. He made the following analogy: "A man will choose his legislator as he chooses his physician. No man exacts a pledge from his physician that he shall prescribe for him a particular treatment."[16] In essence he wanted the role of legislator to be viewed as a profession. Just as people chose their doctor or lawyer and then trusted him unless they lost faith in his general ability to serve them, so they would elect their legislators and give them the same trust.

After his father's death in 1836 Mill's writings show an even more antidemocratic character. By 1840 he was quite skeptical about the ability of a democracy to function in practice, and he was much influenced by de Tocqueville's writings on the potential tyranny of the majority. By the early 1850s (doubtless under the influence of his new wife, Harriet Taylor, which is discussed below) he even abandoned his long-standing support of the secret ballot. He argued that the risk of control by the privileged classes had become less significant than the fear of selfishness on the part of the masses or that the majority would use its electoral power to oppress the minority. Indeed, as earlier liberal goals of a broader electorate were achieved, some began to feel that the people were not as wise as they had anticipated. One Mill scholar has concluded: "A consistent viewpoint unites Mill's political thought from start to finish; but it is not, in the strict sense he would himself have adopted, the viewpoint of a democrat."[17] This assessment is especially true of Mill's views with regard to conditions in countries he considered more backward than England. Until people in those countries are ready for democracy and liberty, he wrote, "there is nothing for them but implicit obedience to an Akbar or a Charlemagne, if they are so fortunate as to find one."[18]

The association of Mill's name with liberal principles comes most directly from his On Liberty, published in 1859. There he strongly defends the importance of an atmosphere of pluralism and freedom to permit the kind of creativity which ultimately benefits society. Originality and independence of spirit, never mind genius, are rare enough, and society should welcome rather than repress them whenever they appear. "If all mankind minus one were of one opinion," he wrote, "and only one person was of the contrary opinion, mankind would be no more justified in silencing that one person, than he, if he had the power, would be justified in silencing mankind."[19] Moreover, in On Liberty he expressed optimism that liberty would allow people the experiences and the opportunity for education which would make them act in socially constructive ways. He displayed an unwonted confidence in human rationality, maintaining that people would freely come to see the advantages to all in acting in a utilitarian way.

Yet two points should be made to qualify this picture of Mill's On Liberty liberalism. First, even there he reminded readers that "I am not one of those who set up liberty as an idol to be worshipped, and I am even willing to go farther than most people in regulating and controlling when there is a special advantage to be obtained by regulation and control."[20] In other words, he preferred to see people free to act rationally in a utilitarian way, but he reserved the right to compel them if necessary. Second, Mill's defense of liberty is stronger in On Liberty than it is in his other writings before it and after.

Gertrude Himmelfarb argues that On Liberty was very much influenced by the thinking of Mill's wife, Harriet Taylor.[21] She was something of a rebel against the social conventions of her time, particularly those regarding the role of women. Moreover, the extended unconventional relationship between Mill and Mrs. Taylor, while she was still married to John Taylor, led to a degree of social ostracism (at least they felt themselves to be ostracized) even after they were married following Mr. Taylor's death. Himmelfarb cogently argues that "in a sense it [On Liberty] was the philosophical expression of their own existential situation. . . . They exalted in On Liberty all the qualities they valued in themselves: an individuality that was the prerequisite of genius, a hostility to the society they felt to be hostile to them, a contempt for the conventions they had been compelled to flout, and an overwhelming solicitude for the liberty that permitted them to cultivate their tastes and talents in defiance of the pressures toward conformity and mediocrity."[22] In sum, there is good evidence for the conclusion that there were two Mills, the "On Liberty Mill" (much influenced by his wife) and the earlier and later "other Mill" (thinking his own thoughts). If this is true, then On Liberty, which many people take as an expression of Mill's views, is a special item not truly representative of his ideas when seen in a broader context.

It is similarly useful to broaden the context by briefly analyzing some nineteenth-century English political figures and their connection with the gradual enactment of liberal programs. As mentioned above, the liberal programs that were put in place during this century resulted from a variety of motives and historical factors. It wasn't only liberal ideology and liberals which brought about liberal programs. For example, Robert Peel's biographer points out that he was far from a democrat.[23] Basically, he was afraid that once the door was opened it couldn't be closed and a small increase in the electorate would eventually lead to everyone voting. This possibility scared him badly. But, like many others, he was also afraid that a revolution by the masses, as had occurred on the Continent, was imminent unless some response was made to the new political forces of the time. The result was the Reform Bill of 1832, a significant liberal measure brought about by the wish to avoid more radical steps rather than a positive commitment to liberalism. The 1846 repeal of the Corn Laws was a slightly different story. Peel had thought for some time that the Corn Laws, and protectionism in general, should be abolished. But there is no doubt that the timing of his political tactics was heavily influenced by an unanticipated historical event--the 1850 potato blight and famine in Ireland.

William Gladstone has the distinction of being the dominant liberal politician of the Victorian period, but he wasn't always so liberal.[24] As a young man, Gladstone was quite conservative, venerated the aristocracy, and feared that reform might open the door to a return of the papacy. He was opposed to the Reform Bill of 1832. His father owned slaves, and Gladstone defended slavery on the grounds that slaves were not yet ready for emancipation. He supported continued restrictions against Dissenters gaining admission to Oxford and Cambridge Universities, wanting to protect the religious status quo at the two institutions. In the 1840s Gladstone began to develop a more liberal outlook. In 1847 he supported the right of Jews to enter Parliament, a policy which was not formally enacted until 1858. In the winter of 1850 Gladstone visited Italy and saw the cruelties associated with the rule of the Bourbon king of Naples, particularly his mistreatment of political prisoners. His growing liberal sentiments are usually traced to this experience. But in the early 1850s he still saw himself as a liberal conservative--"I thought that a Liberal policy would be worked out with the greatest security to the country through the medium of the Conservative party, and I thought a position like Peel's on the Liberal side of that party preferable . . . to the Conservative side of the Liberal party."[25] In 1853, as chancellor of the exchequer, he removed the tax on about 130 food items, abolished the soap tax, and reduced the tea duty. From then on, rightly or wrongly, he was viewed as a champion of the common people and an enemy of the privileged.

In 1864 Gladstone issued his famous statement: "I venture to say that every man who is not presumably incapacitated by some consideration of personal unfitness or of political danger is morally entitled to come within the pale of the Constitution."[26] There were many qualifications in the rest of his speech, but the people remembered this sensational line and he became the champion of the masses in their eyes. Gladstone had gradually come to believe that the vote should be extended to the working class, though not to its lowest, more ignorant segment. In 1865 he introduced a reform bill toward that end, but it was defeated. In 1867 an even more radical version passed, but it did so with a Conservative government in power and Benjamin Disraeli skillfully maneuvering it through the House of Commons.

It is certainly ironic, but also very instructive, that electoral reform and other liberal reforms came at the hands of one as conservative as Disraeli. In debates in the late 1850s he argued that "if you establish a democracy you must in due course reap the fruits of a democracy."[27] These unpleasant fruits included resistance to taxation, emotionalism leading to unnecessary wars, a decline in property values, and less freedom. Disraeli preferred an aristocratic system, and he made no effort to keep his predilections secret. Yet he ended up working for a broadened electorate, with the expectation that the artisan class would vote Conservative in support of the monarchy, empire, and traditional values. It was political expediency, not liberal values, which motivated Disraeli. His biographer writes: "It would be absurd to claim that Disraeli viewed the matter other than first and foremost in the light of party expediency. The prolonged arguments of 1858-9 and 1866-7 all boil down in the end to that."[28] The substantial list of social reforms enacted by Disraeli's government in the session of 1875 (Trade Union Act, Public Health Act, Artisans Dwellings Act, Factory Act, Food and Drugs Act) were all a political response to the growing power of the working class enfranchised in 1867. They were not the result of Disraeli's philosophical commitment to liberal ideas.

The point, for comparative purposes, is that liberal programs often come about in the most piecemeal, catch-as-catch-can fashion if the political circumstances are conducive.

Even many of those liberal reforms associated with Gladstone might be attributed to something other than a coherent liberal philosophy. Scholars of late-Victorian political history suggest a number of contributing factors, which indicate that the texture of the period is far richer than a simple liberal versus conservative dichotomy. For one thing, the Liberal party of the time was a "coalition of convenience," composed of a diverse group of single-issue factions.[29] Liberal politicians were continually searching for an issue or issues that would establish some common ground to unify these diverse elements. Gladstone especially was always on the alert for "worthy causes," especially ones with a high moral tone, to unite the party. So, his anti-Beaconsfieldism, his speeches against the Bulgarian atrocities, and especially his Irish policy might be seen in this light. This is not to suggest hypocrisy on Gladstone's part, but only that he frequently had a twofold purpose in advocating liberal positions. As one scholar has suggested, form was often as important as content in determining Liberal political strategy.[30] That is, a certain issue might be taken up to pacify a particular, single-issue segment of the party. Preservation of a fragile unity, rather than commitment to a coherent philosophy, was the overriding consideration. In other words, "questions were often taken up not only because those who did so believed in them but also because the very process of taking them up and concentrating on them was expected to have beneficial consequences for Liberal political life in general."[31]

In like manner, it is quite possible that many of those who voted for Liberal politicians, or otherwise supported them, were often motivated by personal rather than ideological reasons.[32] Part of the appeal of the Liberal program was that it purported to liberate individuals from domination by the privileged establishment (the landed aristocracy, the rich, the church). Those who had always been subordinates had a chance to lessen the traditional authority of those who had always ruled over them. If townspeople voted out a Tory M.P. in their town and replaced him with a Liberal, it was an assertion of their manhood. They had expressed their determination to be free of domination. They had stood up.

There were still other factors in the complex mixture of historical forces. One was the Christian impulse.[33] For many, the Corn Laws were simply immoral and sinful. Similarly, other Victorian reforms very likely won support because of strong Christian sentiments rather than any carefully formulated liberal philosophy. Yet another factor was the deep distrust which many Gladstonian Liberals felt for the Tories.[34] From their perspective, the Tories were incompetent as administrators and crude political opportunists. So the Liberals thought it important to introduce programs which would win public favor and thereby prevent victory for the irresponsible Tories.

In sum, the progress of liberal ideas in nineteenth-century England resulted from a most varied set of historical circumstances. Liberals played a role, but they were not always as liberal as they seemed. Conservatives sometimes produced liberal reforms for their own purposes. The internal dynamics of the Liberal party played their part. Psychological impulses exerted an influence. Moral and religious impulses influenced many people. The complex tapestry is far too rich in texture to reduce it to a single thread. As G. Kitson Clark writes:

> The trouble is that far too much of the legislative and administrative development which helped create Victorian England has been simply labelled "applied Benthamism," as if it were simply the unfolding of Bentham's political philosophy, and as if Bentham's followers were the only systematic thinkers of the day. . . . In fact, . . . a great deal of administrative and legislative development was the result of the empirical actions and hard-bought experience of a number of officials, many of whom had probably never heard of Bentham, but on whom public demands had imposed novel and very difficult tasks.[35]

As the nineteenth century wore on, British liberalism made its gradual transition from its classical laissez-faire form to its more activist or "constructive" form. Many liberals began arguing that the government should play a more active role in alleviating social problems, thereby enhancing people's freedom to develop to their fullest potential. This line of thought seemed appropriate to many, especially given the economic depression which began in 1873 and lasted practically to the end of the century. Each year the economy was expected to improve, and yet it did not. Many in government thought that these circumstances required a positive response. In some respects both the Liberal and Conservative parties were quite similar during this period. As one scholar puts it: "Both consisted of three kinds of members: a small group of standpatters, a large group of supporters of mild changes, and a small group of advanced reformers."[36] Yet quite definitely a wing of the Liberal party, labeled the New Liberals, sponsored social reforms in education, housing, old age pensions. The names of Rosebery, Asquith, Haldane, and Grey are usually associated with this position. But some, while sympathetic to some of the specific reforms, had grave reservations about the direction which liberalism was taking. These individuals were disturbed that the constructive approach would foster class conflicts and interest-group politics which ultimately would be harmful to the welfare of all citizens.

This point of view is quite similar to that held by Chinese New Culture liberals, and it deserves further consideration. William Gladstone, for example, was definitely not opposed to reform. He certainly felt differently from Palmerston who, as early as 1864, had opined: "We cannot go on adding to the Statute Book ad infinitum. Perhaps we may have a little law reform, or bankruptcy reform; but we cannot go on legislating forever."[37] But Gladstone was disturbed at the trend toward constructionism which he saw developing in the Liberal party, particularly the extreme position of Joseph Chamberlain. Labor's desire for an eight-hour day was seen by Gladstone as "the labouring class beginning to be corrupted by the semblance of power as the other classes have been tainted and warped by its reality."[38] For liberals like Gladstone, the goal was to find a road to reform which maintained social harmony and social cohesion. The whole idea of class consciousness, labor unions, and socialism was anathema to them. They wanted to deal with the pressing need for social reform, but in a way that did not exacerbate class divisions. For them, the Liberal party should serve as a mechanism to mute class conflicts, bringing the classes together so that the entire community could prosper rather than having certain classes benefit at the expense of others.

John Morley, a Liberal politician best known for his service in Ireland and India, was someone who explicitly defended this view of liberalism. In 1874 he wrote: "Do let us try to give a national, not a class tone to English politics."[39] He earnestly hoped that voters would be able to substitute a national perspective for any parochial self-interest. He was a long-time friend and supporter of Joseph Chamberlain, but broke with him in the mid-1880s because he feared that Chamberlain's policies would evoke radical and perhaps socialist sentiments in the masses. He worried about interest-group politics developing a momentum which would be impossible to stop, leading ultimately to the fragmentation of British society into self-seeking classes disinterested in the welfare of the total community. So Morley urged patience upon the working class and, like Gladstone and others, searched for a big issue or cohering principle which would provide a comprehensive framework for liberal reform that would unify rather than divide the population. The Irish Question seemed to some to offer this prospect, but in fact it had quite the opposite effect. In the end Liberals neither found a cohering principle nor succeeded in preventing the development of class interests. And gradually the Liberal party was displaced by the Labour party which was less reluctant to appeal to such interests.

In essence the liberal reservations, for those who held them, were twofold. First, they were not too confident of the rationality (defined as seeing the larger community interest) of the masses. As the electorate expanded, with electoral reform, many liberals began to worry where democracy would lead. Second, they were deeply worried that the natural parochialism of the masses, especially if aggravated by opportunistic appeals from unscrupulous politicians, would fragment the nation into contending interest groups. They feared the country could never recover from such divisiveness. A number of liberal intellectuals discussed these concerns most eloquently. L. T. Hobhouse, for example, wrote that: "We need less of the fanatics of sectarianism and more of the unifying mind."[40] He urged the importance of what he called the "harmonic conception." J. A. Hobson viewed all of society as a total organism with a collective consciousness.[41] He was concerned for individuals, but as part of the collective welfare and not the atomized individualism of the old liberalism. Like Hobhouse, Hobson opposed class solutions to problems because such an approach would not enhance the welfare of the total society.

Graham Wallas, though a Fabian Socialist, also expressed similar concerns. He wondered whether democracy wasn't too advanced for the primitive instincts of the people. Clever politicians could play upon those instincts and so manipulate them for their own purposes. Yet his solution, very much like that of the Chinese New Culture liberals, was education. Education would develop a sense of public-spiritedness in all citizens, so as to "increase the margin of safety in our democracy."[42] Wallas also recognized that the growing complexity of society had a dislocating effect on people. It increased the sense of alienation. Once again, one of Wallas's main solutions to these problems was education. He suggested that education could inculcate a sense of belonging, an affection for the larger group which might otherwise be seen as an impersonal mass. In other words, once again like the Chinese, he thought that education would create a new social ethic. Indeed, he even thought that the Chinese and Japanese experience might provide a model. Japan especially impressed him, particularly with its victory in the Russo-Japanese War. The Japanese seemed to have found a way to combine energy with social cohesion in an ideal mixture worthy of emulation.

This brief look at British liberalism offers some insights which help shed light on the Chinese experience. First the progress of liberal principles in nineteenth-century Britain was erratic, with the emplacement of liberal programs resulting from a most varied combination of historical forces. Certainly, liberals and liberal ideology do not deserve all the credit for whatever liberal progress occurred. Similarly, it would be unfair to place all the blame on New Culture liberals for the absence of success in China. Second, British liberals were as naive, or idealistic, as their Chinese counterparts with respect to the prospects for harmonizing the classes and making reforms without destroying social cohesion. John Stuart Mill, writing in 1839, suggested that the middle class, religious dissenters, skilled craftsmen, and the working class could form an alliance to work for reform.[43] Mill thought that these diverse groups could find common ground as "the people" working against the aristocracy. This simplistic expectation ignored differences within the aristocracy. But of even greater importance was its misjudgment of the many conflicting interests which would divide "the people." The British liberal ideal (of a unified "people" thinking of the collective goal rather than their own "partial" interests) proved to be a misguided illusion. They cherished high hopes, expecting the middle and working classes to act as "rationally" as they thought they themselves were acting, but the result was eventual impotence and isolation. The Chinese liberals had a very similar experience, though their period of influence (the May Fourth period) was far shorter than that enjoyed by their British counterparts.

Conclusion

I am not attracted to the kind of historicism which dooms Chinese liberals to failure because of the absence of a middle class.[44] But one should recognize the daunting prospects which they faced. The Kuomintang was not the Tory or Whig party, and Chinese liberals experienced only a decade of relative stability before all-out war began in 1937. Even in better times, as indicated by the British experience, the achievement of liberal principles is an extremely precarious undertaking. One can hardly be too critical of Chinese liberals, given the conditions under which they labored.

New Culture liberals did push against the current, and they succeeded in building a beachhead. They did solidly establish the New Culture perspective, which overturned long-standing traditions and opened the gates for a flood of new ideas. Minds were opened, and Chinese intellectuals began to contemplate all kinds of new solutions to their nation's problems. New Culture liberals finally laid to rest the Confucian polity and replaced it with a more pluralistic society. Ironically, in doing so they planted the seeds of their own future destruction, or at least isolation, but they were undeniably a vital link in the chain of twentieth-century Chinese history. Lucien Bianco puts it well: "Liberalism had one hour of glory, one hour of life; whereupon, having accomplished the indispensable work of ground-clearing, it was trampled to death by the hardy children to whom it had helped give birth and whose further growth it could only inhibit."[45]

Certainly it is true that liberalism played little part in shaping policies in Mao Tse-tung's China. Liberalism in the sense of tolerance of dissent, protection of civil rights, and the encouragement of a qualified individualism was considered an obstacle to progress in post-1949 China. A People's Daily editorial in early 1966 stated: "If one could utterly ignore wo (I), one would dare to climb a mountain of swords and climb into a sea of fire."[46] Hu Shih, Lo Lung-chi and other New Culture liberals were periodically subjected to criticism campaigns.[47] Their liberal and pragmatic viewpoint was condemned as bourgeois idealism and antiscientific. This meant that they were too individualistic and subjective, rather than basing their ideas on the objective realities. On the surface these seem like unfair charges against men who prided themselves on their rational analysis of the evidence. Yet, as has been discussed, New Culture liberals operated within a certain self-imposed framework of ideas. They were iconoclastic compared to earlier generations, but they were a transitional generation whose attitudes were still influenced by traditional inclinations. They were idealists in hoping that rational persuasion, education, and other culturalistic reforms could transform Chinese society. Their intellectual framework did prevent them from appreciating the potential of mass organization or the justification for class struggle. Their paternalism did reinforce their sense of elitism, however much they might write about the condition of the masses or the need for democracy. They did, thus, represent ideas inimical to the objectives of the People's Republic of China. The campaigns against them have a logical basis, however regrettable might be the excesses and the humiliations endured by some intellectual figures.

Maoist criticisms fit the familiar pattern of attacks by winners against losers. Post-Mao China may well adopt more sympathetic attitudes toward New Culture liberals. Much depends on one's perspective and on subjective judgments about certain practical and moral dilemmas inherent in the liberal philosophy. Both British and Chinese liberals experienced frustration, isolation, and ultimate failure because they could neither escape nor resolve these dilemmas.

Throughout history liberals have advocated moderate reform, trying to steer a careful path between conservatism and radicalism and thus avoid the deficiencies of both. As they saw it, conservatism offered stability and continuity, but it didn't respond to the needs of large segments of the population; radicalism did try to respond to those needs, but at the risk of stirring up class conflict and interest-group politics. Liberals searched for ways to bring about reform while preserving class harmony and social cohesion.

One difficulty with the liberal philosophy has always been practical implementation in concrete historical settings. To implement nondivisive reform, avoiding class conflicts and harmonizing class divisions, requires an exceptional level of public-spiritedness. Liberals themselves might manifest the proper attitude, or at least might think they were doing so, but that didn't necessarily mean others could or would. Liberals hoped to develop such attitudes gradually, through education. But until education produced its leavening effect, pressing social problems might go unaddressed by liberals as they worked toward the distant goal of a new spirit of collective consciousness. In both China and Britain other political groups, focusing on existing conditions, responded to immediate problems and gained political advantages as a result.

Liberals were caught in the inherent contradiction of desiring an organized coalition of like-minded individuals so that socially harmonious reforms could occur, while fearful that the conventional approach of organizing a political coalition of interest groups would jeopardize the chances for such reform. Education was offered as the solution to this dilemma. It would instill a spirit of collective consciousness throughout society, and a coalition of broad-minded rather than self-interested individuals would somehow take shape. This is theoretically feasible, but the historical record does not offer much reason for optimism. Certainly it did not happen in China or Britain.

In addition to questions regarding practicality, the liberal philosophy also contains some inherent moral dilemmas. Is it justifiable to postpone responding to serious social and economic problems from fear of stimulating class conflict? Class conflict and fragmentation into narrow interest groups admittedly carry with them undesirable consequences. But are these worse than the perpetuation of existing injustices or inequities until the proper, socially harmonious reform can be implemented (assuming it is a practical, if distant, possibility)? Beyond this, when circumstances required a choice perceived by liberals as being between conservativism and radicalism, liberals have usually opted for the former. As Japanese threats to Chinese security intensified, many New Culture liberals muted their criticism of the Kuomintang and became more tolerant of dictatorship. But when forced to choose between two illiberal dictatorships, they refused to associate with the radical one. A left-wing Communist dictatorship, which openly advocated class conflict for the benefit of the lower classes, was unacceptable to Chinese liberals. However reluctantly, they became supporters of a government which was sympathetic to few if any of their liberal values. Still, by liberal standards the danger of class warfare, as represented by the Communists, was greater than the risk that social problems would go unsolved because of the conservative inclinations of the Kuomintang. Unwilling to mobilize political pressure to exert influence on Kuomintang policies, Chinese liberals were left with moral suasion in their role as independent critics. When their criticism went unheeded, liberals were rendered impotent.

In Britain liberals such as Morley, Hobhouse, Hobson, and Wallas were similarly reluctant to risk aggravating class tensions by offering programs responsive to the demands of the working class. Their advice, too, proved ineffectual, and Britain has since built an extensive structure of legislation and institutions modeled on the "constructive" liberalism so distressing to the liberals examined in this study. Any assessment of the correctness of the viewpoint of Chinese liberals and Morley et al. depends on one's conclusions about the course of events in China and Britain subsequent to the time when their advice went unheeded.

Both British and Chinese liberals functioned in unique cultural settings, but their experiences contained common elements which seemed to transcend cultural boundaries. One purpose of comparative studies is to define those points of transcendence, thereby enriching our understanding of the human condition. Any political philosophy confronts its adherents with practical and moral dilemmas, but certainly one of the most frustrating of all political circumstances is to be a liberal in an illiberal age.

Abbreviations Used in the Notes

CTFHC	Chiang T'ing-fu hsuan-chi (Selected works of Chiang T'ing-fu)
FSNHC	Fu Ssu-nien hsuan-chi (Selected works of Fu Ssu-nien)
HTPL	Hsien-tai p'ing-lun (Contemporary Review)
KTST	Chiang Meng-lin, Kuo-tu shih-tai chih ssu-hsiang yü chiao-yü (Thought and education in a transitional age)
MHWT	Meng-ho wen-ts'un (Collected writings of T'ao Meng-ho)
MLWT	Meng-lin wen-ts'un (Collected writings of Chiang Meng-lin)
NLCP	Nu-li chou-pao (The Endeavor)
TLPL	Tu-li p'ing-lun (Independent Critic)
TYPCC	Sun Ch'ang-wei, ed., Ts'ai Yuan-p'ei hsien-sheng ch'uan-chi (Complete works of Mr. Ts'ai Yuan-p'ei)
TYPLC	Sun Te-chung, ed., Ts'ai Yuan-p'ei hsien-sheng i-wen lei-ch'ao (Categorized materials on Mr. Ts'ai Yuan-p'ei)

Notes

1. Introduction

1. From a selection in David Sidorsky, ed., The Liberal Tradition in European Thought (New York: G. P. Putnam's Sons, 1970), p. 98.

2. John Plamenatz, Readings from Liberal Writers: English and French (London: George Allen and Unwin, 1965), pp. 16-17.

3. Donald Munro, The Concept of Man in Early China (Stanford: Stanford University Press, 1969), pp. 15-16, 163-67; Barry Keenan, The Dewey Experiment in China: Educational Reform and Political Power in the Early Republic (Cambridge: Harvard University Press, 1977).

4. Liang Ch'i-ch'ao, Intellectual Trends in the Ch'ing Period (Cambridge: Harvard University Press, 1959).

5. Mary Backus Rankin, Early Chinese Revolutionaries: Radical Intellectuals in Shanghai and Chekiang, 1902-1911 (Cambridge: Harvard University Press, 1971), p. 7; Ernest P. Young, "The Reformer as a Conspirator: Liang Ch'i-ch'ao and the 1911 Revolution," in Albert Feuerwerker, ed., Approaches to Modern Chinese History (Berkeley: University of California Press, 1967), pp. 239-67. Michael Gasster, Chinese Intellectuals and the Revolution of 1911 (Seattle: University of Washington Press, 1969.

6. Benjamin I. Schwartz, Reflections on the May Fourth Movement: A Symposium (Cambridge: East Asian Research Center, Harvard University, 1972), pp. 5-10.

7. Three useful studies of Liang Ch'i-ch'ao, listed by date of publication, are: Joseph R. Levenson, Liang Ch'i-ch'ao and the Mind of Modern China (Cambridge: Harvard University Press, 1953); Chang Hao, Liang Ch'i-

ch'ao and Intellectual Transition in China, 1890-1907 (Cambridge: Harvard University Press, 1971); and Philip C. Huang, _Liang Ch'i-ch'ao and Modern Chinese Liberalism_ (Seattle: University of Washington Press, 1972).

8. Jerome Grieder, "The Question of 'Politics' in the May Fourth Era," in Schwartz, _Reflections_, pp. 97-101.

9. Laurence A. Schneider, _Ku Chieh-kang and China's New History_ (Berkeley: University of California Press, 1971), pp. 119-20.

10. Liu Chun-jo, _Controversies in Modern Chinese Intellectual History_ (Cambridge: East Asian Research Center, Harvard University, 1964).

11. Jerome Grieder, _Hu Shih and the Chinese Renaissance: Liberalism in the Chinese Revolution, 1917-1937_ (Cambridge: Harvard University Press, 1970), p. 259.

2. Ts'ai Yuan-p'ei, 1898-1919: The Making of a New Culture Liberal

1. Chou Hsin, "Ts'ai Chieh-min hsien-sheng ti tsui-hou i-yen" (Mr. Ts'ai Chieh-min's last words), TYPCC, p. 1753.

2. The most useful account of Ts'ai's childhood and early career is Huang Shih-hui, "Ts'ai Chieh-min hsien-sheng chuan-lueh" (A short biography of Mr. Ts'ai Chieh-min), Chuan-chi wen-hsueh 10, no. 2 (1967): 107-14 (hereafter cited as "Ts'ai Chieh-min"). Also see Hsiao Yü, "Ts'ai Yuan-p'ei hsien-sheng tzu-chuan i chang" (A chapter of Ts'ai Yuan-p'ei's autobiography; told to Hsiao Yü by Ts'ai in Hong Kong in 1940), Chuan-chi wen-hsueh 10, no. 1 (1967): 43-44; and the "Nien-p'u" (Chronological biography), TYPLC, pp. 1-20.

3. Arthur Hummel, ed., Eminent Chinese of the Ch'ing Period (Washington, D.C.: Government Printing Office, 1943), pp. 532-33. For the best indication of Ts'ai's attitude toward neo-Confucian moralism see his "Chi Shao-hsing chih hsueh-hui ti san ta-yuan" (Recalling the three great wishes of a Shaohsing study society), TYPCC, pp. 646-47.

4. Ch'en Liang-yu, "Chui-tao Ts'ai hsien-sheng wo-men ying-yang ti jen-shih" (The attitude we should adopt in mourning Mr. Ts'ai), Tung-fang tsa-chih 37, no. 8 (15 April 1940): 66-67; Sun K'o, "Hsiao-fa Ts'ai Yuan-p'ei hsien-sheng ti ching-shen" (Imitate Mr. Ts'ai's spirit; 14 January 1968 speech), TYPCC, p. 1401; Sun Te-chung, "I wei-ta chiao-yü-chia" (A great educator), TYPCC, pp. 1501-05.

5. Li Chi, "Li Chi po-shih t'an Ts'ai Yuan-p'ei ti hsueh-shu kung-hsien" (Li Chi talks of Ts'ai Yuan-p'ei's contribution to scholarship; Chung-hua jih-pao, 11 January 1967), TYPCC, p. 1508; Sun-Ch'ang-wei, "Ts'ai Chieh-min hsien-sheng chuan-chi" (A biography of Mr. Ts'ai Chieh-min), TYPCC, p. 7.

6. Lin Yü-t'ang, "Chi Ts'ai Chieh-min hsien-sheng" (Remembering Mr. Ts'ai Chieh-min; Taiwan hsin-sheng pao, 9 April 1965), TYPCC, p. 1407.

7. TYPCC, pp. 662-64.

8. It is a tribute to Ts'ai that he did not succumb to the escapism of scholarship or aesthetics. As John Dewey remarked: "It is very easy to see how cultivated people take refuge in art and spirituality when politics are corrupt and the general state of social life is so

discouraging." Letters from China and Japan (New York: E. P. Dutton, 1920), p. 195.

9. She Lun, "Ts'ai Chieh-min hsien-sheng ti tou-cheng ching-shen" (Mr. Ts'ai Chieh-min's fighting spirit), TYPCC, p. 1814; Sun, "Hsiao-fa Ts'ai," pp. 1402-3.

10. Chou Hsin, "Ts'ai Chieh-min hsien-sheng ti tsui-hou i-yen," TYPCC, p. 1745.

11. Ch'en Hsi-jung, "Kuan-yü Ts'ai hsien-sheng ti hui-i" (Memories regarding Mr. Ts'ai), TYPCC, p. 1536; Chiang Meng-lin, Hsi-ch'ao (Tides from the West) (Taipei: Chung-hua jih-pao, 1960), p. 87.

12. Ch'en, "Kuan-yü Ts'ai," p. 1536.

13. Who's Who in China, 3d ed. (Shanghai: China Weekly Review, 1925), pp. 732-33; Sun Te-chung, "Nien p'u," TYPLC, pp. 2-3. See Weng T'ung-ho's appreciative remarks on the young Shaohsing scholar's abilities, in his diary citation in TYPCC, p. 1665.

14. "Ts'ai Chieh-min," p. 108; Ts'ai Shang-ssu, Ts'ai Yuan-p'ei hsueh-shu ssu-hsiang chuan-chi (The life and thought of Ts'ai Yuan-p'ei) (Shanghai: T'ang ti ch'u-pan she, 1950), p. 49; Ma Ts'ai, "Ts'ai Yuan-p'ei ti ssu-hsiang" (The thought of Ts'ai Yuan-p'ei), in Chung-kuo chin-tai ssu-hsiang shih lun-wen-chi (Symposium on modern Chinese history) (Shanghai: Shanghai jen-min ch'u-pan she, 1958), p. 163.

15. "Ts'ai Chieh-min," p. 108; Ts'ai Yuan-p'ei, "Wo tsai chiao-yü-chieh ti ching-yen" (My experiences in educational circles), in Ts'ai Yuan-p'ei tzu-shu (Ts'ai Yuan-p'ei's autobiography) (Taipei: Chuan-chi wen-hsueh ch'u-pan she, 1967), pp. 36-37 (hereafter cited as TS).

16. "Ts'ai Chieh-min," p. 109; Ts'ai Yuan-p'ei, Wo tsai chiao-yü-chieh ti ching-yen," TS, pp. 37-39; Chiang Wei-ch'iao, "Chung-kuo chiao-yü-hui chih hui-i" (Recollections of the Chinese Education Society), Hsin-hai ko-ming (Shanghai: Shanghai jen-min ch'u-pan she, 1961), 1: 485-96; Feng Tzu-yu, "Chung-kuo chiao-yü-hui yü ai-kuo hsueh-she" (The Chinese Education Society and the Patriotic School), Hsin-hai ko-ming, 1: 481-84.

17. Sun Te-chung, "Nien-p'u," TYPLC, p.5; Li Shu-hua, "Reminiscences," (Chinese Oral History Project, Columbia University), p. 206. However, Ts'ai was apparently not a very charismatic revolutionary leader. See Mary Backus Rankin, "The Revolutionary Movement in Chekiang," in Mary Wright, ed., China in Revolution:

The First Phase, 1900-1913 (New Haven: Yale University Press, 1968), pp. 331-33.

18. "Ts'ai Chieh-min," pp. 109-10; Ma Chien, "Chi-nien Ts'ai Chieh-min hsien-sheng" (Recalling Mr. Ts'ai Chieh-min), Tung-fang tsa-chih 37, no. 8 (15 April 1940): 65; Y. C. Wang, "The Su-pao Case: A Study of Foreign Pressure, Intellectual Fermentation and Dynastic Decline," Monumenta Serica 24 (1965).

19. Ts'ai Yuan-p'ei, "Shih ch'ou-Man" (Explaining revenge against the Manchus), TYPLC, pp. 462-64; Chiang Wei-ch'iao, "Min-kuo chiao-yü tsung-chang Ts'ai Yuan-p'ei" (Minister of Education Ts'ai Yuan-p'ei), TS, p. 100. See the perceptive comments in Ts'ai Shang-ssu, Ts'ai Yuan-p'ei, p. 2.

20. "Ts'ai Chieh-min," p. 111; Sun Te-chung, "Nien-p'u," TYPLC, p. 8.

21. George L. Mosse, The Culture of Western Europe (Chicago: Rand McNally and Co., 1961), pp. 213-30; Gerhard Masur, Prophets of Yesterday: Studies in European Culture, 1890-1914 (London: Weidenfeld and Nicolson, 1963).

22. Ts'ai Yuan-p'ei, Chung-kuo lun-li hsueh shih (A History of Chinese Ethics), TYPCC, pp. 1-102.

23. D. W. Y. Kwok, Scientism in Chinese Thought, 1900-1950 (New Haven: Yale University Press, 1965). Kwok defines scientism as "that view which places all reality within a natural order and deems all aspects of this order, be they biological, social, physical, or psychological, to be knowable only by the methods of science," p. 21.

24. Ts'ai Yuan-p'ei, "Wo tsai chiao-yü-chieh ti ching-yen," TS, p. 41. For a statement of his five-theme curriculum see "Tui-yü chiao-yü fang-chen chih i-chien" (My view of the direction of education), TYPLC, pp. 77-84. For a summary of Ts'ai's ideas, in English translation, see Ts'ai Yuan-p'ei, "The New Education," China Mission Year Book, 1913 (Shanghai: Christian Literature Society for China, 1913), pp. 252-57.

25. "Ts'ai Chieh-min," p. 112; Lo Chia-lun, "Ts'ai Yuan-p'ei hsien-sheng yü Pei-ching ta-hsueh" (Ts'ai Yuan-p'ei and Peking University), Chuan-chi wen-hsueh 10, no. 1 (1967): 31.

26. Chow Tse-tsung, The May Fourth Movement (Cambridge: Harvard University Press, 1960), pp. 36-40.

27. Hua-kung hsueh-hsiao chiang-i (Lectures for the Chinese Workers School), TYPCC, pp. 190-251.

28. Ts'ai Yuan-p'ei, "Wo tsai Pei-ching ta-hsueh ti ching-li" (My experiences at Peking University), TYPLC, pp. 308-09; idem, "Chui-jen Pei-ching ta-hsueh hsiao-chang chih yen-shuo-tz'u" (Speech on assuming the chancellorship of Peking University; 9 January 1917), TYPLC, pp. 316-18; "Ts'ai Chieh-min cheng-tun ta-hsueh chih pan-fa" (Ts'ai Chieh-min's plans for reordering the university), Chiao-yü tsa-chih 9, no. 2 (1917): 11.

29. Ts'ai Yuan-p'ei, "Pei-ching ta-hsueh chih Chin-te-hui chih ch'u-shu" (On the objectives of the Peita Chin-te hui), TYPLC, pp. 325-28. For Ts'ai's speeches on the founding of similar study societies in art, literature, journalism, etc., see TYPLC, pp. 341-47.

30. A brief list of some of the illustrious figures associated with Peita would include Ch'en Tu-hsiu, Hu Shih, Ch'ien Hsuan-t'ung, Chou Tso-jen and his brother Lu Hsun, Li Ta-chao, Shen Yin-mo, Ku Hung-ming, and Huang K'an. Foreign notables such as John Dewey, Bertrand Russell, Hans Driesch, and Rabindranath Tagore also visited.

31. Ts'ai Yuan-p'ei, "Kao Pei-ching ta-hsueh hsueh-sheng yü ch'uan-kuo hsueh-sheng lien-ho-hui shu" (A letter to the Peita and National Student Association; 9 July 1919), TYPLC, pp. 334-36; idem, "Hui-jen Pei-ching ta-hsueh hsiao-chang tsai ch'uan-t'i hsueh-sheng huan-ying-hui yen-shuo-tz'u" (Speech to the student welcome meeting on resuming Peita's Chancellorship), TYPLC, pp. 337-38; idem, "Hung-shui yü meng-shou" (Floods and wild beasts), TYPLC, pp. 51-52.

32. Ts'ai Yuan-p'ei, "Chung-kuo ti wen-i chung-hsing) (China's literary and artistic renaissance), TYPLC, pp. 5-12.

3. Breakdown of the New Culture Consensus and Emergence of a New Liberal Posture

1. See the articles in Benjamin I. Schwartz, ed., Reflections on the May Fourth Movement: A Symposium (Cambridge: East Asian Research Center, Harvard University, 1972).

2. Jerome B. Grieder, Hu Shih and the Chinese Renaissance (Cambridge: Harvard University Press, 1970), pp. 181-83; Li Lung-mu, "I-ko wu-ssu shih-ch'i ti cheng-chih k'an-wu--Mei-chou p'ing-lun" (A May 4 political publication--Mei-chou p'ing-lun); Chang Ching-lu, Chung-kuo hsien-tai ch'u-pan shih-liao (Materials on the history of contemporary Chinese publishing) (Peking: Chung-hua shu-chü, 1954-1959), 4: 40-43.

3. Grieder, Hu-Shih, pp. 183-88; Chang, Chung-kuo hsien-tai, I: 7.

4. Chow Tse-tsung, The May Fourth Movement (Cambridge: Harvard University Press, 1960), pp. 251-53; Chan Lau Kit-ching, The Chinese Youth Party, 1923-1945 (Hong Kong: University of Hong Kong Press, 1972), p. 5; Tso Shun-sheng, "Chi Shao-nien Chung-kuo hsueh-hui" (Recalling the Young China Association), Tso Shun-sheng hsuan-chi (Selected writings of Tso Shun-sheng) (Taipei: Atlantic Books Co., 1968), 1: 5-12.

5. Tso, Tso Shun-sheng, 1: 11-12.

6. Chow, May Fourth Movement, pp. 239-40.

7. NLCP 1 (7 May 1922): 1.

8. The letter and Hu's reply are in NLCP 4 (28 May 1922): 8.

9. NLCP 2 (14 May 1922): 1-2; Grieder, Hu Shih, p. 190, fn. 36.

10. The letters and Hu's reply are in NLCP 4 (28 May 1922): 1-5.

11. Hu Shih, "Cheng-lun-chia yü cheng-tang" (Political commentators and political parties), NLCP 5 (4 June 1922): 1.

12. "Wo ti ch'i-lu" (My crossroads), NLCP 7 (18 June 1922): 3-4 (paraphrase by the author).

13. Ch'en Heng-che, "Kuan-yu Nu-li pen-shen ti i-ko

wen-t'i" (A question regarding the Nu-li chou-pao), NLCP 15 (13 August 1922): 4.

14. Kao I-han, "Cheng-chih yü she-hui" (Politics and society), NLCP 3 (21 May 1922): 2-3.

15. Chang Wei-tz'u's articles appear in NLCP 8, 9, 10, and 12.

16. T'ao Meng-ho, "Tsen-yang chieh-chueh Chung-kuo ti wen-t'i" (How to solve China's problems), NLCP 65 (12 August 1923): 1-2; "Chung-kuo ti jen-min ti fen-hsi" (An analysis of China's people; 2 September 1923), MHWT 1: 19-20.

17. Chiang Meng-lin, "Hsueh-feng yü t'i-kao hsueh-shu" (The academic atmosphere and improving scholarship; Ch'en-pao, 2 December 1922), KTST, pp. 97-99; "Chih-shih chieh-chi ti tzu-jen wen-t'i" (The responsibilities of the intellectuals; Ch'en-pao, November, 1924), KTST, pp. 44-48.

18. Charlotte Furth, Ting Wen-chiang: Science and China's New Culture (Cambridge: Harvard University Press, 1970), pp. 69-74.

19. Ibid., pp. 140-45.

20. Ting Wen-chiang, "Shao-shu-jen ti tzu-jen" (The responsibility of the few), NLCP 67 (26 August 1923): 2-4.

21. "Arrest of Minister of Finance," North China Herald, 25 November 1922, pp. 498-99.

22. This is the conclusion of Andrew Nathan in his Peking Politics, 1918-1923: Factionalism and the Failure of Constitutionalism (Berkeley: University of California Press, 1976), p. 199.

23. Ibid., p. 200.

24. Hu Shih, "Che-i-chou" (This week), NLCP 15 (13 August 1922): 1.

25. See, for example, "Che-i-chou" (This week), NLCP 22 (1 October 1922): 1.

26. Grieder, Hu Shih, p. 204, fn. 58.

27. Hu Shih, "Che-i-chou" (This week), NLCP 30 (26 November 1922): 1; "P'eng Yün-i tai-piao shen-ma?" (What does P'eng Yün-i represent?), NLCP 40 (4 February 1923):1.

28. Kao I-han, "Kuo-fa ho-tsai?" (Where is the na-

tional law?), NLCP 30 (26 November 1922): 2.

29. Ts'ai Yuan-p'ei, "Wo tsai Pei-ching ta-hsueh ti ching-li," TYPLC, p. 315.

30. Ts'ai's brief resignation memorandum is in TYPCC, p. 1115. A somewhat longer letter of resignation is in TYPLC, p. 495.

31. Ts'ai Yuan-p'ei, "Min-kuo shih-erh-nien i-yueh erh-shih-san-jih wei Lo Wen-kan tsao fei-fa tai-pu an k'ang-i hsuan-yen" (23 January 1923 protest of the illegal arrest of Lo Wen-kan), TYPLC, pp. 496-99.

32. Ibid., p. 496; Hu Shih, "Ts'ai Yuan-p'ei i tz'u-chih wei k'ang-i" (Ts'ai Yuan-p'ei's use of resignation as a protest; January, 1923), TYPCC, pp. 1428-29; Lin Yü-t'ang, "Chi Ts'ai Chieh-min hsien-sheng" (Remembering Mr. Ts'ai Chieh-min), TYPCC, p. 1470.

33. Ts'ai Yuan-p'ei, "Wo tsai Pei-ching," p. 315; idem, "Min-kuo shih-erh-nien," pp. 496-98.

34. "Pei-ching ti hsueh-ch'ao" (The student atmosphere in Peking), Tung-fang tsa-chih 20, no. 1 (10 January 1923): 17-19.

35. Hu Shih, "Ts'ai Yuan-p'ei ti pu-ho-tso chu-i" (Ts'ai Yuan-p'ei's theory of noncooperation; January, 1923), TYPCC, pp. 1431-32; idem, "Ts'ai Yuan-p'ei yü Pei-ching chiao-yü-chieh" (Ts'ai Yuan-p'ei and Peking educational circles), TYPCC, pp. 1432-34.

36. Hu Shih, "Hu Shih hsien-sheng tao-ti tsen-yang?" (How is Mr. Hu Shih after all?), NLCP 36 (7 January 1923), p. 4.

37. Chang Wei-tz'u, "Ko-ming ho cheng-chih kai-ko" (Revolution and political reform), NLCP 64 (5 August 1923): 2 and NLCP 66 (19 August 1923): 3.

38. Kao I-han, "Wo-men tsui-hou ti hsi-wang" (Our last hope), NLCP 64 (5 August 1923): 1.

39. Hu Shih, "Yü I-han teng ssu-wei ti hsin" (A letter to Kao I-han et al.), Hu Shih wen-ts'un (Selected works of Hu Shih) (Shanghai: Ya-tung t'u-shu kuan, 1924), 2: iii, 153-56. The translation is from Grieder, Hu Shih, p. 205.

40. NLCP 75 (21 October 1923): 1.

4. The Dilemmas of the Warlord Period

1. See, for example, the report of the annual meeting of the Chinese Social and Political Science Association, 8 December 1922, in the Chinese Social and Political Science Review 7, no. 1 (January 1923): 111-12. Also see Nelson Nai-cheng Shen, "The Changing Chinese Social Mind," in ibid. 8, no. 1 (January 1924): 80-82, as well as the article by Y. S. Tsao, ibid. 10, no. 1 (January 1926): 62-91.

2. Chang Ching-lu, Tsai ch'u-pan-chieh erh-shih nien (Twenty years in the publishing world) (Shanghai: Shang-hai tsa-chih kung-ssu, 1938), pp. 133-34.

3. For the general picture see Andrew J. Nathan, Peking Politics, 1918-1923 (Berkeley: University of California Press, 1976). For information on teacher strikes see Chow Tse-tsung, The May Fourth Movement (Cambridge: Harvard University Press, 1960), pp. 260-62; Grover Clark, "The New Issue in the Teachers' Strike," Millard's Review, 26 March 1921, pp. 183-84; and "Peking Teachers' Strike," North China Herald, 30 July 1921, p. 312.

4. Several such speeches are in KTST, pp. 196, 203, 207.

5. "Chiao-yü ching-fei tao-ti tsen-ma-yang?" (What about educational expenses?), HTPL 4, no. 88 (14 August 1926): 1.

6. Chiang Monlin, Tides from the West (New Haven: Yale University Press, 1947), p. 135.

7. "Ching-hsueh-chieh chiao-yü-fei tu-li chih yün-tung (The movement for financial independence by the Peking educational community), Chiao-yü tsa-chih 13, no. 4 (1921): 2-6; Ma Hsü-lun, Wo tsai liu-shih sui i-ch'ien (My life before sixty) (Shanghai: Sheng-huo shu-tien, 1947), p. 93; "Chiao-yü hsiao-hsi" (Educational news), HTPL 1, no. 5 (10 January 1925): 3.

8. Wang Shih-chieh, "Hsueh-hsiao yü cheng-chih" (Government and the schools), HTPL 4, no. 81 (26 June 1926): 4-6.

9. Ts'ai Yuan-p'ei, "Chiao-yü tu-li i" (On the independence of education; March 1922), TYPLC, pp. 100-102.

10. Allen B. Linden, "Politics and Education in Na-

tionalist China: The Case of the University Council, 1927-1928," Journal of Asian Studies 27, no. 4 (August 1968): 766.

11. Lee-hsia Hsu Ting, Government Control of the Press in Modern China, 1900-1949 (Cambridge: East Asian Research Center, Harvard University, 1974); Yin Fa-lu, "Pei-yang chün-fa tui chin-pu k'an-wu ti ts'ui-ts'an" (The northern warlords' destruction of progressive publications) in Chang Ching-lu, Chung-kuo hsien-tai ch'u-pan shih-liao (Peking: Chung-hua shu-chü, 1954), 1: 45-50.

12. Lee Hsia Hsu Ting, Government Control of the Press in Modern China, 1900-1949 (Cambridge: East Asian Research Center, Harvard University, 1974), p. 211, fn. 27. Also see the special announcement in HTPL 1, no. 19 (18 April 1925): 2.

13. T'ao Meng-ho, "Yen-lun tzu-yu" (Freedom of discussion), HTPL 1, no. 19 (18 April 1925): 4-7.

14. Wang Shih-chieh, "Ching-chih yü fa-chih" (Police rule and the rule of law), HTPL 1, no. 21 (2 May 1925): 8-10; Kao I-han, "Ko-ming-chün yü yen-lun tzu-yu" (Revolutionary warlords and freedom of speech), HTPL 3. no. 64 (27 February 1926): 4-5.

15. Ting, Government Control, pp. 58-59; Wu Hsiang-hsiang, Min-kuo pai jen-chuan (One hundred biographies of the Republican period) (Taipei: Chuan-chi wen-hsueh ch'u-pan she, 1971), 1: 78-79; "K'o-lien ti yen-lun-chieh" (The pitiful press community), HTPL 4, no. 88 (14 August 1926): 1.

16. Chang, Tsai ch'u-pan-chieh, pp. 126-27.

17. John Dewey and Alice Chipman Dewey, Letters from China and Japan (New York: E. P. Dutton, 1920), p. 195.

18. Laurence A. Schneider, Ku Chieh-kang and China's New History (Berkeley: University of California Press, 1971), pp. 73-77, 99, 115-20.

19. Fu Ssu-nien, "Tzu-jan" (Spontaneity), FSNHC (Shu-hsin), pp. 26-31; Schneider, Ku Chieh-kang, pp. 110-15.

20. FSNHC (Shu-hsin), pp. 11, 64.

21. T. F. Tsiang, CTFHC 6: 1084-85.

22. Jean Chesneaux, "The Federalist Movement in

China, 1920-3" in Jack Gray, ed., Modern China's Search for a Political Form (New York: Oxford University Press, 1969), pp. 123-27.

23. Hu Shih, "Lien-sheng tzu-chih yü chün-fa ko-chü" (Federalism and warlord separatism), NLCP 19 (10 September 1922): 1-4.

24. Kao I-han, "Tsui-chin ti kuo-chia hsing-chih hsin-lun" (Recent discussion of the nature of the state), NLCP 37 (14 January 1923): 1-2 and "Hsi-wang Hsien-fa hui-i hsiu-kai Hsien-fa tsao-an chung ti Ta tsung-t'ung hsuan-chü-fa" (I hope the Constituent Assembly reforms the Presidential Election Law in the Draft Constitution), NLCP 36 (7 January 1923): 1-2.

25. Chang Wei-tz'u, "Chih-hsien wen-t'i" (The question of drafting a constitution), NLCP 3 (21 May 1922): 3-4 and "Cheng-chih kai-ko mu-piao" (The objective of political reform), NLCP 63 (29 July 1923): 2-3.

26. HTPL 1, no. 1 (13 December 1924): 2.

27. For example, see Yen Shu-ch'ang's article in HTPL 1, no. 1 (13 December 1924): 5-7; or the discussion of the Aftermath Conference in nos. 3, 5, 8, 10, and 14.

28. Chou Keng-sheng, "Yueh-fa wen-t'i ti chih-chueh" (A decision on the constitutional question), HTPL 1, no. 3 (27 December 1924): 4-7; idem, "Shih-chü ti wei-chi" (A dangerous situation), HTPL 1, no. 13 (7 March 1925): 4-6; idem, "Min-chung shih-li ti tzu-chih" (Organizing the people's strength), HTPL 1, no. 24 (23 May 1925): 4-5.

29. Kao I-han, "Shan-hou-hui-i i-yuan ti ch'u-hsi t'i-t'i" (Notice on the delegates to the Aftermath Conference), HTPL 1, no. 5 (10 January 1925): 4-5 and "P'ing-min ko-ming ti mu-ti yü shou-tuan" (The objectives and tactics of mass revolution), HTPL 2, no. 53 (12 December 1925): 2-3.

30. T. F. Tsiang, "T'ung-i fang-fa ti t'ao-lun" (On methods of unification; HTPL no. 65, 6 March 26), CTFHC 1: 21-27.

31. T'ao Meng-ho, "Wo-men hsiao-min ti hsi-wang" (The hope of us little people), HTPL 3, no. 73 (1 May 1926): 3-4.

32. T'ao Meng-ho, "Cheng-chih ti kung-tso" (Political work), HTPL 5, no. 105 (11 December 1926): 3-6.

33. T'ao Meng-ho, "K'o-hsueh yen-chiu--li-kuo chi-

ch'u" (Scientific research--the foundation of the nation), HTPL 5, no. 117 (5 March 1927): 4-7.

34. Ch'en Heng-che and Jen Hung-chün, "I-ko kai-liang ta-hsueh chiao-yü ti t'i-i" (Some suggestions on reform of university education), HTPL 2, no. 39 (5 September 1925): 10-13.

35. Hu Shih, "Wo-men tui-yü hsi-yang chin-tai wen-ming ti t'ai-tu" (Our attitude toward modern Western civilization), HTPL 4, no. 83 (10 July 1926): 6-10.

36. Jean Chesneaux, The Chinese Labor Movement, 1919-1927 (Stanford: Stanford University Press, 1968), pp. 151-233.

37. Ts'ai Yuan-p'ei, "Lao-kung shen-sheng" (The divinity of labor), TYPLC, p. 469.

38. Ts'ai Yuan-p'ei, "Kuo-wai ch'in-kung chien-hsueh-hui yü kuo-nei kung-hsueh hu-chu-t'uan" (The workers' frugal study society and the workers' study assistance association; 31 August 1920), TYPCC, p. 521.

39. Chang Kuo-t'ao, The Rise of the Chinese Communist Party (Lawrence: University of Kansas Press, 1971), 1: 108.

40. Ts'ai Yuan-p'ei, "She-hui chu-i shih hsü" (Preface to the History of Socialism), Hsin-ch'ing-nien 8, no. 1 (September 1920): 14-15.

41. Ts'ai Yuan-p'ei, "Tsai p'ing-min yeh-hsiao k'ai-hsueh-jih ti yen-shuo" (Speech on the opening of night school; 18 January 1920), TYPLC, pp. 129-30; Grover Clark, "Passing on Their Education," Weekly Review, 21 October 1922, pp. 259-60.

42. Hu Shih, "Shang-hai pa-shih ch'ü-hsiao" (The cancellation of the Shanghai shut-down), NLCP 42 (4 March 1923): 1.

43. Yang Ch'uan, "Chung-kuo tsui-chin pa-kung wen-t'i chih fen-hsi yü pu-chiu" (China's recent strikes: An analysis and remedy), NLCP 53 (20 May 1923): 3-4 and 54 (27 May 1923): 3-4.

44. Kao I-han, "Chung-kuo ken-pen ti she-hui wen-t'i" (China's basic social problems), NLCP 51 (6 May 1923): 1.

45. Li Ching-han, "Pei-ching la-ch'e ti k'u-kung" (The bitter toil of the Peking rickshaw puller), HTPL 3, no. 62 (13 February 1926): 4-6.

46. Li Ching-han, "Shu-shih-nien lai Pei-ching kung-tzu ti pi-chiao" (A comparison of wages in Peking over the last few decades), HTPL 4, no. 80 (19 June 1926): 6-8.

47. Yang Tuan-liu, "Shang-hai pa-kung ti chen-hsiang chi ch'i ying-hsiang" (The reality and influence of the Shanghai strike), HTPL 2, no. 35 (8 August 1925): 4-5.

48. "Wai-kuo-jen kan-she wo-men ti yen-lun" (Foreigners interfere with our speech), HTPL 1, no. 4 (3 January 1925): 3.

49. P'i Hao-po, "Shang-hai Jih-pen sha-ch'ang ti kung-ch'ao" (Workers' movement at the Shanghai Japanese textile factories), HTPL 1, no. 11 (21 February 1925): 16-17.

50. "Shih-shih tuan-p'ing" (Short items), HTPL 1, no. 10 (14 February 1925): 4-5.

51. Ibid. pp. 3-4.

52. Ch'en Hsi-ying, "Chung-kuo pao-chih ti wai-wen" (The foreign news in Chinese newspapers), HTPL 1, no. 11 (21 February 1925): 20.

53. "Shih-shih tuan-p'ing" (Short items), HTPL 1, no. 26 (6 June 1925): 2.

54. Wang Shih-chieh, "Shang-hai tsu-chieh ti ts'an-chü" (The tragedy of the Shanghai Concession), HTPL 1, no. 26 (6 June 1925): 4-5.

55. Chou Keng-sheng, "Shang-hai tsu-chieh ti hsing-chih chi tzu-chih" (The form and organization of the Shanghai Concessions), HTPL 2, no. 27 (13 June 1925): 4-7 and "Cheng-fu tui Hu-an ti wai-chiao" (The government's diplomacy regarding the Shanghai affair), HTPL 2, no. 28 (20 June 1925): 5-7.

56. See articles by Tang Po-huang, T'ang Yu-jen, Yang Tuan-liu, Ting Wen-chiang, and Ma Yin-chu in HTPL 2, no. 27, 28, 30, 33, 35.

57. Yen Shu-ch'ang, "Hu-an chin-hsing ying-ts'ai chih t'u-ching" (The path we should follow in Shanghai), HTPL 2, no. 27 (13 June 1925): 7-8.

58. T'ao Meng-ho, "Tai-chiu ti ai-kuo yün-tung" (Long lasting patriotic movements), HTPL 2, no. 29 (27 June 1925): 6-7.

59. Ts'ai Yuan-p'ei, "Wei Hu-an ko-kuo hsuan-yen" (A proclamation to the whole world on the Shanghai in-

cident), TYPCC, pp. 915-20.

60. Lo Chia-lun, "Hsien-tai hsueh-jen Ting Tsai-chün hsien-sheng ti i-chiao" (One side of the modern scholar Mr. Ting Tsai-chün), Shih-che ju-ssu chi (It passes away like this) (Taipei: Chuan-chi wen-hsueh ch'u-pan she, 1967), pp. 226-27.

61. Leo Ou-fan Lee, The Romantic Generation of Modern Chinese Writers (Cambridge: Harvard University Press, 1973), pp. 177-78.

62. "Shih-shih tuan-p'ing" (Short items), HTPL 1, no. 22 (9 May 1925): 2.

63. T'ao Meng-ho, "Wu-ch'i shih-chien kan-yen" (Impressions of the May 7 affair), HTPL 1, no. 23 (16 May 1925): 3.

64. Chou Keng-sheng, "Ch'ing-nien hsueh-sheng ti cheng-chih yün-tung" (Student political movements), HTPL 1, no. 22 (9 May 1925): 4.

65. T'ao Meng-ho, "Chiu-kuo yü ch'iu-hsueh" (Saving the nation and seeking an education), HTPL 2, no. 37 (22 August 1925): 5-6.

66. Hu Shih, "Ai-kuo yün-tung yü ch'iu-hsueh" (Patriotic movements and seeking an education), HTPL 2, no. 39 (5 September 1925): 5-8.

5. The Early Nationalist Period, 1927-1933

1. "Mei-kuo tui Hua t'ai-tu ti mao-tun" (The contradictions in America's attitude toward China), HTPL 4, no. 102 (20 November 1926): 1.

2. Yang Tuan-liu, "Kuang-chou ti hsien-ch'uang" (Present conditions in Canton), HTPL 4, no. 93 (18 September 1926): 5-8.

3. Ch'i-kung, "Nan-fang cheng-ch'ao ti kuan-ch'a" (An examination of political currents in the South), HTPL 5, no. 123 (16 April 1927): 2-3.

4. Hsü-p'ing, "Nan-ching cheng-fu" (The Nanking government), HTPL 5, no. 125 (30 April 1927): 1-4; Ch'i-kung, "Ch'ing-Tang yün-tung" (The Party Purification Movement), HTPL 5, no. 126 (7 May 1927): 3; Sung-tzu, "Kuo-min ko-ming lun" (On the national revolution) HTPL 6, no. 138 (30 July 1927): 2-3.

5. Erh-wang, "'Nan-fang cheng-ch'ao ti kuan-ch'a' ti fan-ying" (A response to "An examination of political currents in the South"), HTPL 5, no. 125 (30 April 1927): 18-19. Ch'i-kung's response is in ibid., pp. 19-20.

6. Lo Jen-kung, "Kuan-yü nan-fang cheng-ch'ao ti nei-mu" (The inside story of southern political currents), HTPL 5, no. 126 (7 May 1927): 18-19. This letter is followed by an editor's note, refuting its charges.

7. Ts'ai Yuan-p'ei, "Yueh-Ning-Han chih fen-lieh yü chung-yang t'e-pieh wei-yuan-hui ch'eng-li ching-kuo ch'ing-hsing" (The Hankow-Nanking split and the special Central Committee), TYPCC, pp. 815-16.

8. "Chu Chia-hua Fu Ssu-nien chih Li Shih-tseng Wu Chih-hui shu" (A letter from Chu Chia-hua and Fu Ssu-nien to Li Shih-tseng and Wu Chih-hui; 16 May 1927), FSNHC, (Shu-hsin), pp. 10-13.

9. T'ao Meng-ho, "Chün-shih shih-ch'i chung ti cheng-shih (Political affairs in a period of military affairs), HTPL 5, no. 129 (28 May 1927): 2-3. Also see Ch'ien Tuan-sheng's favorable assessment in "Tang-chih yü yü-lun" (Party government and public opinion), HTPL 6, no. 139 (6 August 1927): 7-9.

10. Howard L. Boorman, ed., Biographical Dictionary of Republican China (New York: Columbia University Press, 1967), 1: 75.

11. Allen B. Linden, "Politics and Higher Education in China: The Kuomintang and the University Community, 1927-1937" (Ph.D. thesis, Columbia University, 1969), p. 55.

12. China Weekly Review 43, no. 2 (10 December 1927): 50.

13. Linden, "Politics and Higher Education," pp. 64-66, 75-77 and "Politics and Education in Nationalist China," Journal of Asian Studies 27, no. 4 (August 1968): 763-64.

14. Linden, "Politics and Higher Education," pp 118-20, 141-49; Albert Borowitz, "Chiang Monlin," Papers on China 8 (1954): 130-33; Sun Te-chung, "Meng-lin hsien-sheng ti sheng-p'ing yü chih-ch'ü," Chuan-chi wen-hsueh 5, no. 2 (August 1964): 50.

15. Linden, "Politics and Higher Education," pp. 154-58; John Israel, Student Nationalism in China, 1927-1937 (Stanford: Stanford University Press, 1966), p. 39; Chiang Meng-lin, Hsin-ch'ao (Taipei: Chuan-chi wen-hsueh ch'u-pan she, 1967), p. 78.

16. Lo Chia-lun, "Wo so jen-shih ti Tai Chi-t'ao hsien-sheng" (The Tai Chi-t'ao I knew), Shih-che ju-ssu chi (It passes away like this) (Taipei: Chuan-chi wen-hsueh ch'u-pan she, 1967), pp. 145-48.

17. Lo Chia-lun, "Hsueh-shu tu-li yü hsin Ch'ing-hua" (Education independence and the new Tsinghua), Shih-che ju-ssu chi, pp. 7-15.

18. "Tsing Hua Alumni and the New President," China Critic 1, no. 16 (13 September 1928): 307-8; "Ch'ing-hua feng-ch'ao" (The atmosphere at Tsinghua), Kuo-wen chou-pao 7, no. 27 (14 July 1930).

19. Howard L. Boorman, ed., Biographical Dictionary of Republican China (New York: Columbia University Press, 1970), 3: 335-36; Lo Chia-lun, "Shu-i t'ien-hsia ts'ai--wo wei ts'ang-sheng k'u" (The talented Shu-i--I cry for the people), Shih-che ju-ssu chi, pp. 159-60; Hung-mao Tien, Government and Politics in Kuomintang China, 1927-1937 (Stanford: Stanford University Press, 1972), p. 49.

20. Chang Po-ling, "Ssu-shih nien Nan-k'ai hsueh-hsiao chih hui-ku" (Forty years at Nankai), in Wang Wen-t'ien et al., Chang Po-ling yü Nan-k'ai (Chang Po-ling and Nankai University) (Taipei: Chuan-chi wen-hsueh ch'u-pan she, 1968), p. 103.

21. Patrick Cavendish, "The 'New China' of the Kuomintang," in Jack Gray, ed., Modern China's Search for a Political Form (New York: Oxford University Press, 1969), p. 139.

22. Lau Kit-ching Chan, Chinese Youth Party 1923-1945 (Hong Kong: University of Hong Kong, 1972), pp. 25-26.

23. Lloyd E. Eastman, The Abortive Revolution: China under Nationalist Rule, 1927-1937 (Cambridge: Harvard University Press, 1974), p. 8.

24. Ibid., pp. 24-28; Lee Hsia Hsu Ting, Government Control of the Press in Modern China, 1900-1949 (Cambridge: East Asian Research Center, Harvard University, 1974), pp. 82-89.

25. Ting, Government Control, pp. 97-98.

26. Hu Shih, "Jen-ch'uan yü yueh-fa" (Human rights and the provisional constitution), Hsin-yueh 2, no. 2 (10 April 1929): 1-7; idem, "Wo-men shen-ma shih-hou ts'ai k'o-yu hsien-fa?" (When can we have a constitution?), ibid. 2, no. 4 (10 June 1929): 1-8; idem, "Chih-nan hsing i pu-i" (Knowing is difficult, but action is also not easy), ibid., pp. 1-15; idem, "Hsin wen-hua yün-tung yü Kuo-min-tang (The Kuomintang and the New Culture Movement), ibid. 2, nos. 6-7 (10 September 1929): 1-15.

27 Jerome B. Grieder, Hu Shih and the Chinese Renaissance (Cambridge: Harvard University Press, 1970), pp. 239-44.

28. Liang Shih-ch'iu, "Lun ssu-hsiang t'ung-i" (On thought unification), Hsin-yueh 2, no. 3 (10 May 1929): 1-10.

29. Lo Lung-chi, "Lun jen-ch'uan" (On human rights), Hsin-yueh 2, no. 5 (10 July 1929): 1-25; idem, "Kao ya-p'o yen-lun tzu-yu che" (Repressors of free speech), ibid. 2, nos. 6-7 (10 September 1929): 1-17; idem, "Wo tui tang-wu-shang ti 'chin-ch'ing p'i-p'ing'" (My "penetrating criticism" of Party affairs), ibid. 2, no. 8 (10 October 1929): 1-15.

30. "The Arrest of Dr. Lo Lung-chi," China Critic 3, no. 46 (13 November 1930): 1084.

31. Lo Lung-chi, "Wo ti pei-pu ti ching-kuo yü fan-kan" (My arrest and my response), Hsin-yueh 3, no. 3 (10 May 1930): 1-17. Although this issue was dated 10 May 1930, Hsin-yueh was always far behind in its publication schedule and this issue actually appeared after Lo's

arrest in November, 1930.

32. Eastman, Abortive Revolution, pp. 21-22; C. T. Hsia, A History of Modern Chinese Fiction, 1917-1957 (New Haven: Yale University Press, 1961), pp. 265-66; Tsi-an Hsia, The Gate of Darkness (Seattle: University of Washington Press, 1968), p. 229.

33. Ting, Government Control, p. 96; "The Murder of Liu Yu-sheng," China Forum 2, no. 1 (11 February 1933): 13; "China's Civil Rights," China Critic 2, no. 5 (2 February 1933): 117-18.

34. Eastman, Abortive Revolution, pp. 160-63.

35. T. F. Tsiang, "Nan-ching ti chi-hui" (Nanking's opportunity), CTFHC 1: 169.

36. T. F. Tsiang, "Ts'an-chia kuo-nan hui-i ti hui-ku" (Reflections on participating in the National Emergency Conference), TLPL 1 (22 May 1932): 9.

37. Fu Ssu-nien, "Chung-kuo hsien-tai yao yu cheng-fu" (The government China needs today), FSNHC (Cheng-lun), p. 129.

38. Ting Wen-chiang, "Chung-kuo cheng-chih ti ch'u-lu" (The road for Chinese politics), TLPL 11 (31 July 1932): 4.

39. Fu Ssu-nien, "Kung-ch'an-tang ti hsi-yin-li" (The appeal of the Communist Party; Tzu-yu Chung-kuo, 16 April 1950), FSNHC (Cheng-lun), pp. 155-64, Also see comments on Fu's anti-Communist sentiments in Lo Chia-lun, Shih-che ju-ssu chi, pp. 183-84; and Mao Tzu-shui, Shih-yu chi (Record of teachers and friends) (Taipei: Chuan-chi wen-hsueh ch'u-pan she, 1967), p. 99.

40. Chiang Meng-lin, KTST, p. 2, and Hsin-ch'ao (New tide) (Taipei: Chuan-chi wen-hsueh ch'u-pan she, 1967), pp. 126-29.

41. Fu Ssu-nien, "Chen Tu-hsiu an" (The case of Ch'en Tu-hsiu; TLPL 24, 30 October 1932), FSNHC (Jen-wu), pp. 43-51.

42. Lo Lung-chi, "Wo-men yao shen-ma-yang ti cheng-chih chih-tu?" (What kind of political system do we want?), Hsin-yueh (10 February 1930): 2-5; idem, "Lun kung-ch'an chu-i" (On Communism), ibid. 3, no. 1 (10 March 1930): 1-22; idem, "Lun Chung-kuo ti kung-ch'an" (On Chinese Communism) ibid. 3, no. 10 (n.d.): 1-18.

43. Ts'ai Yuan-p'ei, "Chiao-ch'ih hou chih hsiao-tu

kung-tso" (The work of disinfection after overthrowing the Reds; 27 July 1931), TYPCC, pp. 862-64.

44. T. F. Tsiang, "Tui Kung-ch'an-tang pi-hsü ti cheng-chih cheng-ts'e" (Necessary political plans regarding the Communists; TLPL 11, 31 July 1932), CTFHC 1: 103-7, and "Wei-shih ti ch'iang-t'u shih wo-men ti ch'u-lu" (The unlost land is our outlet; TLPL 47, 23 April 1933), CTFHC 2: 289-91.

45. Ting Wen-chiang, "So-wei 'chiao-fei' wen-t'i" (The so-called "Exterminate Bandits" question), TLPL 6 (26 June 1932): 2-3 and "P'ing-lun kung-ch'an chu-i ping chung-kao Chung-kuo kung-ch'an-tang yuan" (Criticism of Communism and advice to the Chinese Communist Party members), TLPL 51 (21 May 1933): 5-15.

46. "Madam Sun's Statement on Civil Liberty," China Critic 5, no. 44 (3 November 1932): 1168.

47. "For a Civil Liberty Union," Ibid., p. 1157.

48. Sung Ch'ing-ling, Sung Ch'ing-ling hsuan-chi (Selected writings of Sung Ch'ing-ling) (Hong Kong: Chung-hua shu-chü, 1967), p. 56.

49. Boorman, Biographical Dictionary 3: 142-46; Anna Louise Strong, "Mrs. Sun Yat-sen Flees from Victory," China Weekly Review 46, no. 9 (27 October 1928): 287-88.

50. The quote is in Sung, hsuan-chi, pp. 58-59. For some of Soong Ch'ing-ling's radical statements see ibid., pp. 68-78. Also see Harold Isaacs, ed., Straw Sandals (Cambridge: MIT Press, 1974), pp. xxxiv-xxxvi.

51. Sung, hsuan-chi, pp. 65-66.

52. Agnes Smedley, Battle Hymn of China (New York: Alfred A. Knopf, 1943), p. 111.

53. China Forum 2, no. 1 (11 February 1933): 2, 8.

54. Ibid., pp. 1-10.

55. Grieder, Hu Shih, pp. 277-79.

56. China Forum 2, no. 2 (1 March 1933): 14.

57. Ibid.

58. Ibid., no. 4 (13 April 1933): 2 and no. 5 (4 May 1933): 4.

59. Ibid., no. 5 (4 May 1933): 9.

60. Ibid., no. 7 (19 June 1933): 1-3.

61. "Shanghai Shocked by Murder of Noted Scholar, Yang Chuan," China Weekly Review 4 (24 June 1933): 146-47; Ting, Government Control, pp. 96-97; Lin Yutang, A History of the Press and Public Opinion in China (New York: Greenwood Press, 1968), p. 174.

62. Boorman, Biographical Dictionary 3: 299. Ts'ai's public announcement of his 1935 resignation is in TYPCC, pp. 662-64.

63. T. F. Tsiang, "An-sha yü cheng-chih" (Assassination and politics), TLPL 57 (2 July 1933): 2.

64. Sung, hsuan-chi, p. 79.

65. China Forum, 2, no. 7 (19 June 1933): 9.

6. Liberal Periodicals during the Nationalist Period, 1928-1937

1. For some representative liberal thinking regarding the importance of public opinion see T. F. Tsiang, "Cheng-fu yü yü-lun" (Government and public opinion; TLPL 55, 18 June 1933), CTFHC 2: 317-19 and "Wai-chiao yü yü-lun" (Foreign affairs and public opinion; TLPL 70, 1 October 1933), CTFHC 3: 409-14.

2. Leo Ou-fan Lee, The Romantic Generation of Modern Chinese Writers (Cambridge: Harvard University Press, 1973), pp.17-19, 147-48; Jerome B. Grieder, Hu Shih and the Chinese Renaissance (Cambridge: Harvard University Press, 1970), pp. 224-25; C. T. Hsia, A History of Modern Chinese Fiction (New Haven: Yale University Press, 1961), p. 121; Nieh Hua-ling, Shen Ts'ung-wen (New York: Twayne Publishers, 1972), p. 52.

3. "Hsin-yueh ti t'ai-tu" (The attitude of Hsin-yueh), Hsin-yueh 1, no. 1 (10 March 1928): pp. 3-10.

4. "Ching-kao tu-che" (Announcement to readers), Hsin-yueh 2, nos. 6-7 (10 September 1929). The announcement was on a special green insert, with no page number.

5. Lo Lung-chi, "Chuan-chia cheng-chih" (Government by specialists), Hsin-yueh 2, no. 2 (10 April 1929): 1-7; idem, "Wo-men yao shen-ma yang ti cheng-chih chih-tu?" (What kind of political system do we want?), ibid. (10 February 1930): 1-24; idem, "Tui hsün-cheng shih-chi yueh-fa ti p'i-p'ing" (Criticism of the Period of Tutelage Constitution), ibid. 3, no. 8 (n.d.): 1-18.

6. Hu Shih, "Wo-men tsou na-t'iao-lu?" (Which road do we travel?), Hsin-yueh 2, no. 10 (10 December 1929): 1-16. Liang Sou-ming's letter of criticism and Hu's reply are in ibid, 3, no. 1 (10 March 1930): 12-14.

7. Hu Shih, "Chieh-shao wo tzu-chi ti ssu-hsiang" (Introducing my own thought), Hsin-yueh 3, no. 3 (10 June 1930): 1-18.

8. Y. C. Wang, Chinese Intellectuals and the West, 1872-1949 (Chapel Hill: University of North Carolina Press, 1966), p. 409.

9. T. F. Tsiang, "Wo so-chi-te ti Ting Tsai-chün" (The Ting Wen-chiang I remember), CTFHC 6: 1085; Ch'en Chih-mai, Chiang T'ing-fu ti chih-shih yü p'ing-sheng (Taipei: Chuan-chi wen-hsueh ch'u-pan she, 1967), pp. 25-26.

10. Ch'en Heng-che, "Jen-ts'ai yü cheng-chih (Human talent and politics), TLPL 29 (4 December 1932): 6-8.

11. Weng Wen-hao, "Wo-ti i-chien pu-kuo ju-tz'u (My opinion doesn't go beyond this), TLPL 15 (28 August 1932): 2-5.

12. T. F. Tsiang, "Wo-men hsien-tai hai yu shen-ma hua k'o-shuo?" (What can we say now? TLPL 35, 15 January 1933), CTFHC 2: 251-53 and "Chih-shih chieh-chi yü cheng-chih" (Intellectuals and politics; TLPL 51, 21 May 1933), CTFHC 2: 299-306.

13. Wu Ching-ch'ao, "Chih-shih fen-tzu hsia-hsiang nan" (The difficulties of intellectuals going to the countryside), TLPL 62 (6 August 1933): 8-12.

14. Yen Shu-ch'ang, "P'ing-chiao-hui yü Ting-hsien" (Mass Education Society and Ting-hsien), TLPL 74 (29 October 1933): 3-8.

15. T. F. Tsiang, "Po Yen hsien-sheng ti lun-wen" (An epilogue to Mr. Yen's essay), TLPL 74 (29 October 1933): 8-11.

16. T. F. Tsiang, "P'ing-chiao-hui ti shih-tsai kung-hsien" (The real contribution of the Mass Education Society; Ta Kung pao, 13 May 1934), CTFHC 3: 487-91.

17. Hu Shih, "Wei Hsin-sheng-huo yün-tung chin-i-chieh" (A note on the New Life Movement), TLPL 95 (8 April 1934): 17-20.

18. Wu Ching-ch'ao, "Chiao-fei ch'ü-chung ti lao-kung cheng-ts'e" (Labor policies in the bandit suppression areas), TLPL 100 (13 May 1934): 5-9 and "Ching-che ho-shih yu ch'i t'ien?" (When will those who till the fields have their own land?) TLPL 165 (25 August 1935): 5-9.

19. Chang Hsi-jo, "Kuo-min jen-ko chih p'ei-yang" (Developing the national personality), TLPL 150 (12 May 1935): 14-17; Hu Shih, "Ko-jen tzu-yu yü she-hui chin-pu" (Individual freedom and social progress), TLPL 150 (12 May 1935): 2-5.

20. Hu Shih, "Cheng-chih kai-ko ti ta-lu" (The road to reform of the political system), TLPL 163 (11 August 1935): 3 and "Ts'ung i-tang tao wu-tang ti cheng-chih" (From a one party to a no party government), TLPL 171 (6 October 1935): 10-12.

21. Ch'en Chih-mai, "Cheng-chih kai-ko ti pi-yao" (Necessary reforms in the political system), TLPL 162

(4 August 1935): 2-5, and "Tsai lun cheng-chih kai-ko" (Again on political reform), TLPL 166 (1 September 1935): 3-4.

22. Lo Lung-chi, "Hsün-cheng ying-kai chieh-shu-le" (Tutelage should be ended), TLPL 171 (6 October 1935): 5-8.

23. Hu Shih, "Tu-li p'ing-lun ti ssu-chou-nien" (The fourth anniversary of the Tu-li p'ing-lun), TLPL 201 (17 May 1936): 3-5.

24. T. F. Tsiang, "Kuo-min-tang yü Kuo-min-tang tang-yuan" (The Kuomintang and its party members), TLPL 176 (10 November 1935): 11-14.

25. "Students and Politics," China Critic 1, no. 17 (20 September 1928): 325.

26. "Education and Politics," ibid. 3, no. 45 (6 November 1930): 1058-59.

27. "The Raid on the Soviet Consulate," ibid. 2, no. 24 (13 June 1929): 468-69.

28. "Generalissimo Chiang Kai-shek to the Front," ibid. 3, no. 51 (18 December 1930): 1205.

29. "Two ways to Deal with Communists," ibid. 5, no. 24 (16 June 1932): 593.

30. "Courageous Youth," ibid. 4, no. 49 (3 December 1931): 1169; "Declaration of War," ibid. 4, no. 53 (31 December 1931): 1266-67.

31. "The Students Again," ibid. 5, no. 2 (14 January 1932): 35.

32. "Three R's of National Emergency Conference," ibid. 5, no. 14 (7 April 1932): 311.

33. "The Toast for a Free Press," ibid. 2, no. 29 (18 July 1929): 567-68; "Freedom of the Press," ibid. 2, no. 35 (29 August 1929): 685; "The Deportation of Mr. Sokolsky," ibid. 2, no. 17 (25 April 1929): 327.

34. "A Bill of Rights for China," ibid. 3, no. 6 (6 February 1930): 123.

35. "Press Regains Freedom," ibid. 4, no. 44 (29 October 1931): 1047-48.

36. "The Constitutionalist Movement," ibid. 5, no. 27 (7 July 1932): 676-77.

37. "China League of Civil Rights," ibid. 5, no. 52 (29 December 1932): 1377.

38. "The Assassination of Yang Chien," ibid. 6, no. 26 (29 June 1933): 638-39.

39. "The Attempt on Lo Lung-chi's Life," ibid 6, no. 42 (19 October 1933): 1024.

40. "Fukien's Independence," ibid. 6, no. 48 (30 November 1933): 1156-57.

41. "The New Life Movement," ibid. 7, no. 12 (12 March 1934): 273-74.

42. "Y. S. Tsao, "China Needs a Dictator," ibid. 7, no. 32 (9 August 1934): 773-75.

43. "Students Active Once More," ibid. 11, no. 12 (19 December 1935): 268; "A Word to the Students," ibid. 12, no. 1 (2 January 1936): 6.

44. "The Arrest of Six Intellectuals," ibid. 15, no. 11 (10 December 1936): 245-46.

45. "Chang Hsueh-liang's Rebellion," ibid. 15, no. 13 (24 December 1936): 295.

7. The Japanese Threat and Gravitation toward the Government

1. Wang Wen-t'ien et al., Chang Po-ling yü Nan-kai (Taipei: Chuan-chi wen-hsueh ch'u-pan she, 1968), p. 16.

2. Wu Hsiang-hsiang, Min-kuo pai jen-chuan (Taipei: Chuan-chi wen-hsueh c'hu-pan she, 1971), 1: 44-45; John Israel, Student Nationalism in China, 1927-1937 (Stanford: Stanford University Press, 1966), pp. 75-76; TYPCC, pp. 870-79.

3. Ts'ai Yuan-p'ei, "Shou Pei-p'ing hsueh-sheng-t'uan wei-kun hou ta chi-che wen" (Interview after the Peiping student demonstration), TYPCC, p. 869.

4. Lo Chia-lun, "Wei-ta yü ch'ung-kao" (Great and lofty), Shih-che-ju-ssu chi (Taipei: Chuan-chi wen hsueh ch'u-pan she, 1967), p. 52; Ts'ai Yuan-p'ei, "Hsi-sheng hsueh-yeh sun-shih yü shih-t'u hsiang-teng" (The similarity between losing land and the loss through sacrificing schoolwork; 14 December 1931 speech), TYPCC, pp. 866-68.

5. Hu Shih, "Lun tui-Jih wai-chiao fang-chen" (The direction of our diplomacy toward Japan), TLPL 5 (19 June 1932): 2-5, and "Ts'an-t'ung ti hui-i yü fan-hsing" (Sorrowful memories and introspection), TLPL 18 (18 September 1932): 8-13.

6. Jerome B. Grieder, Hu Shih and the Chinese Renaissance (Cambridge: Harvard University Press, 1970), p. 252.

7. T. F. Tsiang, "Chiu-i-pa ti tse-jen wen-t'i" (The question of responsibility for 18 September; TLPL 18, 18 September 1932), CTFHC 1: 109-15, and "Kuo-lien t'iao-ch'a-t'uan so-chih ti lu" (The road indicated by the League Investigation Commission; TLPL 22, 16 October 1932), CTFHC 1: 131-38.

8. Ch'en Chih-mai, Chiang T'ing-fu ti chih-shih yü p'ing-sheng" (Chiang T'ing-fu's life and goals) (Taipei: Chuan-chi wen-hsueh ch'u-pan she, 1967), p. 28.

9. T. F. Tsiang, "Yu i-ko Lo-ssu-fu chin pai-kung" (Another Roosevelt in the White House; TLPL 27, 20 November 1932), CTFHC 1: 145-52.

10. Weng Wen-hao, "Wo ti i-chien pu-kuo ju-tz'u" (My opinion doesn't go beyond this), TLPL 15 (28 August 1932): 2-3.

11. Ch'en Heng-che, "Ta i-wei shao-nien nü-p'eng-yu" (Answering a young girl), TLPL 13 (14 August 1932): 20-22.

12. Lo, "Cha-t'an hsia chang-ta ti Chung-yang ta-hsueh" (Central University under increasing bombardment), Shih-che ju-ssu chi, pp. 16-17.

13. Fu Lo-ch'eng, Fu Meng-chen hsien-sheng nien-p'u (The chronological biography of Mr. Fu Meng-chen /Ssu-nien/) (Taipei: Chuan-chi wen-hsueh ch'u-pan she, 1969), p. 33.

14. Ibid.; Fu Ssu-nien, "Tung-pei-shih kang yin-yü" (An introduction to An Outline of Manchurian History), FSNHC (Shih-hsueh), pp. 99-101.

15. Fu Ssu-nien, "Chiu-i-pa i nien le!" (One year after 18 September; TLPL 18, 18 September 1932), FSNHC (Cheng-lun), pp. 17-28.

16. Fu Ssu-nien, "Kuo-lien t'iao-ch'a-t'uan pao-kao shu i-p'ieh" (A glance at the Commission Report; TLPL 22, 16 October 1932). FSNHC (Cheng-lun), pp. 29-32.

17. T. F. Tsiang, "Je-ho shih-shou i-hou" (After the loss of Jehol, TLPL 43, 26 March 1933), CTFHC 2: 275-77, and "Ch'ang-ch'i ti-kang chung ju-ho yün-yung kuo-lien yü kuo-chi" (Using the League and other nations in our long-term resistance), TLPL 45 (9 April 1933): 2-5.

18. Hu Shih, "Po Chiang T'ing-fu hsien-sheng ti lun-wen" (An epilogue to Mr. Chiang T'ing-fu's essay), TLPL 45 (9 April 1933): 6-8.

19. Hu Shih, "Wo-men k'o-yi teng-hou wu-shih nien" (We can wait fifty years), TLPL 44 (2 April 1933): 2-4.

20. Hu Shih, "Wo ti i-chien yeh pu-kuo ju-tz'u" (My opinion is just this), TLPL 46 (16 April 1933): 2-4.

21. Wu, Min-kuo pai, p. 134; Fu Lo-ch'eng, "Fu Meng-chen hsien-sheng ti min-tsu ssu-hsiang" (The nationalist thought of Mr. Fu Meng-chen), Chuan-chi wen-hsueh 2, no. 5 (May 1963): 19; Grieder, Hu Shih, p. 252.

22. T. F. Tsiang, "Ch'iang-k'ou tui-wai pu k'o-luan" (Pointing a gun won't solve anything; TLPL 60, 23 July 1933), CTFHC 2: 364; idem, "Kuo-chi ti feng-yün ho wo-men ti chün-pei" (The international situation and our preparation; TLPL 59, 16 July 1933), CTFHC 2: 355-57; idem, "Lun t'o-hsieh ping ta T'ien-chin I-shih-pao" (On compromise and in response to the Tientsin I-shih-pao; TLPL 62, 6 August 1933), CTFHC 2: 375-80.

23. Hu Shih, "Chin-jih ti wei-chi" (Today's crisis), TLPL 99 (6 May 1934): 4.

24. T. F. Tsiang, "Lun Jih-pen ho-p'ing" (On the Pax Japanica), TLPL 100 (13 May 1934): 2-5.

25. Fu Ssu-nien, "Cheng-fu yü tui-Jih wai-chiao" (The government's diplomacy toward Japan; Ta kung pao, 10 June 1934), FSNHC (Cheng-lun), pp. 51-52.

26. T'ang Erh-ho, "Ts'ung Jih-pen kuei-lai" (Returning from Japan), TLPL 101 (20 May 1934): 5-10.

27. Fu, Fu Meng-chen hsien-sheng nien-p'u, p. 38.

28. Ibid., pp. 37-38.

29. Chang Hsi-jo, "Tung-ya ta-chü wei-lai ti t'ui-ts'e" (Deductions about future East Asian conditions), TLPL 161 (28 July 1935): 6-9.

30. Hu Shih, "Su-o ko-ming wai-chiao-shih ti yu i-yeh chi ch'i chiao-hsün" (Another page in the history of Soviet diplomacy and its lessons), TLPL 163 (11 August 1935): 15-18; Fu Ssu-nien, "I hsi tsa-kan" (Reflections one evening), TLPL 164 (18 August 1935): 8.

31. Fu Ssu-nien, "Kuo-lien yü Chung-kuo" (The League and China; TLPL 17, 27 October 1935), FSNHC (Cheng-lun), pp. 37-41.

32. Hu Shih, "Hua-pei wen-t'i" (The North China question), TLPL 179 (1 December 1935): 2-3; Fu Ssu-nien, "Chung-hua min-tsu shih cheng-ko ti" (The Chinese people are one), TLPL 181 (15 December 1935): 5-8; Weng Wen-hao, "Wo-men ying nu-li yung-hu t'ung-i" (We must work hard to preserve unity), TLPL 180 (8 December 1935): 2-4.

33. Chiang Monlin, Tides from the West (New Haven: Yale University Press, 1947), pp. 202-6; Lo Chia-lun, "Chiang Meng-lin hsien-sheng chuan-lueh" (A biography of Chiang Meng-lin), Shih-che ju-ssu chi, pp. 99-102.

34. Grieder, Hu Shih, p. 257, fn. 29.

35. Ma Hsü-lun, Wo tsai liu-shih sui i-ch'ien (Shanghai: Sheng-huo shu-tien, 1947), pp. 114-18.

36. Hu Shih, "Wei hsueh-sheng yün-tung shih i-yen" (A word concerning the student movement), TLPL 182 (22 December 1935): 4-7, and "Tsai lun hsueh-sheng yün-tung" (Again on the student movement), TLPL 183 (29 December 1935): 2-4.

37. Israel, Student Nationalism, pp. 133-34.

38. Grieder, Hu Shih, p. 250. Faculty and administrators at Yenching University, most notably John Leighton Stuart, wrestled with the same dilemmas. See Philip West, Yenching University and Sino-Western Relations, 1916-1952 (Cambridge: Harvard University Press, 1976), pp. 146-54.

39. Allen B. Linden, "Politics and Higher Education in China" (Ph.D. diss., Columbia University, 1969), pp. 66-76; Israel, Student Nationalism, pp. 24-27.

40. Ts'ai Yuan-p'ei, "Tui-yü ch'ing-nien yün-tung t'i-an" (Proposal regarding youth movements; 9 August 1928), TYPLC, pp. 138-42.

41. Linden, "Politics and Higher Education," pp. 164-65.

42. Fu Ssu-nien, "Chiao-yü peng-k'uei chih yuan-yin" (The cause of our educational disorder; TLPL 9, 17 July 1932), FSNHC (Chiao-yü), pp. 63-67, and "Chiao-yü kai-ko chung chi-ko chü-t'i shih-chien" (Some practical considerations in educational reform; TLPL 10, 24 July 1932), FSNHC (Chiao-yü), pp. 75-78.

43. Fu Ssu-nien, "Kai-ko kao-teng chiao-yü chung chi-ko wen-t'i" (Some problems in reforming Chinese higher education; TLPL 14, 21 August 1932), FSNHC (Chiao-yü), pp. 85-88.

44. Fu Ssu-nien, "Hsien-t'an li-shih chiao-k'o-shu" (Casual talk on history textbooks; 1 October 1935), FSNHC (Shih-hsueh), pp. 21-35.

45. T. F. Tsiang, "Ch'en Kuo-fu hsien-sheng ti chiao-yü cheng-ts'e" (Ch'en Kuo-fu's educational plan; TLPL 4, 12 June 1932), CTFHC 1: 81-85, and "Tui ta-hsueh hsin-sheng kung-hsien chi-tien i-chien" (Some views on the contributions of the new university generation; TLPL 69, 24 September 1933), CTFHC 3: 404-6.

46. H. C. Zen [Jen Shu-yung], "Tang-hua chiao-yü shih k'o-neng ti ma?" (Is it possible to politicize education?), TLPL 3 (5 June 1932): 12-15, and "Tsai lun tang-hua chiao-yü" (Again talking about politicizing education), TLPL 8 (10 July 1932): 10-13.

47. Weng Wen-hao, "I-ko ta-p'o fan-men ti fang-fa" (A method of dispelling gloom), TLPL 10 (24 July 1932): 2-5.

48. Coverage in this study is limited to a brief

survey of some of the key statements by New Culture liberals. For further details on the democracy versus dictatorship debate see Lloyd E. Eastman, *The Abortive Revolution: China under Nationalist Rule* (Cambridge: Harvard University Press, 1974), pp. 140-59, and Grieder, *Hu Shih*, pp. 259-77.

49. Hu Shih, "Chien-kuo yü chuan-chih" (National construction and despotism), *TLPL* 81 (17 December 1933): 2-5; idem, "Tsai lun chien-kuo yü chuan-chih" (Again on national construction and despotism), *TLPL* 82 (24 December 1933): 2-5; idem, "Ta Ting Tsai-chün hsien-sheng lun min-chu yü tu-ts'ai" (Responding to Ting Wen-chiang's essay on democracy and dictatorship), *TLPL* 133 (30 December 1934): 7-9.

50. Lowe Chuan-hua, "China Has a Dictator," *China Critic* 7, no. 33 (16 August 1934): 804-5.

51. Chang Hsi-jo, "Wo wei-shen-ma hsiang-hsin min-chih" (Why I have faith in democracy), *TLPL* 240 (27 June 1937): 2-5; T'ao Meng-ho, "Min-chih yü tu-ts'ai" (Democracy and dictatorship), *Kuo-wen chou-pao* 12, no. 1 (1 January 1935): 1-4.

52. Eastman, *Abortive Revolution*, pp. 146-47; Ch'ien Tuan-sheng, "Min-chu cheng-chih hu? Chi-ch'uan kuo-chia hu?" (Democratic government or a totalitarian state?), *Tung-fang tsa-chih* 31, no. 1 (1 January 1934): 24.

53. Ting Wen-chiang, "Min-chu cheng-chih yü tu-ts'ai cheng-chih" (Democracy versus dictatorship), *TLPL* 133 (30 December 1934): 4-7.

54. Wu Ching-ch'ao, "Ko-ming yü chien-kuo" (Revolution and construction), *TLPL* 84 (7 January 1934): 5, and "Chung-kuo ti cheng-chih wen-t'i" (China's political system), *TLPL* 134 (6 January 1935): 17-19.

55. Ch'en Chih-mai, "Tsai lun cheng-chih ti she-chi" (Again on the planning of a political system), *TLPL* 205 (14 June 1936): 2-6. Ch'en also wrote some general historical surveys of this question in *TLPL* 136 (20 January 1935): 4-11, and in *She-hui k'o-hsueh* 2, no. 2 (January 1937): 211-82.

56. T. F. Tsiang, "Ko-ming yü chuan-chih" (Revolution and despotism; *TLPL* 80, 10 December 1933), *CTFHC* 3: 447-52, and "Lun chuan-chih ping ta Hu Shih-chih hsien-sheng" (On Despotism and in response to Hu Shih; *TLPL* 83, 31 December 1933), *CTFHC* 3: 453-60; Ch'en, *Chiang T'ing-fu*, pp. 28-31.

57. T'ao Hsi-sheng. "Min-chu yü tu-ts'ai ti cheng-

lun" (The debate over democracy versus dictatorship), TLPL 136 (20 January 1935): 12.

58. Howard L. Boorman, ed., Biographical Dictionary of Republican China (New York: Columbia University Press, 1967), 1: 356. Also see the preface in Ch'en, Chiang T'ing-fu, pp. 8-9.

59. Boorman, Biographical Dictionary, 3: 281.

60. See articles by Hu Shih and Chang Hsi-jo in TLPL, nos. 206 and 207.

61. Fu Ssu-nien, "Lun Chang-tsei p'an-pien" (Concerning the bandit Chang's rebellion), FSNHC (Jen-wu), pp. 71-74, and "T'ao-tsei chung chih ta-lu" (The road to punishing the bandit; Chung-yang jih-pao, 21 December 1936), FSNHC (Jen-wu), pp. 75-78.

62. Lo Chia-lun, "Wo so jen-shih ti Tai Chi-t'ao hsien-sheng" (The Tai Chi-t'ao I knew), Shih-che ju-ssu chi, pp. 148-50; Tien-wei Wu, The Sian Incident: A Pivotal Point in Modern Chinese History (Ann Arbor: Center for Chinese Studies, University of Michigan Press, 1976), p. 123.

63. Wu, Sian Incident, pp. 121-22.

64. Ibid., pp. 123-24.

65. Fu Ssu-nien, "Hsi-an shih-pien chih chiao-hsün" (The lesson of the Sian affair; Kuo-wen chou-pao, February 1937), FSNHC (Cheng-lun), pp. 63-67.

66. Wu, Sian Incident, p. 162.

67. TLPL 130 (18 April 1937).

68. Hu Shih, "Tsai t'an-t'an hsien-cheng" (Again talking about constitutional government), TLPL 236 (30 May 1937): 5-7, and "Wo-men neng hsing ti hsien-cheng yü hsien-fa" (The constitutional government we can implement), TLPL 242 (11 July 1937): 12-13.

69. Chang Hsi-jo, "Min-chu cheng-chih tang-chen shih yu-chih ti cheng-chih ma?" (Is democracy really a kindergarten political system?), TLPL 239 (20 June 1937): 3-6, and "Wo wei-shen-ma hsiang-hsin min-chih" (Why I have faith in democracy), TLPL 240 (27 June 1937): 2-5.

70. T'ao Hsi-sheng, "Pu-Tang-che ti li-liang" (The strength of nonparty members), TLPL 242 (11 July 1937): 9-11.

71. H. C. Zen, "Chin-pu ti chi-ch'u" (The foundation of progress), TLPL 242 (11 July 1937): 16-18.

72. "Pien-chi hou-chi" (Editor's postscript), TLPL 243 (18 July 1937): 19.

73. Grieder, Hu Shih, p. 293.

74. Wang, Chang Po-ling, pp. 33-34, 97-98; Wu, Min-kuo pai, 1: 307-8.

75. Among many sources of information on this period are the following: Suzanne Pepper, "Socialism, Democracy, and Chinese Communism: A Problem of Choice for the Intelligentsia, 1945-49," in Chalmers Johnson, ed., Ideology and Politics in Contemporary China (Seattle: University of Washington Press, 1973); Jessie Lutz, China and the Christian Colleges, 1850-1950 (Ithaca: Cornell University Press, 1971), pp. 430-34; and Carsun Chang, The Third Force in China (New York: Bookman Associates, 1952).

8. Modern Chinese Liberalism in Comparative Perspective

1. Jerome B. Grieder, Hu Shih and the Chinese Renaissance (Cambridge: Harvard University Press, 1970), pp. 319-48; Charlotte Furth, Ting Wen-Chiang: Science and China's New Culture (Cambridge: Harvard University Press, 1970), pp. 232-37; Lloyd E. Eastman, The Abortive Revolution: China under Nationalist Rule (Cambridge: Harvard University Press, 1974), pp. 179-80. Also see the review article: Eugene Lubot, "The Formation of Political Convictions: Liberalism vs. Communism in Modern China," Asian Forum 3, no. 3 (July-September 1971): 175-82.

2. In his study Lau Kit-ching Chan writes, "To conclude, the Chinese Youth party was a tragic attempt at politics by a group of intellectuals of the May Fourth period. . . . However, as intellectuals first and foremost, their outlook, character, and mentality were severe liabilities in the area of hard politics" (The Chinese Youth Party, 1923-1945 /Hong Kong: University of Hong Kong, 1972/, p. 52).

3. Such a theory is usually associated with the writings of Karl Deutsch, Daniel Lerner, C. E. Black, W. W. Rostow, and others. For useful critiques of the trends in modernization scholarship see Alberto Guerreiro-Ramos, "Modernization: Towards a Possibility Model," in Willard A. Beling and George Totten, eds., Developing Nations: Quest for a Model (New York: Van Nostrand Reinhold Co., 1970), pp. 21-59; Chong-Do Hah and Jeanne Schneider, "A Critique of Current Studies on Political Development," Social Research 35, no. 1 (Spring 1968): 130-58; and S. N. Eisenstadt, Tradition, Change and Modernity (New York: John Wiley & Sons, 1973), pp. 14-15.

4. See, for example, Dankwart A. Rustow, A World of Nations: Problems of Political Modernization (Washington, D.C.: Brookings Institution, 1967), p. 227; and Rupert Emerson, From Empire to Nation (Cambridge: Harvard University Press, 1967), p 292.

5. For analyses of the conditions for democracy that were present in the West and generally absent in newly modernizing societies, see: Seymour M. Lipset, "Some Social Requisites of Democracy: Economic Development and Political Legitimacy," American Political Science Review 53, no. 1 (March 1959): 69-105; Barrington Moore, Jr., Social Origins of Dictatorship and Democracy (Boston: Beacon Press, 1966), pp. 413-32; and Karl von Vorys, Democracy without Consensus (Princeton:

Princeton University Press, 1975), pp. 4-7, 10-12.

6. Gunnar Myrdal, Asian Drama: An Inquiry into the Poverty of Nations (New York: Twentieth Century Fund, 1968), 1:65.

7. Gunnar Myrdal, The Challenge of World Poverty (New York: Pantheon Books, 1970), pp. 208-52.

8. Ibid., pp. 49-77.

9. Myron Weiner, "Political Participation: Crisis of the Political Process," in Leonard Binder et al., Crises and Sequences in Political Development (Princeton: Princeton University Press, 1971), pp. 160, 177-81; Samuel Huntington, Political Order in Changing Societies (New Haven: Yale University Press, 1968); and Selig Harrison, The Widening Gulf: Asian Nationalism and American Policy (New York: Free Press, 1978), p. 320.

10. Michael Harrington, The Vast Majority: A Journey to the World's Poor (New York: Simon and Schuster, 1977), pp. 57-59, 90-91, 97-101. Also see his Socialism (New York: Saturday Review Press, 1972), pp. 219-21.

11. David E. Apter, The Politics of Modernization (Chicago: University of Chicago Press, 1965), pp. 393-94; Lucian W. Pye, Aspects of Political Development (Boston: Little, Brown & Co., 1966), pp. 71-88; Richard Lowenthal, Model or Ally? The Communist Powers and the Developing Countries (New York: Oxford University Press, 1977), pp. 34-40; Jean-Francois Revel, The Totalitarian Temptation (Garden City, N.Y.: Doubleday and Co., 1977).

12. Samuel P. Huntington and Joan M. Nelson, No Easy Choice: Political Participation in Developing Countries (Cambridge: Harvard University Press, 1976), p. 3; Francine R. Frankel, "Compulsion and Social Change: Is Authoritarianism the Solution to India's Economic Development Problems?" World Politics 30, no. 2 (January 1978): 215-40.

13. Perhaps an emerging consensus will be to stress the trade-offs involved, and the options that exist, with regard to the democratic and authoritarian models of modernization. See, for example, Apter, Politics of Modernization, pp. 358-59; and Lowenthal, Model or Ally?, pp. 39-40.

14. Charles W. Everett, Jeremy Bentham (London: Weidenfeld and Nicolson, 1966).

15. Alan Bullock and Maurice Shock, The Liberal Tradition from Fox to Keynes (Washington Square: New York

University Press, 1957).

16. J. H. Burns, "J. S. Mill and Democracy, 1829-61," in J. B. Schneewind, ed., Mill: A Collection of Critical Essays (Notre Dame: University of Notre Dame Press, 1969), p. 284.

17. Ibid., p. 328.

18. Edward Alexander, Matthew Arnold and John Stuart Mill (New York: Columbia University Press, 1965), pp. 69-70.

19. Bullock and Shock, Liberal Tradition, p. 109.

20. Pedro Schwartz, The New Political Economy of J. S. Mill (Durham: Duke University Press, 1972), p. 32.

21. Gertrude Himmelfarb, On Liberty and Liberalism: The Case of John Stuart Mill (New York: Alfred A. Knopf, 1974).

22. Ibid., p. 254.

23. Norman Gash, Sir Robert Peel: The Life of Sir Robert Peel After 1830 (Totowa, N. J.: Rowman and Littlefield, 1972).

24. E. J. Feuchtwanger, Gladstone (London: Penguin Books, 1975).

25. Ibid., p. 76.

26. J. L. Hammond and M. R. D. Foot, Gladstone and Liberalism (London: English Universities Press, 1952), p. 99.

27. Robert Blake, Disraeli (New York: St. Martin's Press, 1967), p. 397.

28. Ibid., p. 396.

29. D. A. Hamer, Liberal Politics in the Age of Gladstone and Rosebery (London: Oxford University Press, 1972); John Vincent, The Formation of the British Liberal Party (New York: Charles Scribner's Sons, 1966).

30. Hamer, Liberal Politics, p. xii.

31. Ibid., p. xii.

32. Vincent, British Liberal Party, pp. xiv-xv; Robert Kelley, The Transatlantic Persuasion: The Liberal-Democratic Mind in the Age of Gladstone (New York:

Alfred A. Knopf, 1969), p. 47.

33. G. Kitson Clark, The Making of Victorian England (Cambridge: Harvard University Press, 1963), pp. 38-39.

34. Vincent, British Liberal Party, p. 14.

35. Clark, Victorian England, p. 19.

36. Herman Ausubel, In Hard Times: Reformers among the Late Victorians (New York: Columbia University Press, 1960), p. 140.

37. Hammond and Foot, Gladstone and Liberalism, p. 97.

38. Feuchtwanger, Gladstone, p. 262.

39. D. A. Hamer, John Morley: Liberal Intellectual in Politics (Oxford: Clarendon Press, 1968), p. 81 (Morley's italics).

40. L. T. Hobhouse, Liberalism (New York: Oxford University Press, 1964), pp. 126-27.

41. See Michael Freeden's Introduction in J. A. Hobson, Confessions of an Economic Heretic (Hamden, Conn.: Archon Books, 1976). pp. v-xiv.

42. Martin Wiener, Between Two Worlds: The Political Thought of Graham Wallas (Oxford: Clarendon Press, 1971).

43. Joseph Hamburger, Intellectuals in Politics: John Stuart Mill and the Philosophic Radicals (New Haven: Yale University Press, 1965), p. 218.

44. See Moore, Social Origins of Dictatorship and Democracy.

45. Lucien Bianco, Origins of the Chinese Revolution, 1915-1949 (Stanford: Stanford University Press, 1971), p. 50.

46. Frederic Wakeman, Jr., History and Will: Philosophical Perspectives of Mao Tse-tung's Thought (Berkeley: University of California Press, 1973), p. 44.

47. Chan Lien, "Chinese Communism versus Pragmatism: The Criticism of Hu Shih's Philosophy, 1950-1958," Journal of Asian Studies 27, no. 3 (May 1968): 551-70; Chalmers A. Johnson, "An Intellectual Weed in the Socialist Garden: The Case of Ch'ien Tuan-sheng," China Quarterly 6 (April-June 1961): 29-52.

Bibliography

Alexander, Edward. Matthew Arnold and John Stuart Mill. New York: Columbia University Press, 1965.

Apter, David E. The Politics of Modernization. Chicago: University of Chicago Press, 1965.

Arima, Tatsuo. The Failure of Freedom: A Portrait of Modern Japanese Intellectuals. Cambridge: Harvard University Press, 1969.

Ausubel, Herman. In Hard Times: Reformers among the Late Victorians. New York: Columbia University Press, 1960.

Ayers, William. Chang Chih-tung and Educational Reform in China. Cambridge: Harvard University Press, 1971.

Beling, Willard, and George Totten. Developing Nations: Quest for a Model. New York: Van Nostrand Reinhold Co., 1970.

Benda, Harry J. "Non-Western Intelligentsias as Political Elites," in John H. Kautsky, ed., Political Change in Underdeveloped Countries: Nationalism and Communism. New York: John Wiley & Sons, 1962, 235-51.

Bianco, Lucien. Origins of the Chinese Revolution, 1915-1949. Stanford: Stanford University Press, 1971.

Blake, Robert. Disraeli. New York: St. Martin's Press, 1967.

Boorman, Howard L., ed. Biographical Dictionary of Republican China. 4 vols. New York: Columbia University Press, 1967-1971.

Borowitz, Albert. "Chiang Monlin: Theory and Practice of Chinese Education 1917-1930." Papers on China 8 (1954): 107-35.

Briggs, Asa. "The Political Scene," in Simon Nowell-Smith, ed., Edwardian England, 1901-1914. London: Oxford University Press, 1964, 45-101.

Bullock, Alan, and Maurice Shock. The Liberal Tradition from Fox to Keynes. Washington Square: New York University Press, 1957.

Cavendish, Patrick. "The 'New China' of the Kuomintang," in Jack Gray, ed., Modern China's Search for a Political Form. New York: Oxford University Press, 1969, 138-86.

Chan, Lau Kit-ching. The Chinese Youth Party, 1923-1945. Hong Kong: University of Hong Kong, 1972.

Chang Ch'i-yün. Chung-hua min-kuo ta-hsueh chih (Account of universities in the Chinese Republic). Vol. 1. Taipei: Chung-hua wen-hua ch'u-pan shih-yeh wei-yuan-hui, 1954.

Chang Ching-lu. Chung-kuo ch'u-pan shih-liao pu-pien (Supplementary material on Chinese publishing). Peking: Chung-hua shu-chü, 1957.

_______. Chung-kuo hsien-tai ch'u-pan shih-liao (Material on the history of contemporary Chinese publishing). 4 vols. Peking: Chung-hua shu-chü, 1954-1959.

_______. Tsai ch'u-pan-chieh erh-shih nien (Twenty years in the publishing world). Shanghai: Shanghai tsa-chih kung-ssu, 1938.

Chang Hao. Liang Ch'i-ch'ao and Intellectual Transition in China, 1890-1907. Cambridge: Harvard University Press, 1971.

Ch'en Chih-mai. Chiang T'ing-fu ti chih-shih yü p'ing-sheng (Chiang T'ing-fu's life and goals). Taipei: Chuan-chi wen-hsueh ch'u-pan she, 1967.

Chesneaux, Jean. The Chinese Labor Movement, 1919-1927. Stanford: Stanford University Press, 1968.

_______. "The Federalist Movement in China, 1920-3," in Jack Gray, ed., Modern China's Search for a Political Form. New York: Oxford University Press, 1969, 96-137.

Chiang Meng-lin. Hsi-ch'ao (Tides from the West). Taipei: Chung-hua jih-pao she, 1960.

_______. Hsin-ch'ao (New tide). Taipei: Chuan-chi wen-hsueh ch'u-pan she, 1967.

_______. Kuo-tu shih-tai chih ssu-hsiang yü chiao-yü (Thought and education in a transitional age). Taipei: Shih-chieh shu-chü, 1962.

_______. Meng-lin wen-ts'un (Collected writings of Chiang Meng-lin). Taipei: Cheng-ching shu-chü, 1954.

_______. T'an hsueh-wen (On learning). Taipei: Shih-chieh shu-chü, 1962.

Chiang Monlin /Meng-lin/. Tides from the West. New Haven: Yale University Press, 1947.

Chiang T'ing-fu /T. F. Tsiang/. Chiang T'ing-fu hsuan-chi (Selected works of Chiang T'ing-fu). 6 vols. Taipei: Chuan-chi wen-hsueh ch'u-pan she, 1971.

Chiao-yü tsa-chih (Education Journal). Vols. 9-15. 1917-1923.

China Critic. Vols. 1-18. 1928-1937.

China Forum. Vols. 2, no. 1 - 3, no. 4. 1933-1934.

China Weekly Review. 1927-1937.

Chinese Ministry of Information. China Handbook, 1937-1945. New York: Macmillan Co., 1947.

Chinese Social and Political Science Review. Vols. 1-20. 1916-1937.

Ch'ing-hua hsueh-pao (Tsinghua Journal). Vols. 1-12. 1924-1937.

Chow Tse-tsung. The May Fourth Movement. Cambridge: Harvard University Press, 1960.

Clark, G. Kitson. The Making of Victorian England. Cambridge: Harvard University Press, 1963.

Clarke, Peter. Liberals and Social Democrats. Cambridge: Cambridge University Press, 1978.

Clecak, Peter. Radical Paradoxes: Dilemmas of the American Left, 1945-1970. New York: Harper & Row, 1973.

Commager, Henry Steele. Freedom and Order. New York: George Braziller, 1966.

Coser, Lewis. Men of Ideas. New York: Free Press, 1965.

Crick, Bernard. In Defense of Politics. 2d ed. Chicago: University of Chicago Press, 1972.

Cumming, Robert Denoon. Human Nature and History: A Study of the Development of Liberal Political Thought. 2 vols. Chicago: University of Chicago Press, 1969.

Dahrendorf, Ralf. Society and Democracy in Germany. Garden City, N.Y.: Doubleday & Co., 1969.

Dangerfield, George. The Strange Death of Liberal England. New York: Capricorn Books, 1961.

Davidson, William L. Political Thought in England: The Utilitarians from Bentham to J. S. Mill. London: Thornton Butterworth, 1935.

de Bary, William Theodore. "Individuals and Humanitarianism in Late Ming Thought," in William Theodore de Bary, ed., Self and Society in Ming Thought. New York: Columbia University Press, 1970, 145-247.

de Ruggiero, Guido. The History of European Liberalism. Translated by R. G. Collingwood. London: Oxford University Press, 1927.

Dewey, John, and Alice Chipman Dewey. Letters from China and Japan. New York: E. P. Dutton, 1920.

Dimberg, Ronald G. The Sage and Society: The Life and Thought of Ho Hsin-yin. Honolulu: University of Hawaii Press, 1974.

Dirlik, Arif. "Mass Movements and the Left Kuomintang." Modern China 1, no. 1 (January 1975): 46-74.

Duiker, William J. "Ts'ai Yuan-p'ei and the Confucian Heritage." Modern Asian Studies 5, no. 3 (1971): 207-26.

Dumont, Rene, with Marcel Mazoyer. Socialisms and Development. Translated by Rupert Cunningham. London: Andre Deutsch, 1973.

Eastman, Lloyd E. The Abortive Revolution: China under Nationalist Rule, 1927-1937. Cambridge: Harvard University Press, 1974.

Eber, Irene. "Hu Shih and Chinese History: The Problem of Cheng-li Kuo-ku." Monumenta Serica 27 (1968): 169-207.

Eisenstadt, S. N. "Intellectuals and Tradition." Daedalus, Spring 1972, 1-19.

_______. Tradition, Change, and Modernity. New York: John Wiley & Sons, 1973.

Emerson, Rupert. From Empire to Nation. Cambridge:

Harvard University Press, 1967.

Emy, H. V. Liberals, Radicals, and Social Politics, 1892-1914. Cambridge: At the University Press, 1973.

Evans, R. J. The Victorian Age, 1815-1914. London: Edward Arnold, 1968.

Everett, Charles W. Jeremy Bentham. London: Weidenfeld and Nicolson, 1966.

Fan Yin-nan, ed. Tang-tai Chung-kuo ming-jen (Who's who in China). Shanghai: Liang-yu t'u-shu yin-shua kung-ssu, 1931.

Feuchtwanger, E. J. Gladstone. London: Penguin Books, 1975.

Forcey, Charles. The Crossroads of Liberalism. New York: Oxford University Press, 1961.

Freeden, Michael. The New Liberalism: An Ideology of Social Reform. Oxford: Clarendon Press, 1978.

Fu Lo-ch'eng. Fu Meng-chen hsien-sheng nien-p'u (The chronological biography of Mr. Fu Meng-chen [Ssu-nien]). Taipei: Chuan-chi wen-hsueh ch'u-pan she, 1969.

_______. "Fu Meng-chen hsien-sheng ti min-tsu ssu-hsiang" (The nationalist thought of Mr. Fu Meng-chen). Chuan-chi wen-hsueh 2, no. 5 (May 1963): 17-20; 2, no. 6 (June 1963): 26-31.

Fu Ssu-nien. Fu Ssu-nien hsuan-chi (Selected works of Fu Ssu-nien). Edited by Liu Shao-t'ang. 6 vols. Taipei: Chuan-chi wen-hsueh ch'u-pan she, 1971.

Furth, Charlotte. Ting Wen-chiang: Science and China's New Culture. Cambridge: Harvard University Press, 1970.

_______, ed. The Limits of Change: Essays on Conservative Alternatives in Republican China. Cambridge: Harvard University Press, 1976.

Gash, Norman. Sir Robert Peel: The Life of Sir Robert Peel after 1830. Totowa, N.J.: Rowman and Littlefield, 1972.

Gasster, Michael. Chinese Intellectuals and the Revolution of 1911. Seattle: University of Washington Press, 1969.

Girvetz, Harry K. The Evolution of Liberalism. New York: Collier Books, 1963.

Goldman, Merle, ed. Modern Chinese Literature in the May Fourth Era. Cambridge: Harvard University Press, 1977.

Goldstene, Paul N. The Collapse of Liberal Empire: Science and Revolution in the Twentieth Century. New Haven: Yale University Press, 1977.

Grieder, Jerome B. Hu Shih and the Chinese Renaissance: Liberalism in the Chinese Revolution, 1917-1937. Cambridge: Harvard University Press, 1970.

Hah, Chong-do, and Jeanne Schneider. "A Critique of Current Studies on Political Development." Social Research 35 (Spring 1968): 130-58.

Halevy, Elie. The Growth of Philosophic Radicalism. Translated by Mary Morris. Boston: Beacon Press, 1966.

Hamburger, Joseph. Intellectuals in Politics: John Stuart Mill and the Philosophic Radicals. New Haven: Yale University Press, 1965.

Hamer, D. A. John Morley: Liberal Intellectual in Politics. Oxford: Clarendon Press, 1968.

_______. Liberal Politics in the Age of Gladstone and Rosebery. London: Oxford University Press, 1972.

Hammond, J. L., and M. R. D. Foot. Gladstone and Liberalism. London: English Universities Press, 1952.

Hao Yen-p'ing. "The Abortive Cooperation between Reformers and Revolutionaries (1895-1900)." Papers on China 15 (1961): 91-114.

Harrington, Michael. Socialism. New York: Saturday Review Press. 1972.

_______. The Vast Majority: A Journey to the World's Poor. New York: Simon and Schuster, 1977.

Harrison, Selig S. The Widening Gulf: Asian Nationalism and American Policy. New York: Free Press, 1978.

Heilbroner, Robert L. An Inquiry into the Human Prospect. New York: W. W. Norton & Co., 1974.

Himmelfarb, Gertrude. On Liberty and Liberalism: The Case of John Stuart Mill. New York: Alfred A. Knopf, 1974.

_______. Victorian Minds. New York: Alfred A. Knopf, 1968.

Hobhouse, L. T. Liberalism. New York: Oxford University Press, 1964.

Hobson, J. A. Confessions of an Economic Heretic. Hamden, Conn.: Archon Books, 1976.

Hocking, William Ernest. The Lasting Elements of Individualism. New Haven: Yale University Press, 1937.

Houghton, Walter E. The Victorian Frame of Mind, 1830-1870. New Haven: Yale University Press, 1957.

Hsia, C. T. A History of Modern Chinese Fiction, 1917-1957. New Haven: Yale University Press, 1961.

Hsia, Tsi-an. The Gate of Darkness. Seattle: University of Washington Press, 1968.

Hsien-tai p'ing-lun (Contemporary Review). 1924-1927.

Hsin chiao-yü (New Education). Vols. 1-5. 1919-1923.

Hsin-yueh (Crescent Moon). Vols. 1-4. 1928-1932.

Hu Shih. The Chinese Renaissance. Chicago: University of Chicago Press, 1934.

_______. "Dr. Hu Shih's Personal Reminiscences." Chinese Oral History Project, Columbia University. Tapes recorded, 1958, ed. Hu Shih, 1959.

Hu Shih and Lin Yu-tang. China's Own Critics: A Selection of Essays. Tientsin, Shanghai, and Canton: China United Press, 1931.

Hu Shih, Lo Lung-chi, and Liang Shih-ch'iu. Jen-ch'uan lun-chi (Essays on human rights). Shanghai: Hsin-yueh shu-tien, 1931.

Huang, Philip C. Liang Ch'i-ch'ao and Modern Chinese Liberalism. Seattle: University of Washington Press, 1972.

Huang Shih-hui. "Ts'ai Chieh-min hsien-sheng chuan-lueh" (A short biography of Mr. Ts'ai Chieh-min /Yuan-p'ei/), *Chuan-chi wen-hsueh* 10, no. 2 (1967): 107-14.

Huntington, Samuel P. *Political Order in Changing Societies*. New Haven: Yale University Press, 1968.

Huntington, Samuel P., and Joan M. Nelson. *No Easy Choice: Political Participation in Developing Countries*. Cambridge: Harvard University Press, 1976.

Isaacs, Harold, ed. *Straw Sandals*. Cambridge: MIT Press, 1974.

Israel, John. *Student Nationalism in China, 1927-1937*. Stanford: Stanford University Press, 1966.

Israel, John, and Donald W. Klein. *Rebels and Bureaucrats: China's December 9ers*. Berkeley: University of California Press, 1976.

James, Robert Rhodes. *Rosebery*. New York: Macmillan Co., 1963.

Johnson, Chalmers A. "An Intellectual Weed in the Socialist Garden: The Case of Ch'ien Tuan-sheng." *China Quarterly* 6 (April-June 1961): 29-52.

Keenan, Barry. "Educational Reform and Politics in Early Republican China." *Journal of Asian Studies* 33, no. 2 (February 1974): 225-37.

Kelley, Robert. *The Transatlantic Persuasion: The Liberal-Democratic Mind in the Age of Gladstone*. New York: Alfred A. Knopf, 1969.

Kiang Wen-han. *The Chinese Student Movement*. New York: King's Crown Press, 1948.

Koss, Stephen E. *Lord Haldane: Scapegoat for Liberalism*. New York: Columbia University Press, 1969.

Ku Chieh-kang. *The Autobiography of a Chinese Historian*. Translated by Arthur W. Hummel. Taipei: Ch'eng-wen Publishing Co., 1966.

Kuhn, Philip A. "T'ao Hsing-chih (1891-1946): An Educational Reformer." *Papers on China* 13 (1959): 163-95.

Kwok, D. W. Y. Scientism in Chinese Thought, 1900-1950. New Haven: Yale University Press, 1965.

Lang, Olga. Pa Chin and His Writings: Chinese Youth between the Two Revolutions. Cambridge: Harvard University Press, 1967.

Lasch, Christopher. The New Radicalism in America, 1889-1963: The Intellectual as a Social Type. New York: Vintage Books, 1965.

Laski, Harold J. The Rise of Liberalism: The Philosophy of a Business Civilization. New York: Harper & Brothers, 1936.

Lawson, R. Alan. The Failure of Independent Liberalism, 1930-1941. New York: G. P. Putnam's Sons, 1971.

Lee, Leo Ou-fan. The Romantic Generation of Modern Chinese Writers. Cambridge: Harvard University Press, 1973.

Leontief, Wassily, et al. The Future of the World Economy. New York: Oxford University Press, 1977.

Levenson, Joseph R. Liang Ch'i-ch'ao and the Mind of Modern China. Cambridge: Harvard University Press, 1953.

Li Chien-nung. The Political History of China, 1840-1928. Stanford: Stanford University Press: 1967.

Li Shu-hua. "The Reminiscences of Li Shu-hua." Chinese Oral History Project, Columbia University.

Lien Chan. "Chinese Communism versus Pragmatism: The Criticism of Hu Shih's Philosophy, 1950-1958." Journal of Asian Studies 27, no. 3 (May 1968): 551-70.

________. "The Criticism of Hu Shih's Thought in Communist China." Ph.D. dissertation, University of Chicago, 1965.

Lin Yu-sheng, "The Crisis of Chinese Consciousness: Iconoclasm in the May Fourth Era." Ph.D. dissertation, University of Chicago, 1970.

Lin Yutang. A History of the Press and Public Opinion in China. New York: Greenwood Press, 1968.

_______. "Hsiang-nien Ts'ai Yuan-p'ei hsien-sheng" (Recalling Mr. Ts'ai Yuan-p'ei). Chuan-chi wen-hsueh 10, no. 2 (1967): 17-23.

Linden, Allen B. "Politics and Education in Nationalist China: The Case of the University Council, 1927-1928." Journal of Asian Studies 27, no. 4 (August 1968): 763-76.

_______. "Politics and Higher Education in China: The Kuomintang and the University Community, 1927-1937." Ph.D. dissertation, Columbia University, 1969.

Lipset, Seymour M. "Some Social Requisites of Democracy: Economic Development and Political Legitimacy." American Political Science Review 53, no. 1 (March 1959): 69-105.

Liu Chun-jo. Controversies in Modern Chinese Intellectual History. Cambridge: East Asian Research Center, Harvard University, 1964.

Lo Chia-lun, Shih-che ju-ssu chi (It passes away like this). Taipei: Chuan-chi wen-hsueh ch'u-pan she, 1967.

_______. "Ts'ai Yuan-p'ei hsien-sheng yü Pei-ching ta-hsueh" (Ts'ai Yuan-p'ei and Peking University). Chuan-chi wen-hsueh 10, no. 1 (1967): 30-34.

Lowenthal, Richard. Model or Ally? The Communist Powers and the Developing Countries. New York: Oxford University Press, 1977.

Lubot, Eugene. "Peking University Fifty-five Years Ago: Perspectives on Higher Education in China Today." Comparative Education Review 17, no. 1 (February 1973): 44-57.

_______. "Ts'ai Yuan-p'ei and Chiang Meng-lin during the May Fourth Period: The Dilemma of Modern Chinese Liberalism." Journal of Asian and African Studies 7, nos. 3-4 (July-October 1972): 161-75.

_______. "Ts'ai Yuan-p'ei and the May Fourth Incident: One Liberal's Attitude toward Student Activism." Chinese Culture 13, no. 2 (June 1972): 73-82.

Lutz, Jessie Gregory. China and the Christian Colleges, 1850-1950. Ithaca: Cornell University Press, 1971.

Ma Hsü-lun. Wo tsai liu-shih sui i-ch'ien (My life before sixty). Shanghai: Sheng-huo shu-tien, 1947.

Mack, M. P. A Bentham Reader. New York: Pegasus, 1969.

_______. Jeremy Bentham: An Odyssey of Ideas. New York: Columbia University Press, 1963.

MacKenzie, Norman, and Jeanne MacKenzie. The Fabians. New York: Simon and Schuster, 1977.

Manning, D. J. Liberalism. London: J. M. Dent & Sons, 1976.

Mao Tzu-shui. "Fu Meng-chen hsien-sheng chuan-lueh" (A short biography of Mr. Fu Meng-chen). Tzu-yu Chung-kuo 4, no. 1 (1 January 1951): 16-17, 27.

_______. "Kuan-yü Meng-lin hsien-sheng ti tsa-i" (Memories of Mr. Chiang Meng-lin). Chuan-chi wen-hsueh 5, no. 1 (July 1964): 6.

_______. Shih-yu chi (Record of teachers and friends). Taipei: Chuan-chi wen-hsueh ch'u-pan she, 1967.

_______. "Tui yü Ts'ai hsien-sheng ti i-hsieh hui-i" (Some memories of Mr. Ts'ai Yuan-p'ei). Chuan-chi wen-hsueh 10, no. 1 (1967): 35-36.

Mazlish, Bruce. James and John Stuart Mill. New York: Basic Books, 1975.

Moore, Barrington, Jr. Social Origins of Dictatorship and Democracy. Boston: Beacon Press, 1966.

Moore, Charles A., ed. The Status of the Individual in East and West. Honolulu: University of Hawaii Press, 1968.

Myrdal, Gunnar. The Challenge of World Poverty. New York: Pantheon Books, 1970.

Nathan, Andrew J. Peking Politics, 1918-1923: Factionalism and the Failure of Constitutionalism. Berkeley: University of California Press, 1976.

Neill, Thomas P. The Rise and Decline of Liberalism. Milwaukee: Bruce Publishing Co., 1953.

Nieh Hua-ling. Shen Ts'ung-wen. New York: Twayne Publishers, 1972.

Nisbet, Robert. Twilight of Authority. New York. Oxford University Press, 1975.

North China Herald. 1919-1937.

Nu-li chou-pao (The Endeavor). 1922-1923.

Orton, William Aylott. The Liberal Tradition. New Haven: Yale University Press, 1946.

Packe, Michael St. John. The Life of John Stuart Mill. New York: Macmillan Co., 1954.

Pao Tsun-p'eng. Chung-kuo chin-tai ch'ing-nien yün-tung shih (History of modern Chinese youth movements). Taipei: Pamir Shu-tien, 1953.

Peake, Cyrus H. Nationalism and Education in Modern China. New York: Columbia University Press, 1932.

Pepper, Suzanne. "Socialism, Democracy, and Chinese Communism: A Problem of Choice for the Intelligentsia, 1945-49," in Chalmers Johnson, ed., Ideology and Politics in Contemporary China. Seattle: University of Washington Press, 1973, 161-218.

Perleberg, Max. Who's Who in Modern China. Hong Kong: Ye Olde Printerie, 1954.

Plamenatz, John. Readings from Liberal Writers: English and French. London: George Allen and Unwin, 1965.

Pye, Lucian W. Aspects of Political Development. Boston: Little, Brown & Co., 1966.

Rankin, Mary Backus. Early Chinese Revolutionaries: Radical Intellectuals in Shanghai and Chekiang, 1902-1911. Cambridge: Harvard University Press, 1971.

Reitman, Alan, ed. The Pulse of Freedom: American Liberties, 1920-1970s. New York: W. W. Norton & Co., 1975.

Revel, Jean-Francois. The Totalitarian Temptation. Translated by David Hapgood. Garden City, N.Y.: Doubleday & Co., 1977.

Roy, David Tod. Kuo Mo-jo: The Early Years. Cambridge: Harvard University Press, 1971.

Rustow, Dankwart A. A World of Nations: Problems of Political Modernization. Washington, D.C.: Brookings Institution, 1967.

Saari, Jon. "The Passage to Modernity: The Early Years of a Disinherited Generation of Chinese Intellectuals." Ph.D. dissertation, Harvard University, 1973.

Sakai, Robert K. "Ts'ai Yuan-p'ei as a Synthesizer of Western and Chinese Thought." Papers on China, 3 (1949): 170-92.

Schapiro, J. Salwyn. Liberalism and the Challenge of Fascism. New York: McGraw-Hill, 1949.

Schneewind, J. B., ed. Mill: A Collection of Critical Essays. Notre Dame: University of Notre Dame Press, 1969.

Schneider, Laurence A. Ku Chieh-kang and China's New History. Berkeley: University of California Press, 1971.

Schwartz, Benjamin I. "The Limits of 'Tradition versus Modernity' as Categories of Explanation: The Case of the Chinese Intellectuals." Daedalus, Spring 1972, 71-88.

_______, ed. Reflections on the May Fourth Movement: A Symposium. Cambridge: East Asian Research Center, Harvard University, 1972.

Schwartz, Pedro. The New Political Economy of J. S. Mill. Durham: Duke University Press, 1972.

She-hui k'o-hsueh (Social Sciences). Vols. 1, 2. 1935-1937.

Sheridan, James E. China in Disintegration: The Republican Era in Chinese History, 1912-1949. New York: Free Press, 1975.

Shih, Vincent Y. C. "A Talk with Hu Shih." China Quarterly 10 (April-June 1962): 149-65.

Shils, Edward. The Intellectuals and the Powers and Other Essays. Chicago: University of Chicago Press, 1972.

Shu Hsin-ch'eng, ed. Chung-kuo chin-tai chiao-yü shih tzu-liao (Materials on the history of modern Chinese education). 3 vols. Peking: Jen-min chiao-yü ch'u-pan she, 1961.

Sidorsky, David, ed. The Liberal Tradition in European Thought. New York: G. P. Putnam's Sons, 1970.

Steel, Ronald. Walter Lippmann and the American Century. Boston: Little, Brown & Co., 1980.

Stephan, Leslie. The English Utilitarians. New York: Augustus M. Kelley, 1968. Vol. 1, Jeremy Bentham.

Stillinger, Jack, ed. The Early Draft of John Stuart Mill's Autobiography. Urbana: University of Illinois Press, 1961.

Sun Ch'ang-wei. Ts'ai Yuan-pei hsien-sheng ch'uan-chi (Complete works of Mr. Ts'ai Yuan-p'ei). Taipei: Taiwan Commercial Press, 1968.

Sun Te-chung. "Meng-lin hsien-sheng ti sheng-p'ing yü chih-ch'ü" (The life and personality of Mr. Chiang Meng-lin). Chuan-chi wen-hsueh 5, no. 2 (August 1964): 48-52.

_______, ed. Ts'ai Yuan-p'ei hsien-sheng i wen lei ch'ao (Categorized materials on Mr. Ts'ai Yuan-p'ei). Taipei: Fu-hsing shu-chü, 1961.

Sung Ch'ing-ling. Sung Ch'ing-ling hsuan-chi (Selected writings of Sung Ch'ing-ling). Hong Kong: Chung-hua shu-chü, 1967.

Tai Chin-hsieo. "The Life and Work of Ts'ai Yuan-p'ei." Ed.D. dissertation, Harvard University, 1952.

Talmon, J. L. The Origins of Totalitarian Democracy. New York: Frederick A. Praeger, 1960.

Tan, Chester. Chinese Political Thought in the Twentieth Century. Garden City, N.Y.: Doubleday & Co., 1971.

T'ao Meng-ho. Meng-ho wen-ts'un (Collected writings of T'ao Meng-ho). 3 ch'uan. Shanghai: Ya-tung t'u-shu-kuan, 1925.

Thomson, James C., Jr. While China Faced West: American Reformers in Nationalist China, 1928-1937. Cambridge: Harvard University Press, 1969.

T'ien Hsia Monthly. Vols. 1-5. 1935-1937.

Tien Hung-mao. Government and Politics in Kuomintang China, 1927-1937. Stanford: Stanford University Press, 1972.

Ting, Lee Hsia Hsu. Government Control of the Press in Modern China, 1900-1949. Cambridge: East Asian Research Center, Harvard University Press, 1974.

Totten, George O. III. The Social Democratic Movement in Prewar Japan. New Haven: Yale University Press, 1966.

Treadgold, Donald W. The West in Russia and China. Cambridge: At the University Press, 1973. Vol. 2, China, 1582-1949.

Ts'ai Shang-ssu. Ts'ai Yuan-p'ei hsueh-shu ssu-hsiang chuan-chi (The scholarship and thought of Ts'ai Yuan-p'ei). Shanghai: T'ang ti ch'u-pan she, 1950.

Tso Shun-sheng. "The Reminiscences of Tso Shun-sheng," Chinese Oral History Project, Columbia University.

_______. Tso Shun-sheng hsuan-chi (Selected writings of Tso Shun-sheng). 5 vols. Taipei: Atlantic Book Co., 1968.

Tu-li p'ing-lun (Independent Critic). 1932-1937.

Vincent, John. The Formation of the British Liberal Party. New York: Charles Scribner's Sons, 1966.

Vorys, Karl von. Democracy without Consensus. Princeton: Princeton University Press, 1975.

Wakeman, Frederic, Jr. History and Will: Philosophical Perspectives of Mao Tse-tung's Thought. Berkeley: University of California Press, 1973.

_______. "The Price of Autonomy: Intellectuals in Ming and Ch'ing Politics." Daedalus, Spring 1972, 35-70.

Wang, Tsi C. The Youth Movement in China. New York: New Republic, 1927.

Wang Wen-t'ien et al. Chang Po-ling yü Nan-k'ai (Chang Po-ling and Nankai University). Taipei: Chuan-chi wen-hsueh ch'u-pan she, 1968.

Wang, Y. C. Chinese Intellectuals and the West, 1872-1949. Chapel Hill: University of North Carolina Press, 1966.

Watkins, Frederick. The Political Tradition of the West: A Study in the Development of Modern Liberalism. Cambridge: Harvard University Press, 1948.

Weiner, Myron. "Political Participation: Crisis of the Political Process," in Leonard Binder et al., eds., Crises and Sequences in Political Development. Princeton: Princeton University Press, 1971, 159-204.

West, Philip. Yenching University and Sino-Western Relations, 1916-1952. Cambridge: Harvard University Press, 1976.

Wheeler, Harvey. Democracy in a Revolutionary Era. New York: Frederick A. Praeger, 1968.

Wiener, Martin. Between Two Worlds: The Political Thought of Graham Wallas. Oxford: Clarendon Press, 1971.

Wolfe, Alan. The Seamy Side of Democracy: Repression in America. New York: David McKay, 1973.

Wolff, Robert Paul. The Poverty of Liberalism. Boston: Beacon Press, 1968.

Wright, Mary C., ed. China in Revolution: The First Phase, 1900-1913. New Haven: Yale University Press, 1968.

Wu Hsiang-hsiang. Min-kuo pai jen-chuan (One hundred biographies of the Republican period). 4 vols. Taipei: Chuan-chi wen-hsueh ch'u-pan she, 1971.

Wu, Tien-wei. The Sian Incident: A Pivotal Point in Modern Chinese History. Ann Arbor: Center for Chinese Studies, University of Michigan Press, 1976.

Young, G. M. Portrait of an Age. London: Oxford University Press, 1977.

Index

About the Author

Eugene Lubot is Vice-President for Academic Affairs and Professor of History at Albright College in Reading, Pennsylvania. He has authored numerous articles on Chinese intellectual history, which have appeared in publications such as *Asian Forum*, *The Journal of Asian Studies*, *The Journal of Asian and African Studies*, and *Comparative Education Review*.